Representing Segregation

Representing Segregation

Toward an Aesthetics of Living Jim Crow,
and Other Forms of Racial Division

Edited by

BRIAN NORMAN

and

PIPER KENDRIX WILLIAMS

Cover photo courtesy of the Library of Congress

Published by State University of New York Press, Albany

For information, contact State University of New York Press, Albany, NY
www.sunypress.edu

Production by Diane Ganeles
Marketing by Michael Campochiaro

Library of Congress Cataloging-in-Publication Data

Representing segregation : toward an aesthetics of living Jim Crow, and other forms
  of racial division / edited by Brian Norman and Piper Kendrix Williams.
       p. cm.
  Includes bibliographical references and index.
  ISBN 978-1-4384-3033-1 (hardcover : alk. paper)
  ISBN 978-1-4384-3032-4 (pbk. : alk. paper)
   1. American literature—African American authors—History and criticism.
2. American literature—20th century—History and criticism.   3. Segregation in
literature.   4. Race in literature.   5. African Americans in literature.   6. African
Americans—Segregation—Historiography.   I. Norman, Brian, 1977–   II. Williams,
Piper Kendrix, 1972–

  PS153.N5R47 2010
  810.9'896073—dc22   2009022997

10 9 8 7 6 5 4 3 2 1

Contents

Illustrations

Foreword

Joycelyn Moody

Segregation usually connotes racialized discrimination in the twentieth-century public sphere—on public conveyances, in public venues ranging from churches to hospitals, even to graveyards. Utter the word *segregation,* and one might envision Rosa Parks as a young woman, perhaps recall Parks's coy smile in her now famous mug shot, taken on the December night she was arrested for violating Chapter 6, Section 11 of the 1955 segregation law of Montgomery, Alabama. It bears remembering, however, that the origins of segregation were formed in the institution of slavery as legislated and practiced in colonial America and as persistent in the nascent United States. Before the colonies severed themselves from England, Africans—enslaved and nominally free—were barred from social interactions with Europeans and gravely punished for overstepping the bounds erected to create and maintain a binaristic society of unequal opportunity.

One of the earliest legal acts penalizing those who would violate fiercely guarded codes of black separation from whites punished "free-borne English" women for "shameful Matches" with African men. Contemporaneous with Virginia's notorious 1661 Act that made bastards of all children borne of African mothers, Maryland's 1664 Act punished with slavery for life "divers English women forgetful of their free Condicon [who] to the disgrace of our Nation doe intermarry with Negro Slaves" (Morgan 48). This act of the white elite against white women of the servant class who loved black men determined the condition of the child according to that of the father, to punish white mothers' sex acts across the color line with bondage and ignominy. By the time the nation was constituted, then, its prescribed legacy of race separation—and female subjugation—was more than a century old.

Thomas Jefferson's posthumously published, negrophobic *Notes on the State of Virginia* (1784) cemented many of the early informal practices of discrimination against African Americans. This influential pseudoscientific volume from the third president of the United States became among the most prominent in a long line of European and European American "natural histories" to argue for the innate inferiority of persons of African descent. Jefferson's *Notes* contributed to the shift in U.S. laws from sanctions against problematic white women and their mixed-race sons and daughters to penalties against blacks who trespassed beyond their appointed sphere.

At the beginning of the nineteenth century, the disadvantaged but "good women of Wethersfield, Conn. [who] toiled in the blazing sun, year after year, weeding onions, then sold the seed and procured money enough to erect them a house of worship" inspired black orator Maria W. Stewart—ironically, because the "good women" apparently erected a *segregated* church. In an 1831 essay, Stewart would appeal to other black women to emulate the white women's spiritual self-determination: "and shall we not imitate their examples, as far as they are worthy of imitation?" ("Religion" 15–16). A year later, Stewart would once more underscore white women's complicity in race and/or class segregation—specifically barring blacks from education and schooling. Anticipating Harriet Jacobs's 1861 entreaties, Stewart pleads: "O, ye fairer sisters, whose hands are never soiled, whose nerves and muscles are never strained, go learn by experience! Had we the opportunity that you have had, to improve our moral and mental faculties, what would have hindered our intellects from being as bright, and our manners from being as dignified as yours?" ("Lecture" 54–55).

And so it went throughout the nineteenth and twentieth centuries, and so it persists in the twenty-first. In the post-black era, the binary is broken, exploded, so that now segregations split Americans by zig-zagging color and gender lines through bizarre swatches of the population. Now, "the hardest things" that render life in the United States divisive and nearly unbearable might well be, as Saidiya Hartman grieves, "the terrible things we [blacks] do to one another" (198). Terrible things we learned from masters of domination and cruelty.

Works Cited

Hartman, Saidiya. *Lose Your Mother: A Journey Along the Atlantic Slave Route.* New York: Farrar, Straus and Giroux, 2006.

Morgan, Kenneth, ed. "Maryland Establishes Slavery for Life." *Slavery in America: A Reader and a Guide.* Athens: U of Georgia P, 2005. 48.

Stewart, Maria W. "Lecture, Delivered at the Franklin Hall, Boston, Sept. 21, 1832." *Productions of Mrs. Maria W. Stewart.* 1835. *Spiritual Narratives.* Ed. Sue Houchins. New York: Oxford UP, 1988. 51–56.

———. "Religion and the Pure Principles of Morality, The Sure Foundation on Which We Must Build." 1831. Ed. Susan Houchins. *Spiritual Narratives.* New York: Oxford UP, 1988. 3–24.

Acknowledgments

We are grateful to the contributors who made this collection possible, and who are helping to stake out new terrain in studies of representations of segregation. We are grateful in particular to Joycelyn Moody, who provided steadfast support of this project in its earliest stages when she was editor of *African American Review*; Cheryl Wall, who signed on early to help us see the possibilities opened up by this line of inquiry; Trudier Harris who leant her discerning mind to the task of thinking about segregation today in light of segregation yesterday; and Shawn Michelle Smith who chose this endeavor to début her original visual art series. Our student research assistants JoSann Lien, JoLynn Graubart, and Angeline Henrickson provided valuable help during the process. We are fortunate that this project found a home at SUNY Press. We are thankful to our editor Larin McLaughlin for her enthusiastic support, as well as the rest of the folks at SUNY, especially Andrew Kenyon, Gary Dunham, Michelle Alamillo, Diane Ganeles, Michael Campochiaro, and Robin Weisberg. We are also grateful to Aileen Keenan at *African American Review* for her gracious assistance at each phase.

A special issue of *African American Review* 42.1 (2008) featured earlier versions of the pieces by Elizabeth Abel, Shawn Michelle Smith, Trudier Harris, Lori Robison and Eric Wolfe, Anne P. Rice, Michelle Y. Gordon, GerShun Avilez, Gary Totten, Eve Dunbar, Zoe Trodd, Vince Schleitwiler, and Cheryl A. Wall. Tess Chakkalakal's "Wedded to the Color Line: Charles Chesnutt's Stories of Segregation" first appeared in *Studies in American Fiction* (2008).

Introduction

To Lie, Steal, and Dissemble
The Cultural Work of the Literature of Segregation

BRIAN NORMAN
PIPER KENDRIX WILLIAMS

Segregation is a touchstone issue in African American history, and it profoundly shapes how we think about group identity and belonging in the United States. How have writers represented experiences of racial segregation in literary venues? Segregation comprises a diverse set of cultural practices, ethnic experiences, historical conditions, political ideologies, municipal planning schemes, and racialized social systems, although it is primarily associated with the Jim Crow South and the era between court cases *Plessy v. Ferguson* (1896) and *Brown v. Board of Education* (1954), when segregation was no longer the law of the land but a persistent *de facto* condition. In 1896, when the Supreme Court decided in a seven to one decision to enter the fray of post-Reconstruction race relations, it upheld the infamous separate-but-equal doctrine. This decision also helped set the parameters of a literary predicament: How to represent race segregation without necessarily reinscribing it? More than an ideological question, this aesthetic challenge infuses the literature that follows as writers differently approach what W.E.B. Du Bois famously declared the twentieth-century's defining dilemma: the problem of the color line.

The collection's title is inspired by the work of perhaps the most key literary figure associated with Jim Crow segregation: Richard Wright. In his famous essay "The Ethics of Living Jim Crow" (1937), Wright dramatizes his "Jim Crow education." As he matures into adulthood and takes on employment, Wright notes, "It was no longer brutally cruel, but subtly cruel. Here I learned to lie, to steal, to dissemble. I learned to play that dual role which every Negro must play if he wants to eat and live" (1418). In this moment, Wright gets at not only what it means to be a colored citizen under Jim Crow, but also the tactics, ingenuity, and acrobatics required by the aesthetic project of representing segregation. For Wright, this meant telling stories about what happens when exemplary figures like Bigger Thomas or Big Boy cross color lines, be they *de jure* or *de facto*. Other writers, too, developed narratives, characters, plots, and a plethora of fictional strategies to play Wright's dual role, from Charles Chesnutt's learned narrator relaying Uncle Remus tales, to W.E.B. Du Bois's invitation to join him on the Jim Crow car at the turn of the twentieth century, to Nella Larsen's African American women passing as white during the heyday of the Harlem Renaissance, all the way to Lorraine Hansberry's cramped Chicago apartment at the tail end of *de jure* segregation in *A Raisin in the Sun* (1959) in which the white community association representative Karl Linder intrudes on the Younger family with a rather mundane message of racial intolerance. Perhaps Wright's dual role is most starkly illustrated by Chesnutt's often remarked tactics to foster ambiguity around his own racial identity in his early career. In any case, writers across political, racial, and social spectra develop narrative strategies to lie, steal, and dissemble to get at the truth of the experiences of race segregation, but also to tell us something about how and why race segregation works, often with the hopes of influencing a change of heart or mind.

Wright's essay works on both these levels, revealing how segregation operates at the same time that he joins a literary tradition that rises to the aesthetic challenge of representing segregation. In the first few sentences of his essay, Wright employs symbolic geographies to reveal how segregation shapes spaces in society: "My first lesson in how to live as a Negro came when I was quite small. We were living in Arkansas. Our house stood behind the railroad tracks. Its skimpy yard was paved with black cinders. Nothing green ever grew in that yard. The only touch of *green* we could see was far away, beyond the tracks, over where the white folk lived" (1411). With this opening, Wright establishes the importance of the way space is organized in segregated spaces, even at the level of foliage within a color palette for a segregated landscape.

We should caution at the outset that this collection will not offer an exhaustive catalog or chronology of something we would call a segregation narrative tradition. Such a task would greatly exceed the confines of one book. Instead, we offer a series of illustrative approaches and studies of texts, periods, writers, and spaces that instigate conversations about reordering how we think about the periods and practices of race segregation. In his provocative study of what he calls "beautiful democracy," Russ Castronovo also asks aesthetic questions about traditionally political concerns and events, such as Du Bois's anti-lynching work at *The Crisis*, ultimately finding "a sort of political alchemy that tried to wring an activist methodology out of aesthetic formalism" (110). He cautions, "In rearticulating 'the beautiful,' the men and women at *The Crisis* walked dangerous ground, trying to recuperate forms of representation that had done so much injury to black people. Worse still, they risked their own irrelevance, opening themselves up to the accusation that effeminate dabbling in art did little to abate black victimization" (110). Far beyond *The Crisis* and anti-lynching activities, such "dangerous ground" lies underneath the wide-ranging literary tradition associated with race segregation in its multiple forms.

A Segregation Narrative Tradition?

What does it mean to propose the existence of a segregation narrative? And are we ready for that? We now universally recognize "the slave narrative." Of course, that, too, required similar intellectual work to create a category that we can so easily use to describe a coherent tradition. After Reconstruction hopes faded when federal troops left the South in 1877, Jim Crow segregation became the nation's wallpaper and eventually the last citizens with direct experiences of being slaves passed away. In that wake, literary critics synthesized the archive of texts, tracts, and testimonials and identified something called a "slave narrative." More so than the institution of slavery, complex and changing as it was, race segregation comprises an even more disparate set of laws, practices, beliefs, and policies, even if we start from Jim Crow segregation and work outward. So, the literary archive is also much more varied and the task of identifying something called a "segregation narrative" is challenging, one whose merits are in question. We think it is useful to use "segregation" as a literary category that holds the promise of creating coherence across different regions, historical experiences, and genres associated with segregation. The special issue of *African American Review* on which this collection builds asked more questions than it answered while beginning the project of identifying some of the writers, approaches, and locations that should probably inform conversations about a segregation narrative tradition. This collection goes a bit further in some of those directions, including identifying foundational figures, such as a section on Chesnutt (a potential bookend to the tradition, with Wright and Lorraine Hansberry on the other), providing a framework on the place of Jim Crow within a larger segregation narrative tradition, and taking comparative ethnic and transnational approaches a bit further. The essays in the collection also attend to how segregation narratives involve formal innovation in response to the social and political institutions of compulsory race segregation. Pushing the question of aesthetics, conceived broadly, the collection focuses on the very nature of literary and theoretical representations of segregation. Moreover, in this introduction, we also offer a few generalizations that we think might withstand scrutiny when other scholars think about what other literary figures, experiences, and texts could fall under the umbrella of segregation literature.

I. Racial Cartographies

The first generalization concerns the spatialization of race. In segregation narratives, race infuses the landscape. In this way, writers dramatize the process of how Jim Crow and other kinds of segregation are naturalized. Each text must invent a geography of race to denote where certain bodies belong and the various sociolegal codes that attend such geographic inscriptions. Drawing from the same palette as Richard Wright's spatial aesthetic of segregation, for instance, Toni Morrison's first novel, *The Bluest Eye* (1970), represents segregated spaces with visual metaphors closely akin to Wright's colored spaces. In Morrison's novel, we experience a symbolic geography through a child's perspective when Claudia, Frieda, and Pecola walk to Pauline Breedlove's place of employment, where she is a domestic for a white family:

> We walked down tree-lined streets of soft gray houses leaning like tired ladies. . . . The streets changed; houses looked more sturdy, their paint newer, porch posts straighter, yards deeper. Then came brick houses set well back from the street, fronted by yards edged in shrubbery clipped into smooth cones and balls of velvet green. . . .
>
> The orange-patched sky of the steel mill section never reached this part of town. This sky was always blue.
>
> We reached Lake Shore Park, a city park laid out with rosebuds, fountains, bowling greens, and picnic tables. It was empty now, but sweetly expectant of clean, white well behaved children and parents who would play there. . . . Black people were not allowed in the park, and so it filled our dreams. (105)

Morrison's signature voice and deceptively simple words are a particularly insightful take on segregation and echo Wright in a manner that begins to reveal a discrete aesthetic practice in representing segregation. Likewise, Morrison lays out how, if people are colored (white and black), so, too, are the spaces in which they live. Blacks live in "gray" and "black" places; in these passages the spaces are also hard, worn down, and seemingly inferior. Whites in contrast live in "green," lush, and open spaces, obviously superior. For these children it is not a far leap: inferior gray and black spaces become synonymous with the people that live within. Although Wright highlights the absence of anything green where he resides, focusing instead on the "black cinders" and "skimpy yard," Morrison spends time revealing the reverse in white spaces. Here everything is better: "newer," "sturdier," "straighter," and yards "deeper." Morrison's passage also articulates the deep longings of children not yet conditioned in the ways of segregation; they desire equality, figured here in terms of access to the "city" (read: "public") park to which blacks are denied entrance. Other literary and political figures take up this aestheticization of racial geographies, such as Martin Luther King Jr.'s famous "Letter from Birmingham Jail" (1963) in which he talks about what segregation must seem like to his young daughter who is denied access to "Funtown," another "public" amusement park.

Wright and Morrison exemplify the way symbolic geographies, especially as understood by children, work well to represent segregation. Before either the young Wright or Morrison's children may know the concrete laws of segregation, *de jure* or *de facto*, they know the discrepancies informing the spaces in which they live. Whether it is Arkansas or Lorraine, Ohio, these differences are deeply encoded in the geography, in contrast to the difference between North and South that shapes traditional understandings of American spaces. "The Ethics of Jim Crow" and *The Bluest Eye* together challenge this conventional wisdom, which somehow suggests that guilt and innocence, access and denial of such, opportunity and disadvantage can be mapped using the Mason-Dixon Line. Rather, as Morrison's insightful narrator understands, the phenomenon of difference embedded in segregated societies transcends physical ground and instead encapsulates the entire world within which these children live. To repeat: "The orange-patched sky of the steel mill section never reached this part of town. This sky was always blue."

II: Fear

The second generalization we offer follows from the first: the spatialization of fear. Wright's essay reveals this common aspect of segregation literature, now telling us something about how and why race segregation works: fear becomes part and parcel of segregated lives. After fighting with some white boys, young Richard returns to his home and his mother beats him, imparting yet another "gem of Jim Crow wisdom" (1411). She wants him to realize how dangerous it is for him to fight with whites, telling him he "ought to be thankful to God as long as (he) lived that they didn't kill (him)" (1412). For the younger Wright, another truism of segregated living comes into full focus: fear is essential to survival. "All that night I was delirious and could not sleep," Wright reports. "Each time I closed my eyes I saw monstrous white faces from the ceiling, leering at me" (1412).

Once a text portrays geographies of race, including across public and private or domestic spaces, the narrative must enforce such demarcations, often through an atmosphere of fear. Much as lynching and other practices enforced Jim Crow boundaries, literary texts dramatize the fear and consequences related to marking, crossing, or not crossing lines of segregation, including characters on both sides of such lines, from modernist narratives of passing to socialist polemics against lynching. Just as Morrison draws from a similar color palette as Wright, other key writers pick up this aesthetic of fear when representing segregation. For instance, in his long polemic essay *The Fire Next Time* (1963), James Baldwin excoriates:

> This world is white and they are black. . . . Long before the Negro
> child perceives this difference, and even longer before he understands
> it, he has begun to react to it, he has begun to be controlled by
> it. Every effort made by the child's elders to prepare him for a fate
> from which they cannot protect him causes him secretly, in terror,
> to begin to await, without knowing he is doing so, his mysterious
> and inexorable punishment. (26)

Wright and Baldwin begin to define the shape of representing fear in the way segregation works, and it would not be difficult to further trace this line through lynchings, mob violence, and the psychological terror of passing that infuse African American literary representations of segregation. Taken together, the passages exemplify the utter control necessary to maintain a segregated society; here black parents must become part of the project of maintaining segregation, tragically in the effort to keep their children "safe."

III: Cross-Racial Contact

The third and final generalization we offer concerns how narratives set in motion the geography of race and the climate of fear: key scenes of cross-racial contact. The foundational passages from Wright and Baldwin discussed earlier point to a key device common to nearly all segregation literatures: representative scenes of cross-racial contact that underscore the effects and basic injustices—from petty to fatal—of segregated societies. These scenes might be stark and violent, such as the lynching Big Boy witnesses before "leaving home" to go North in Wright's early short story or the murder of the Emmett Till figure in Baldwin's *Blues for Mister Charlie* (1964). They might be subtle psychological wrestling matches such as the drawing room scene in Larsen's *Passing* when a white husband unknowingly bullies three passing African American women into colluding in his habit of teasing his wife about her nig-ness, or they might be almost off-scene or segmented into flashbacks such as Janie's humorous account of recognizing herself as the sole black girl in a school photo at age six in Zora Hurston's *Their Eyes Were Watching God* (1937). But these necessary scenes of cross-racial contact also signal other kinds of crossings for which the stark color line is an inadequate formulation. For instance, Chesnutt's learned narrator's contact with Uncle Remus also represents meetings of North and South, Reconstruction and slavery, cosmopolitan and rooted, voyeuristic and experiential knowledge, among others. Or another good example is how the meeting between Karl Lindner and the Younger Family in *A Raisin in the Sun* allows a solidarity among heretofore-divergent positions of Beneatha's youthful revolutionary stances, Walter Lee's small capitalist dreams, Mama's migration narrative and generational hopes, and Ruth's conflicted motherhood.

By identifying a literary tradition associated with U.S. practices of race segregation, this collection sees Jim Crow as more than historical backdrop. That way, we attend to conscious strategies of representing compulsory race segregation. Historians have identified the cultural and political practices of Jim Crow.[1] Lynching in particular has captured their attention[2] and literary and visual critics have begun to bring aesthetic considerations to this practice of segregation,[3] especially the notorious history of spectacle lynching photographs brought back into popular circulation in James Allen's 2000 collection *Without Sanctuary*. Now is the time to follow the lead of scholars who are thinking about a segregation aesthetic writ large.[4] African American and Southern literature scholars have long shown great interest in how collective experiences such as slavery, migration, and diaspora, impact the literary imagination. But scholars have rarely and only recently used segregation as a term to describe the literature of the Jim Crow period. This is surprising given segregation's looming presence in the lives and institutions of postbellum America to the present. We offer this edited collection to trace the outlines of this absence. The collection brings together writers, locations, concerns, and movements to prompt a conversation about what happens when we think about race segregation as giving rise to a distinct literary tradition. What does that tradition look like? Is it primarily associated with a specific practice or location, such as the Jim Crow South, or does it reach to the urban North and the American West or further? Do writings about racial division or segregation practices share aesthetic properties, as well as political concerns? What happens when other ethnic groups compare their experiences to African Americans living under Jim Crow? The articles in this collection begin to answer these questions so that we can propose a multiregional and multi-era understanding of literatures of U.S. racial segregation, with African American literature and the Jim Crow South at the center. Future work will be able to pursue further questions. For instance, what happens when Jim Crow enters transnational projects? Do the aesthetics of segregation shift when the project is designed to inscribe racial separation, rather than reject such practices? In this vein, what is the aesthetic difference between antiracist texts like Chesnutt's *The Marrow of Tradition* (1901) and white supremacist texts like Thomas Dixon's clan trilogy?

Because twentieth-century concerns so often frame our understanding of segregation in the U.S. context, Joycelyn Moody, a scholar of nineteenth-century African American literature and culture, opens the collection by considering the rise of Jim Crow segregation from longstanding racial ideologies that both buttressed slavery and preceded the nation's founding. By tracing the practices and ideologies of segregation through the long centuries of slavery, Moody shows us, we can better understand the ever-shifting manifestations of segregation practices in the United States. Moreover, Trudier Harris reminds us, in a "sound-off," that attempted desegregation is an unfinished, and perhaps failed, project, so a study of segregation narratives is both urgent and tricky. Indeed, a wide-ranging scholarly conversation about literary representation of Jim Crow and other forms of race segregation is necessarily ambitious. So, we have taken care to balance our desire for a specific focus on Jim Crow at the center of U.S. race segregation with the need to facilitate a scholarly conversation that is open to the many directions, times, locations, and political sensibilities that emerge from the moment race segregation became the law of the land in 1896.

The first section of the collection, "The Aesthetic Challenge of Jim Crow Politics," considers the legacy of Jim Crow segregation and its lessons for a *de facto* era. Along with Harris's sound-off, Elizabeth Abel's provocative study of Jim Crow signage and their post-civil rights legacy delineates some of the aesthetic challenges raised by curiously stylized artifacts of some of the most notorious—and mundane—practices of policing race segregation. The second section, "Imagining and Subverting Jim Crow in Charles Chesnutt's Segregation Fiction," places Chesnutt as a key figure in accepting the challenge of representing newly forming and contested ideas about the bright line of race segregation and the institutionalization of Jim Crow practices in the wake of the failures of Reconstruction. The third section, "Inside Jim Crow and His Doubles," comprises analyses of representative writers, eras, and texts that in some way tell the story of Jim Crow and related practices of racial division with an eye toward not only representing racial segregation, but also protesting it and imaging alternative systems of racial interaction. The following section, "Exporting Jim Crow," approaches Jim Crow in other contexts: transnational, pan-African and cross-ethnic. In this way, the section illustrates how Jim Crow participates in a cross-cultural imaginary of race relations. The final section, "Jim Crow's Legacy," provides suggestive models for how to approach the ambitious project of talking about segregation's legacy in a *de facto*, post-civil rights era, moving from visual studies of civil rights representation of segregation to a comparative ethnic literary studies meditation on what it means to talk about a practice that is officially dead but persists in memory and social institutions. We also included some suggestive images that further reflect on Jim Crow's legacy and challenge with pieces from Shawn Michelle Smith's visual art series heading each section.

This collection is necessarily speculative; it could not possibly cover all eras, locations, practices, and aesthetic sensibilities that we could usefully group under the rubric of representing segregation. Cheryl Wall's afterword meditates on what we gain when we think about representations of Jim Crow and other forms of race segregation as a distinct literary tradition. Wall extends the work of the final section to underscore how Jim Crow's legacy continues to haunt U.S. race relations and literature. Wall also challenges future scholars to carry further some of the questions raised by this collection, including perhaps some of the inevitable omissions and threadbare spots. Let the conversation begin.

Notes

1. See for example Dailey, Gilmore, Simon; Gilmore; Hale.
2. See for example Dray, Gonzales-Day, Markovitz, Pfeifer, Waldrep.
3. See for example Apel, Goldsby, Gunning, Rice, Smith and Apel.
4. See for example Duck, McCaskill and Gebhard.

Works Cited

Allen, James, ed. *Without Sanctuary: Lynching Photography in America*. Santa Fe: Twin Palms, 2000.

Apel, Dora. *Imagery of Lynching: Black Men, White Women, and the Mob*. New Brunswick, NJ: Rutgers UP, 2004.

Baldwin, James. *The Fire Next Time*. 1963. New York: Vintage International, 1993.

Castronovo, Russ. *Beautiful Democracy: Aesthetics and Anarchy in a Global Era*. Chicago: U of Chicago P, 2007.

Dailey, Jane Elizabeth, Glenda Elizabeth Gilmore, and Bryant Simon, eds. *Jumpin' Jim Crow: Southern Politics from Civil War to Civil Rights*. Princeton, NJ: Princeton UP, 2000.

Dray, Philip. *At the Hands of Persons Unknown: The Lynching of Black America*. New York: Modern Library, 2003.

Duck, Leigh Anne. *The Nation's Region: Southern Modernism, Segregation, and U.S. Nationalism*. Athens: U of Georgia P, 2006.

Gilmore, Glenda. *Gender and Jim Crow*. Chapel Hill: U of North Carolina P, 1996.

Goldsby, Jacqueline. *A Spectacular Secret: Lynching in American Life and Literature*. Chicago: U of Chicago P, 2006.

Gonzales-Day, Ken. *Lynching in the West: 1850–1935*. Durham, NC: Duke UP, 2006.

Gunning, Sandra. *Race, Rape, and Lynching: The Red Record of American Literature, 1890–1912*. New York: Oxford UP, 1996.

Hale, Grace Elizabeth. *Making Whiteness: The Culture of Segregation in the South, 1890–1940*. New York: Pantheon, 1998.

King, Martin Luther, Jr. "Letter from Birmingham City Jail." 1963. *A Testament of Hope: The Essential Writings and Speeches of Martin Luther King, Jr.* Ed. James M. Washington. San Francisco: HarperCollins, 1986. 289–302.

Markovitz, Jonathan. *Legacies of Lynching: Racial Violence and Memory*. Minneapolis: U of Minnesota P, 2004.

McCaskill, Barbara and Caroline Gebhard. *Post-Bellum, Pre-Harlem: African American Literature and Culture, 1877–1919*. New York: New York UP, 2006.

Morrison, Toni. *The Bluest Eye*. 1970. New York: Plume, 1994.

Pfeifer, Michael J. *Rough Justice: Lynching and American Society, 1874–1947*. Urbana: U of Illinois P, 2004.

Rice, Anne P. *Witnessing Lynching: American Writers Respond*. New Brunswick, NJ: Rutgers UP, 2003.

Smith, Shawn Michelle and Dora Apel. *Lynching Photographs*. Berkeley: U of California P, 2008.

Waldrep, Christopher, ed. *Lynching in America: A History in Documents*. New York: New York UP, 2006.

Wright, Richard. "The Ethics of Living Jim Crow." 1937. *The Norton Anthology of African American Literature*. Ed. Henry Louis Gates and Nellie McKay. New York: Norton, 2004. 1411–19.

In the Crowd

Artist's Statement

SHAWN MICHELLE SMITH

In the last decades of the nineteenth century and the first decades of the twentieth, thousands of men and women were murdered by mobs in the United States. The victims of lynching included people of all races and ethnicities, but the majority of them were African American men who died at the hands of white men, women, and children. The perpetrators of lynching were rarely prosecuted, and in the twentieth century lynching was so implicitly condoned that it became a public spectacle—crowds numbered in the thousands for planned and advertised murders.

The mob gained community consent largely through a pervasive discourse that suggested lynching was a response to a black man's rape of a white woman. Even when rape was not an explicit accusation, people believed lynching was committed as retribution for a sexual attack. In other words, lynching was perpetuated through the rhetoric of protecting the purity of white womanhood.

In this series of images I explore the legacy of lynching for the white women in whose name lynching was performed. Working with photographs of lynchings, I have isolated actual white women and girls in the crowds. Reducing these figures to their minimal forms, I have made white silhouettes that recall the projections of nineteenth-century phantasmagorias, spectacles of light and shadow that created ghostly apparitions. The series plays upon and inverts the registers of black and white so powerfully set forth in Kara Walker's silhouettes, and engages in a visual dialogue about white women and lynching elicited by Kerry James Marshall's *Heirlooms and Accessories* (2002). Ultimately, I am interested in the ways white womanhood haunts lynching, and also in the ways in which white women must, in turn, be haunted by the horrors performed in their name.

৫৯

Five images, archival ink prints, 14 × 11 inches. The images from the In the Crowd *series appear throughout the collection, one at the head of each section.*

11

In the Crowd series, Untitled #1 (Indiana, 1930). Archival ink print, 14 × 11 inches. Image courtesy of the artist, Shawn Michelle Smith.

Section I

The Aesthetic Challenges
of Jim Crow Politics

Elizabeth Abel's piece appears at the beginning of this collection because it illustrates the kinds of theoretical approaches that allow us to think about an aesthetics of segregation across periods and historical or political contexts. She focuses on the persistent and curious ways that Jim Crow signs and related memorabilia and images pop up in contemporary U.S. culture, from antique collectors of mammies to anti-immigrant acts of racism to Affirmative Action struggles that draw on Jim Crow iconography on both sides of the debate. Her visual studies approach to political and cultural representations of Jim Crow lead to concerns about memory, complicity, and resignification that are especially urgent in the literary realm, too. Abel alerts us to conscious strategies of representing segregation, even in seemingly inert historical objects, so that we see such items not as passive vessels or repositories of historical meaning, but as cultural texts that require our close attention to how, when, and where they mean. In this way, Abel's sign-makers, activists, and collectors provide a suggestive contrast to the literary figures in later sections who take up the challenge of representing Jim Crow and other kinds of race segregation for their own ends. The section ends with a "sound off" from Trudier Harris, who places scholarly work about segregation into its political context, especially in a post-civil rights era of what Harris prefers to call the project of "attempted desegregation."

American Graffiti

The Social Life of Segregation Signs

ELIZABETH ABEL

A streetcar conductor in a 1945 cartoon in the *Chicago Defender* points to a
sign declaring "FROM HERE BACK FOR nEGROES." Beneath the sign, a
Caucasian-featured woman protests: "... But I'm not! I got this tan out at
the beach" (Figure 1). Playing with case and color, the cartoon shifts attention

Figure 1. July 7, 1945. Courtesy *Chicago Defender*.

from the laws of race to their malleable surfaces. By pairing and mocking the arbitrariness of racial signifiers, graphic and somatic, the cartoon suggests that they both can be resignified, that there is some room for play.

I begin with this unorthodox perspective to propose that critical interest in representations *of* segregation should be complemented by attention to segregation *as* a representation that was consequently subject, as person-to-person interactions were not, to various strategies of back talk.[1] This goes against the grain in several ways. By attending to the letter of segregation's texts, I hope to challenge the assumption that segregation signs were merely transparent tools of a disciplinary technology that impressed racial distinctions on silent bodies. The cartoon offers a twist on a classic trope of African American letters, in which the inaugural encounter with a segregation sign is a defining moment of social inscription, a painful rite of passage that spells the fall into race. To learn to read the "colored" sign, in a scene whose variations are so frequent they have become, in James Forman's words, a "cliché of the black experience," is to learn that one has already been read by a law that writes its terms on a body forever after "branded and tagged and set apart from the rest of mankind upon the public highways, like an unclean thing" (Forman 20; Chesnutt 57). By shifting focus from the invisible and inaccessible source of the signs' authority to their visible and vulnerable bodies, composed like human bodies of multiple and mutable signifiers that don't cohere in a single definition, I hope (in the spirit of the cartoon) to rethink this foundational scenario in terms that allow greater space for agency.

Whereas narrative accounts of encounters with segregation signs have inclined with good reason toward allegory, post-civil rights reconstructions of those moments, also with compelling albeit different reasons, have produced another formulaic structure that constitutes a more persistent foil. The cutting force of signs restricting African Americans has been replaced, for example, at the entryway to the "Field to Factory" exhibit at the National Museum of American History by a pair of separate-but-equal doors that attempts to bring the experience of racialization home for contemporary Americans of all races. There is an almost audible gasp as visitors confront the implications of having to choose between the "White" and "Colored" gateways to the exhibit. The exhibition context may justify reproducing the fiction of racial symmetry, since who would be willing to stoop either literally (on the "Colored" side) or figuratively (on the "White" side) to walk through unequal doors? With less dramatic effect and more conventional purpose, however, other institutions of cultural memory have similarly relied on the symmetrical "White" and "Colored" binary as efficient shorthand for segregation. Juxtaposed in textbooks and political rhetoric as the sanitized and standardized terms of a safely settled history, the formula obscures not only the variation within segregation's textual history, but also the ways that history extends into the present.

The pervasive and tenacious web of segregation signage that stretched across much of the United States for three-quarters of a century constitutes one of American racism's most explicit and under-read texts. Rather than a self-enclosed historical phenomenon securely locked in a formulaic past, these signs serve as vehicles of new articulations in changing ideological contexts and contests. By tracking the social life of segregation signs *as signs*—that is as dense and cryptic nodes of meaning negotiated between producers and consumers—I seek to uncover some of segregation's changing textual body at key junctures across the twentieth century: the proliferation of signs in the century's early decades, their dismantling in the 1960s and 1970s, and their reproduction at the close of the century, when these tools of domination acquire both regressive and progressive functions vis-à-vis the racial politics of postmodernity.

Prioritizing the politics of representation always risks masking or evading the brute realities of subjugation. Without wanting to minimize these, I hope to call attention to a different dynamic that reorients the prevailing theoretical framework in recent accounts of segregation from the Foucauldian model of disciplinarity to the alternative model of consumption elaborated by Michel de Certeau, whose goal (in contradistinction to Foucault's) is "not to make clearer how the violence of order is transmuted into a disciplinary technology, but rather to bring to light the clandestine forms taken by the dispersed, tactical, and makeshift creativity of groups or individuals already caught in the nets of 'discipline.' Pushed to their ideal limits, these procedures and ruses of consumers compose the network of an antidiscipline" (xiv–xv). Certeau's account of consumption as "*another* production"—devious, dispersed, and often invisible "because it does not manifest itself through its own products, but rather through its *ways of using* the products" imposed by a dominant order—gives us a good handle on the tactics of those who diverted segregation signs from their original purposes (xii–xiii, emphasis in original). Once diverted, however, the signs were at risk of becoming simply diversions, as commercial producers, no less resourceful than Certeau's devious consumers. Inspired, perhaps, by some of the signs' tricks, these consumers devised new and profitable uses for middle-class consumption. If the ruses of consumers can comprise a "way of making," those of mass producers can enact and elicit ways of consuming that disturb Certeau's more cleanly divided turf. The complementary nets of discipline and antidiscipline are more intricately intertwined when the marketplace rescripts the social text of segregation signs.

Grace Elizabeth Hale offers a provocative account of this rescripting in *Making Whiteness: The Culture of Segregation in the South, 1890–1940* in which she traces the ways new commercial spaces in the growing towns and cities of the turn-of-the-century South complicated and compromised the rigid structures of segregation that were officially instantiated by Jim Crow signs. Through the development first of general stores and subsequently of towns whose merchants could not afford not to sell to the African Americans who constituted a significant percentage of their potential clientele, there emerged a "shared geography of consumption that belied any absolute racial difference." This "racial messiness of consumer culture" (Hale 186) undermined the authority of segregation signs that became "as much admissions of weakness as labels of power" (193): "Signs blared 'For Colored' and 'For White" on the very streets in which blacks and whites mingled," betraying "the weakness of their ordering claims" (196). My goal is to add a new twist to the unsettling effects of consumer culture by advancing the script to the late twentieth century, when segregation signs themselves enter into and are remade by the marketplace. Energized by consumer desire for a material record of a vanishing history, the marketplace has become an engine of reproductions and reinventions whose diversions can be read, alternatively, as resisting or repressing the burden of that history. Antidisciplinarity takes on greater ambiguity here, for what is weakened by the traffic in reproductions of the signs is not the disciplinary function of the originals, but rather the commemorative function of the copies as a record of that disciplinarity. This entanglements of production and consumption, discipline and antidiscipline, in the latter twentieth century pushes us to revisit the origins of segregation signs, which were created, discarded, and preserved—whether by complicity or agency—between and within divergent groups that took the words of segregation into their own hands.

American Graffiti

Beginning in the closing decades of the nineteenth century inside train cars and outside station doors, segregation signs—"more numerous than magnolia trees," in Gloria Wade-Gayles's wry formulation—quickly spread to courthouses, whorehouses, cemeteries, orphanages, hospitals, libraries, lavatories, eating places, theaters, elevators, laundries, parks, drinking fountains, windows, and then (keeping pace with technology) to telephone booths, vending machines, and airport waiting rooms not only across the South, but also more sporadically up and down both coasts and across much of the Midwest (Wade-Gayles 2). This was a social text inscribed by many hands across a spectrum of regional, class, and even racial positions. Through a variety of tonal and tangible inflections, the signage sought not only to command, but also to persuade, solicit, ingratiate, and humiliate. Whether jotted in faltering penmanship on scraps of paper tacked to private walls, carved in block capitals on the granite thresholds of public buildings, blazoned in neon lights above the entries to movie theaters, crafted in tiffany glass on art deco hotel windows, or commercially printed on framed paper, segregation signs gave race a graphic body that shaped the meaning of the written words.

This signage constituted a collective and flexible articulation whose dimensions were determined more by custom, taste, and convention than by statutory regulation. To the extent that ordinances specified any of their features, they concentrated on the signs' physical dimensions rather than their wording. A Maryland ordinance specifying that railroads must have segregation signs in each coach with "appropriate words, in plain letters, in some conspicuous place" is a characteristically vague formulation. More stringent specifications, such as a South Carolina ordinance requiring trolleys to bear illuminated signs reading "White" or "Colored" clearly visible for three hundred feet after sunset, were exceptional (Kennedy 184).

As a result, there was room for considerable variation, thereby creating a range of corporate and private interests in the field of segregation signs. At one pole was a template that spelled out the component features of the standardized signs commissioned by transportation and entertainment companies, business and merchant organizations, and government agencies. Here, the message stands on a tripod of authority: the name or logo of the commissioning organization, the name of the company that manufactured the sign, and the date or number of the relevant ordinance (Figure 2). The image of social space constructed by

Figure 2. Sample segregation signs.

these standardized signs achieved its ideal form in the restroom and drinking fountain signs that—like the parallel doorways that reiterate them—have become enduring icons of Jim Crow. More carefully balanced than the L & N restroom sign, the Montgomery drinking fountain sign, which was probably distributed to locations around the city, is designed to maximize symmetry. Its idealized representation was almost certainly divorced from the actual location and condition of the "fountain"—even the contraction of two fountains into one betrays this fictionalization—because the "colored" fountain was almost invariably inferior, smaller, lower, older, and as likely to be squeezed into a corner as to be placed next to the white fountain. The sign deploys the materiality of language—the printing and placement of the words—to create an imaginary space in which words supplant substance. Behind the state ordinance it cites by date, the sign implicitly draws a higher mandate for its racial map through a silent quotation of the separate but equal formula of the *Plessy* case.

Such standardized signs provided a conceptual frame for a broad range of individual and sometimes idiosyncratic utterances. The physical frame served as an index of an authorizing social frame, and no other feature of the signage was more significant or seductive. That the frame's symbolic value was widely recognized is suggested by the frequency with which private citizens painted one around the improvised signs they stenciled or scrawled on family stores. The further the verbal content strayed beyond the standard discursive boundaries, the more essential was the legitimating frame, which was especially salient in border states where segregation signs interpolated immigrant populations into the racial framework of Jim Crow. In an exceptionally offensive instance from a Florida café, for example, the sequence of addressees, designed to incorporate Puerto Ricans and Mexican Americans under the inaugural racial slur, is enclosed within an authorizing frame that is painted to appear three dimensional, as if it were a portable object attached to this wall, and thus by implication potentially to others (Figure 3). In a more comical example from a restaurant wall in San Antonio, by contrast, an incompletely painted frame is also insufficient to compensate for a grammatical error—"WE SERVE WHITES ONLY NO SPANISH OR MEXICANS"—that may betray the national origin or economic status of owners eager to proclaim their service to whites as a cover for vulnerabilities of their own. As this case indicates, the frame was a double-edged device that enticed private voices into public expression by offering to divest them of social liabilities that could not be fully purged.

The promise of a social frame was a heady incentive, however, especially for those whose status afforded little access to a public voice, but its effective use required mastering the conventions of public speech. The most obvious taboo was the personal signature, as a signed variant of a standard formula makes clear (Figure.4). This sign, posted on a tree standing sentry over a park, is given some weight by the substantial signboard, but the highly unprofessional,

Figure 3. SCEF Collection. Special Collections and Archives. William Russell Pullen Library Georgia State University Library.

Figure 4. Dorothy Sterling Papers. The Amistad Research Center, Tulane University, New Orleans, Louisiana.

almost childish inscription—uncertain penmanship, uneven lines, smudged paint, misspellings, lack of foresight in spacing—seriously compromises its authority. This poses the question of who—child, semi-literate, or even prankster—could have written it? Perhaps to circumvent that question, and to recuperate some lost authority, the sign is uncharacteristically dignified with a signature of sorts, but the name that is signed has the opposite effect: intentionally or not, the mode of inscription tilts the sign from amateurism to absurdity, and possibly to parody. Whether E.W. Grove is the name of a park commissioner or an area of the park (the east and west groves?), its inclusion creates the impression that the tree is speaking on its own behalf.

What the crudely made sign reveals, moreover, is that signatures could be inscribed in many ways. The anonymity of the signs' discursive form was countered by the individuality of the graphic form, which provided a handprint in the absence of a name. The body of the sign that was intended to replace its author's often betrayed that authorship. Individuals drawn to this mode of self-aggrandizement posed within the legitimating frame by which they were seduced. Consider, for example, the side wall of an outhouse in a field in North Carolina (Figure 5). The racial restriction here appears an exercise in absurdity: who would want to use this collapsing "tolit" whose tilt seems to suggest the precarious structure of white supremacy itself? The broadcasting of racial exclusivity seems transparently, almost pathetically, compensatory, and

Figure 5. "This tolit is for white onley," Harry Golden Papers, University of North Carolina at Charlotte Library.

self-implicating as racial entitlement attempts to remedy a class disadvantage that is visible in both the diction and the spelling.

Segregation signs thus have a unique place in the history of public signage. They share with their commercial counterparts the interrelation that David M. Henkin proposes between private interests and public language, but they work it in reverse. Henkin argues that as commercial signs in the course of the nineteenth century developed a uniform typography and style, they subsumed the competitive interests they served into the semblance of a "single, official voice" that contributed to the evolving perception of a coherent public space (Henkin 55). Segregation signage likewise fostered the impression of impersonal authority from which each individual instance benefited, but this putatively public discourse was inadvertently a vehicle of self disclosure. Because in contrast to commercial signage, nothing was being marketed, there was no shared stake in professionalization, no need to gain credibility in a field of competitive signs, and no immediate penalties for sloppy or casual expression. Whereas the commercial signage played a crucial role in developing the concept of the public sign, the racial signage that was defined as the voice of the public became both intentionally and unintentionally a mode of private expression.

Consequently, in a mode of production that was also a practice of consumption (adapting standard formulas to individual uses), a surprisingly broad cross section of the American public left its racial signature in this perversely democratic mode of articulation. Segregation signage elicited a spectrum of expression, from educated middle-class conservatives who believed in the neutrality of segregation laws, to rednecks, kooks, extremists, and individuals who for reasons of class or psychological disenfranchisement adapted the signage to their needs for self-expression. Before the aerosol can gave anyone the means and incentive to impress a private signature on a public place, segregation signage offered a frame for social writing that encouraged self expression from the fringes as well as the center. This licensing of hate speech had bitter, long-term costs. But in teasing racist attitudes out of hiding, the signage also gave visible form to the spectrum of discourse it encouraged and exposed, producing a trail of evidence. That is, an American graffiti.

Collecting and Consuming

Like more traditional forms of graffiti, this trail is evanescent. Gradually succumbing to the pressures of the civil rights movement, it disappeared in stages through the 1960s and 1970s (and even into the 1980s), sometimes sandblasted or painted over lightly to keep them legible, sometimes reinstated in less explicit versions (such as doors color-coded black or white that continued to mark entries after the signage was removed), sometimes partially dismantled but allowed to remain as broken but decipherable fragments. Some traces continue to linger: symmetrical holes drilled into the marble surface above drinking fountains in civic buildings; decentered or duplicate restroom facilities; and irrelevant and innocuous signage sporting messages, such as "Safety First" whose primary function appears to be occluding prior messages.

The language of the signs is harder to recover, however, except through the lens of the camera that has been a silent partner in this inquiry so far and must, given the constraints of space, unfortunately remain one. For the camera's intervention produced another, more complexly layered and comprehensive text, as the blatant inscription of race across the Southern landscape began in the 1930s to draw the attention of northern photographers whose selection, juxtaposition, and reframing of the signs translated a set of local practices into a national debate.[2] What concerns me here, however, is the tenuous—and repeatedly reinvented—legacy of the physical signs. Typically produced on perishable materials (paper and cardboard more often than metal, glass, or wood), most rapidly deteriorated after they were finally taken down, as the radical southern writer Stetson Kennedy poignantly describes: "I raced around to dumpsters collecting discarded 'White' and 'Colored' signs, thinking they would be of some interest to posterity in a Museum of Horrors. Alas, I stored them under my house, where termites got them, which may be just as well" (Kennedy 234).

As a Southern white, Kennedy was unusual and perhaps unusually careless in his habits. Although his experience undoubtedly speaks for that of countless other ambivalent sign retrievers, in conjunction with that of the intentional sign destroyers who, whether out of anger, bitterness, triumph, or shame, worked to make these hateful reminders disappear, there were some determined and deliberate collectors and preservers. We owe the preservation of the few surviving original signs almost entirely to the courage and foresight of the generation of African Americans who came of age during the civil rights movement and who realized, as an end to the Jim Crow era began to be imaginable, that the signs would become important evidence. Acquiring these signs in the final years of their reign was a form of activism: risking jail to lift them surreptitiously from buses under cover of evening; pilfering them from those hotels or restaurants to which African Americans gained access as employees; snatching them from trash cans after they were taken down by law; or returning to abandoned buildings, gutted by natural disasters, to detach them from walls still reeking of smoke.[3] Those with less audacity but equal foresight scoured flea markets and yard sales for the signs that others had collected, stored in attics, and eventually discarded. By retrieving the tools of their own domination, these activist collectors—Certeau-style consumers—worked a reversal: turn the artifacts around to bear witness against their producers.

This reversal is well named by Whoopi Goldberg, who has mounted her collection of black memorabilia on what she calls her "Wall of Shame." In a calculated shift of context, she and other African American collectors reappropriate segregation signs and other artifacts of discrimination as a burden of proof against their producers. Repossessed, the signs now speak as symptoms; instead of imprinting the bodies they address, they fingerprint the bodies they express. In new hands, these artifacts become, in Julian Bond's words, "sentinels guarding the past, doorkeepers who prevent our ever returning to it. . . . They are our common past; silently, they face the future. They have lost the power to define my world; they have taken on the power to create a new one" (Bond 1996, vii, ix).

As one of the early and most eloquent activist collectors, Bond has become the foremost spokesman for the value of repossessing Jim Crow memorabilia as a resistant and revisionist practice of consuming. This position runs counter to that of cultural critics such as Gerald Early and Lynn Casmier-Paz, who decry what they consider a "bourgeois investment pastime" that mimics the habits of the white middle class; they question the extent to which racist objects can be successfully wrenched from their original contexts (Early 161; Casmier-Paz 43–61; Bond 2003). The distinction hinges both on the signs and on the conditions of their display. The originals that activists salvaged have become extremely rare, their value enhanced by the transgressive acts embedded in their ownership. So what kinds of political statements are available to those who purchase rather than pilfer the signs, who engage in the traditional consumer practices whose potential to transform consumption into production may be, as Susan Stewart argues about middle-class collecting generally, more wishful thinking than reality (158–60)?

The issue is complicated by the fact that the scarcity of the originals has inflated their cost—as high as $2,000 when their provenance is known, which is more than most slave documents—compounding unavailability with unaffordability for all but the wealthiest collectors, a market increasingly dominated by celebrities (not only Whoopi Goldberg, but also Bill and Camille Cosby, Cicely Tyson, Oprah Winfrey, Alan Page, Anita Baker, Sammy Davis Jr., Spike Lee, Anita Pointer, and Juanita Jordan).[4] Because these collections are not open to the public, we have to turn to more modest and accessible exhibits in order to assess the acts of juxtaposition and reframing that might elevate consuming into a *poiesis* (Certeau xii).

For a frame of reference, we could start with ground zero of consumerism: the white-authored catalogues designed to market black memorabilia to white buyers.[5] Jan Lindenberger's *Black Memorabilia Around the House* offers a particularly blatant case of a characteristic tendency to marginalize segregation signs in the general inventory and to recast them as domestic kitsch. One page of the catalogue, for example, displays a decorative pair of 1940s signs for "COLORED MEN" and "COLORED WOMEN" (strategically eliminating the counterparts for whites) as if they were a tribute instead of an affront. Placed above a pair of mammy and butler candles, the signs construct the couple of color as happy household servants presiding over an entourage of little black children in the form of candles, candy dishes, and Christmas tree ornaments. This is a plantation fantasy sufficiently expansive to include a badge of membership in the Ku Klux Klan and a pricey statue of a wizard (his arm detachable to facilitate transportation.)

Against this backdrop of domestication, we can see the organizing principles of a wall of shame across town from Whoopi Goldberg's: the personal collection of Bryan Breyé, which he calls the "Museum in Black." On Breyé's wall, as on the catalogue page, segregation signs are spliced with advertisements for household products, but in a way that draws attention to the power relations that frame the production of domestic iconography (Figure 6). By foregrounding a rod contrived to hold a grinning hobo dangling in the air, the arrangement alludes to a lynching that transforms the grin of the happy servants—splashed across the wall in virtually every ad—into a grimace. Coercion becomes more explicit in the African-American Panoramic Experience museum, dedicated to the history of black Atlanta, which places the signs in the framework of terror: sole items in an expressionistic setting whose painted patterns and shades of black, white, and gray evoke blood-dripping walls for which the signs, hung beneath gun-like metal rods, appear responsible.

Museum walls and consumer catalogues share some common ground, however: both rely on reproductions. Whereas activists from the 1960s and celebrities from the 1990s could gain access to the scarce originals, albeit

Figure 6. Wall from Museum in Black, Los Angeles. Photograph by author.

through divergent channels of consumption, the great majority of collectors and collections, including such august institutions as the Birmingham Civil Rights Institute, must resort to copies.[6] Sometimes meticulously derived from archival photographs, these copies are more often drawn from a supply of inexpensive reproductions that typically sell for fifteen to twenty-five dollars apiece and are produced by a new industry that has emerged to meet recent consumer interest. Although concerns about legislative and social pressure against the dissemination of racist materials have shrouded this industry in secrecy, its products are readily available at memorabilia and secondhand stores in urban black communities, where inexpensive copies of segregation signs share shelf space with movie posters, baseball cards, old copies of *Ebony*, and local bus and movie schedules. Dispensed by ordinary citizens turned street educators, these stores, often located in the heart of the ghetto, function as improvised museums and alternative history centers, repositories of knowledge both arcane and mundane, meeting places, resource centers and communities of memory. The signs educate whether they remain in the stores or travel to private homes or public museums or academic articles such as this one, whose opening examples were scans of reproductions.[7]

With ready access to inexpensive reproductions, we enter slippery political terrain. On the one hand, we must acknowledge that the historical record is being attenuated and, in the worst cases, fabricated by mass-produced and often careless reproductions that tend to recirculate the standardized formulas that are easiest to replicate, and that sometimes sport misspellings and fictional dates—or none.[8] On the other hand, the purchasing power of consumers who are segregation's victims or their descendents has helped to shape this record to express their own concerns. Against the most predictable formulas, they have used the power of the purse to assert a preference for signs that are so extreme they are easy to reappropriate. Hence, it is not the black-owned Lenox Theater's politically courageous but rhetorically tame "FOR COLORED ONLY NO WHITES ALLOWED" sign that is in most demand, but the Lonestar Restaurant Association's outrageous "NO DOGS NEGROES MEXICANS" sign whose popularity has generated multiple versions with diminishing degrees of historical specificity (Figure 7). This sign is the hands-down favorite at Nightmares and Notions in Oakland, California, where young African American and Chicano men buy it to display in their pick-up trucks; so, too, a framed copy hangs on the wall of the director's office at the Museum of African American Life and Culture in Dallas because, in his view, "these things send a message, and the more repulsive, the louder the message."[9]

The Lonestar Restaurant Association sign crystallizes the question posed by the shift from the heroic age of collecting in the 1960s and 1970s to an era of postmodern simulacra in which consumption may devolve into an empty form of play: if contemporary consumers and producers are renegotiating segregation's texts, are there or should there be any constraints?

Figure 7. Three versions of Lonestar Restaurant Association sign.

Pastiche and Politics

A good site to begin to track these negotiations is one of the most successful, controversial, and well documented of the new memorabilia stores: Martha's Crib, an Afrocentric art, crafts, and memorabilia store that opened in 1994 in Matteson, Illinois, a predominantly African American community south of Chicago, and subsequently moved to a tonier mall in Country Club Hills, where it remained until 2005. Initially uncertain whether segregation signs would be too painful to include in her inventory, its owner Marchel'le Renise Barber polled her regular clientele. Almost everyone urged her to make the signs available and asked to be placed on a waiting list to ensure that they would be among the first to purchase them. Because not only the originals but also *copies* of the signs were in short supply, Barber expanded her merchandise by designing her own line: the Martha's Crib Jim Crow Sign Series.

Barber, whose goal is to keep alive the pain of the past for a generation that has "no sense of history and no sense of hurt," initially planned to reproduce only one or two of the "less offensive" signs. Her plan changed when one of her African American customers insisted that he wanted to buy a "WHITE ONLY" sign in order "to hang it in his house outside his bathroom so his teenage son might be able to relate to the experience of needing to go to the bathroom—but not having anyplace he could go." That forged Barber's determination to "go all the way": not only to include the sign in her Jim Crow Sign Series, but also to hang it over the bathroom of her own condominium (Jenkins 43; Lenoir 5). In this historical reinscription, the dominant culture's imprinting of the "Colored" sign on the African American body is now administered by a "White" sign in the hands of African American consumers seeking to impress an endangered dimension of their racial heritage on the nerves and flesh of a younger generation.

This weighty, verging on sadomasochistic, method of transcribing history is at odds with its instrument, however, for the "WHITE ONLY" sign that Barber designed to meet the demand of her customers is, like the rest of her series, openly a fake. Deploring the unscrupulous practices of antique dealers who attempt to pass copies off as originals, Barber conscientiously marks her own signs as reproductions. Although she meticulously imitates the lettering, shapes, colors, and borders of originals, she stamps her versions "Historical Reproduction" and sells them at the bargain rate of ten dollars a piece. She also stamps them with the name of the store, the copyright symbol and date (Figure 8). Her signature has replaced

Figure 8. Two signs from Martha's Crib Jim Crow Sign series.

that of the companies that commissioned and produced the originals: it is not the white sign producers that sign—and profit from—the copies of their signs, but their African American reproducer. As white historical production becomes black historical reproduction, the date of the ordinance on the originals is displaced by the date of the copyright. Ownership has changed hands, but what exactly is now owned? It is not the original object or language, but the copy that is copyrighted, reserving to Martha's Crib the exclusive right to continue to make copies. The copy, apparently, is an original, a form of intellectual property, whose originality resides in its conception and execution as a copy. As a copyrighted copy, however, it makes a different claim on its owners. As the ordinance that stamped the signs with public authority is replaced by the copyright that stamps them private property, the signature of the producer is severed from the social body and the sign that was produced to keep alive an experience of the body takes the disembodied form of a commodity. A "retailer of revolution" is Barber's chosen moniker. Bringing the burden of the past to bear on the vision of the future is, she explains, a way of "affecting change" (Jenkins 43). Perhaps some unconscious recognition of the effect of retailing on revolution finds expression in the slip of the tongue: affecting change may be the effect of marketing reproductions.

If the text of segregation is only being lightly traced on the body of future generations despite the best intentions and collaborative efforts of African American producers and consumers, a more serious problem exists in the mass marketplace that also attempts to engage and shape consumer desire by placing new versions of segregation signs into general circulation. Whereas Barber has tried to monitor the uses of her own products by refusing to take phone or e-mail orders in order to ground the traffic in signs in face-to-face encounters, other reproductions travel outside any determinate political frame and are as readily available for purchase in redneck stores as in the African American marketplace. The "WHITE ONLY" sign demanded by Barber's customers is as avidly sought after by white racists to display over *their* bathrooms, swimming pools, and recreation rooms to keep the memory of entitlement alive. Inexpensive copies are for sale not only in such high-profile stores as the Redneck Shop of the Ku Klux Klan Museum, but also in the garden-variety country stores that are a feature of backwoods communities such as Skullbone, Tennessee, whose inhabitants can undoubtedly find them alongside the "Equal Rights for Whites" T-shirts, Confederate flags, and Ku Klux Klan crosses that are so popular there (Strauss 19).

The industry in simulacra serves opposing camps in opposing ways, but at least the political intentions of these opposing camps are clear. In the open marketplace, however, where profit attaches to invention, and production and consumption are politically unconstrained, segregation's charged and concise formulas have become a catalyst and frame for other forms of signifying play. The more extreme the invention, the more it lends itself to reappropriation—which also runs in both directions, as the display of racial entitlement is parodically inverted, and then inverted back again. No sooner did a sign declaring:

PARKING FOR
AFRICAN
AMERICANS
ONLY
ALL OTHERS
WILL BE TOWED
city ord 1082

appear on the market, complete with a fictional ordinance number that mimics the conventions of segregation signs, than copies of the copy sprang up to vaunt the rights of other minority, but hardly parallel, groups. Alamo Flags Company produced variations on the template for (among many others) Greeks, Norwegians, Irish, Italians, Australians, Armenians, Serbians, Danes, and Swiss. Printed as much as possible in the colors of the national flag, the model has been deflected from racial to national groups that, however small their numbers in this country, could hardly be construed as oppressed. Indeed, the list has been constructed to occlude culturally sensitive racial/ethnic categories. There is a "PARKING FOR MEXI-CANS ONLY," but none for Chicanos; a "PARKING FOR CHINESE ONLY," but none for Asian Americans; a "PARKING FOR PERUVIANS ONLY," but none for Latinos; and no acknowledgment that Jews drive cars at all.[10] The sign for African Americans that generated the others designates the only racial category (and conversely no African nationalities are named). As soon as the parodic inversion was in place, it was translated into less volatile forms. Other features of the signs changed accordingly: as segregation ordinances became parking authorizations, their numbers evolved from the plausible 1082 on the African American sign to the fanciful 0007 on the Italian sign, a seeming allusion to James Bond, a superhero powerful enough to commandeer that most prized urban possession: a personal parking space. In the transition from the heroic collecting practices of the generation of Julian Bond to the magical prowess of James Bond, signs are uncoupled from history, and bodies from identity. As racial difference is diluted into national origin and the struggle over social space devolves to the parking lot, the only bodies that matter are the mobile mechanical ones stationed under the sign of nationality—and only when it offers an advantage. Lost in the translation to postmodernity is any recollection that segregation signs were designed to secure racial difference by attaching it to referents in the physical and social body.

This mobility of reference marks an outer limit at which the text of segregation is unmoored from political ground. The uncoupling is overdetermined. The proliferation of signs and the evacuation of meaning on the marketplace are supported by a political climate that proclaims itself "postracial." As the discourse of color blindness launched by Justice Harlan's ringing dissent in the *Plessy* case and reprised by the movement for civil rights has been co-opted by right-wing politicians to justify the dismantling of social programs, the argument that race is a social construction has been exploited to discredit its claims. The political mantra of color blindness, or what Ian Haney Lopez calls "color-blind White dominance," now signals not the critique of segregation but indifference to its legacy, a pretense not to notice race as a pretext for discounting the causes and consequences of racial stratification (Lopez xviii). It is an environment that has encouraged the trivialization of segregation signs, but has also galvanized a new redeployment.

In a pointed challenge to the myth of color blindness, segregation signs are beginning to appear to dramatize the rolling back of the affirmative action policies that had been implemented to redress segregation's effects. In this context, the signs signal both that racial distinctions have *not* vanished from a social order that has prematurely declared their passing; *and* that the dismantling of social programs designed to equalize opportunity will have the effect of reinstating the conditions of segregation. The signs operate negatively as monitory images of what must not return and also positively as indicators of what endures and therefore functions as a goad to change. In this latest turn, these regressive signs are put to the progressive use of puncturing the fiction that color blindness describes a present reality rather than a future goal.

This use has been especially visible in California, which has the dubious distinction of being the first state to pass a proposition barring affirmative action from university admissions and state hiring procedures. Students at the University of California at Berkeley (as well as at other campuses) demonstrated repeatedly against Proposition 209, and on at least two occasions specifically and effectively deployed segregation signs in ways that recall and reject the separate but equal formula that has enjoyed a cultural afterlife as a mnemonic aid. In the more dramatic instance, triggered by the Supreme Court's refusal to review the proposition's constitutionality, Students Against 209 blockaded Sather Gate, the main entry to the campus, forcing everyone to enter through a side gate over which a "WHITE MEN ONLY" sign had been hung in order to demonstrate how the proposition will "narrow the door" for those seeking access to the university (Lou 1). Jesse Ehrman, a *Daily Cal* photographer, shot the scene at a moment that suggests that women of color are reluctantly exiting the campus as white men enter (Figure 9). As this scenario revisits the structure of parallel gateways to propose that there was only ever really one, an earlier image revisits the scenario of parallel drinking fountains to exploit the asymmetry behind its public face. A poster protesting the decision of the University of California Regents that was the precursor to Proposition 209 inserts into one corner a photograph by Danny Lyon of segregated fountains in a courthouse in Albany, Georgia, in 1962. The choice of photographs is telling: in contrast to more familiar images of more nearly symmetrical fountains that

Figure 9. Students Against 209, Berkeley, California, November 7, 1997. Photograph by Jesse Ehrman.

might conceivably be brought into line with segregation's separate-but-equal formula, Lyon (who was deputized to take the photo by James Forman, executive secretary of the Student Nonviolent Coordinating Committee, which on the other side of town was converting Albany into a center of social revolution) documents a travesty of justice that is so entrenched as a piece of legal furniture that the entire system would have to be dismantled to enable change. Imported into the poster, the photograph serves both as a reminder of the past into which the present threatens to devolve, and, provocatively tilted at an angle, as a reinforcement of the poster's call to action.

These students offer a model for reinscribing segregation's text in ways that acknowledge its history. They engage in what John L. Jackson Jr. calls a "post-postracial" practice that contests the end of race, however much that outcome is devoutly desired. Race won't simply die, he says, attack it as we may; it is more productive to uncover and rework, rather than deny, the ways that "racial Americana," those racially invested social relations and representations that are deeply interwoven in the fabric of national life, refuse to go away (Jackson 396–402). Segregation signs are prime examples of racial Americana. Having survived a century of refashioning in the hands of divergent producers and consumers, they don't seem ready to be discarded or enclosed in a museum. Instead, they have a social life that continues to propel them through changing scripts. Appalling and energizing, outrageous and absurd, they remind us that segregation was staged through representations that are still being written and still need to be read.

Notes

1. Those who pushed back, overtly and covertly, against the Jim Crow regime of course displayed agency in numerous ways. For an analysis of these resistant practices, see Kelley. For some firsthand accounts, see Chafe, Gavins, and Korstad.

2. For a discussion of the photographs, see the book from which this essay is drawn, *Signs of the Times: The Visual Politics of Jim Crow* (forthcoming from the University of California Press).

3. My understanding of African American collecting draws from my conversations with the following collectors, to whom I am very grateful: James Allen, Marchel'le Renise Barber, Brian Breyé, Thomas C. Bridge, LaCheryl B. Cillie, Janette Falkner, Rose Fontanella, Mildred Franklin, Sallie Hurt, Virgil J. Mayberry, Chuck McDew, Phillip Merrill, David Pilgrim, and Dan Williams.

4. Out of the thousands of artifacts Phillip Merrill has collected over many years, only one is a Jim Crow sign (P. Merril, pers. comm., 23 June 1997). James Allen, whose persistence and skill in uncovering relics of the racist past captured national attention through his display of lynching postcards, owns only two Jim Crow signs despite years of searching (J. Allen, pers. comm., 4 June 1998). Skip Mason, director of Digging It Up, an African American Research and Consulting Firm in Atlanta, has no Jim Crow signs that are, in his words, "extremely hard to come by" and prohibitively expensive (S. Mason, pers. comm., 4 June 1998). Dusty Rose, who advertises "All Types of Collectible Black Americana For Sale" in her Brooklyn shop, confirms that no original signs have been on the market for a long time (D. Rose, pers. comm., 12 June 1998). Slave papers are rarely more than $1,000 in the Black Americana Price Guide and often considerably less.

5. These catalogues reflect the traditional dominance of white collectors in the field of black memorabilia. In the past two decades, however, the balance has shifted dramatically. According to Jeanette Carson, founder of the Black Memorabilia Collectors Association, fifty to seventy percent of the collectors of black memorabilia are now African Americans, as opposed to thirty percent a decade ago. Carol Hernandez, "Black Memorabilia Finds Big Demand," *The Wall Street Journal* 1996; telephone conversation with Mrs. Mildred Franklin, current president of the Black Memorabilia Collectors Association, December 16, 1997.

6. Florence Davis-Wilson, director of public relations at the Birmingham Civil Rights Institute (F. Davis-Wilson, pers. comm., 17 July 1997). The Black Memorabilia Collectors Association, reluctant to lend its rare originals out for display, commissions

copies for its educational exhibits, according to Mildred Franklin (M. Franklin, pers. comm., 16 December 1997).

7. Some of the stores I have been fortunate to visit are Dan Williams' Nightmares and Notions in Oakland, California; Glenda R. Taylor and Mary Taylor's Aunt Meriam's in Harlem, New York; and Marchel'le Barber's Martha's Crib in Matteson, Illinois. I have also communicated at length with Virgil Mayberry of V.J.M. Unlimited, Inc. in Rock Island, Illinois. I have been unable so far to penetrate the mystery of the reproduction industry, which is also protected by dealers who don't want to reveal their sources to potential competitors. The consensus, however, is that it is run by whites and is probably located abroad, as are the production centers of other kinds of black memorabilia, many of which are based in Japan, Germany, China, England, France, Australia, and parts of Africa, according to P.J. Gibbs in *Black Collectibles Sold in America* (Paducah, KY: Collector Books, 1987).

8. The dangers of fabrication are presented by Richard Jensen about a related case in "'No Irish Need Apply."

9. Based on a conversation with Dan Williams, owner of Nightmares and Notions (January 13, 1998). Carol Hernandez in "Black Memorabilia Finds Big Demand," *The Wall Street Journal*, cites the museum director's claim. David Pilgrim, founder of the Jim Crow Museum of Racist Memorabilia at Ferris State University in Big Rapids, Michigan, comments: "Not surprisingly, signs that have obvious derogatory racist words are the most expensive" (D. Pilgrim, pers. comm., 27 February 2003). "The most offensive" is the criterion used by Marchel'le Barber, owner of Martha's Crib, for choosing signs to stock in her store (M. Barber, pers. comm., 3 March 2001).

10. As of the most recent check, Alamo Flags (http://www.flagline.com) has dropped the Parking for African Americans sign and lists among its offerings only "Country Parking Signs." There are still no African nationalities on its list.

Works Cited

Bond, Julian. "Collecting Black Americana," *Black Americana Price Guide*, ed. Kyle Husfloen. Dubuque, IA: Antique Trader Publications, 1996. vi–ix.

———. "Julian Bond Responds." *Southern Cultures* 9.1 (2003): 62.

Casmier-Paz, Lynn. "Heritage, not Hate? Collecting Black Memorabilia." *Southern Cultures* 9.1 (2003): 43–61.

Chafe, William H., Raymond Gavins, Robert Korstad, eds. *Remembering Jim Crow: African Americans Tell about Life in the Segregated South*. New York: The New Press, in association with Lyndhurst Books of the Center for Documentary Studies of Duke University, 2001.

Chesnutt, Charles W. *The Marrow of Tradition*. 1901. Ann Arbor: U of Michigan P, 1969.

De Certeau, Michel. *The Practice of Everyday Life*. Trans. Steven Rendall. Berkeley: U of California P, 1984.

Early, Gerald. "Collecting 'The Artificial Nigger': Race and American Material Culture." *The Culture of Bruising: Essays on Prizefighting, Literature, and Modern American Culture*. Hopewell, NJ: Ecco Press, 1994. 155–62.

Forman, James. *The Making of Black Revolutionaries.* Washington, DC: Open Hand Publishing, 1985.

Gibbs, P.J. *Black Collectibles Sold in America.* Paducah, KY: Collector Books, 1987.

Hale, Grace Elizabeth. *Making Whiteness: The Culture of Segregation in the South, 1890–1940.* New York: Pantheon, 1998.

Henkin, David M. *City Reading: Written Words and Public Spaces in Antebellum New York.* New York: Columbia UP, 1998.

Hernandez, Carol. "Black Memorabilia Find Big Demand." *The Wall Street Journal* 10 Aug. 1996: B1.

Jackson, John L., Jr. "A Little Black Magic." *Racial Americana,* a special issue of *The South Atlantic Quarterly* 104.3 (2005): 3, 394–402.

Jenkins, Maureen. "Crafting a Positive Image: Store Owner Offers Lessons in History." *Chicago Sun Times* 19 Dec. 1997: 43.

Jensen, Richard. " 'No Irish Need Apply': A Myth of Victimization." *Journal of Social History* 32.2 (2002): 405–29.

Kelley, Robin D.G. *Race Rebels: Culture, Politics, and the Black Working Class.* New York: The Free Press, 1994.

Kennedy, Stetson. *The Jim Crow Guide to the U.S.A.* 1959. Boca Raton: Florida Atlantic UP, 1990.

Lenoir, Lisa. "At Home with . . . shop owner Marchel'le R. Barber." *Chicago Sun Times* 19 Dec. 1997: 5.

Lopez, Ian Haney. *White by Law: The Legal Construction of Race.* New York: New York UP, 1996; rpt 2000.

Lou, Linda. "Students Block Off Sather Gate in Anti-209 Protest." *The Daily Californian* 7 Nov. 1997: 1.

Stewart, Susan. *On Longing: Narratives of the Miniature, the Gigantic, the Souvenir, the Collection.* Durham, NC: Duke UP, 1993.

Strauss, Neil. "Concerts Rock the Tiny Kingdom of Skullbonia." *The New York Times* 1 June 2001: 19.

Wade-Gayles, Gloria. *Pushed Back to Strength: A Black Woman's Journey Home.* Boston: Beacon, 1993.

Smacked Upside the Head—Again

TRUDIER HARRIS

I recently viewed *July '64* (2006), a documentary by Carvin Eison about racial violence in Rochester, New York on July 24 and 25, 1964. It was the first time in history that the U.S. National Guard had to be called out for racial disturbances in a Northern city in the United States. In the midst of the heated desire—on each side—to spill blood, black and white citizens exhibited some of the traditionally expected responses that continue to guide interracial interactions. Black folks were sick and tired of being denied opportunity in a strikingly prosperous city; indeed, one black man with two years of college education had gone to Kodak, one of the major companies in the city, three days a week for six months without being hired. As far as whites were concerned, blacks could not manage to pull themselves up in the same ways that whites had. Whites were complacent in their image of prosperity and planning college educations for their children. As far as blacks were concerned, whites were directly responsible for their economic situations (landlords had slashed larger homes into several "efficiency apartments" and routinely hired blacks for janitorial work in most businesses). Blacks believed that whites considered them near-animals and were ready to exterminate them at the slightest provocation, which many blacks, especially youth, were willing to provide on those two very hot evenings in which dogs and fire hoses were standard weapons of the police.

Today, Rochester's formerly vibrant mixed wards, where most of the blacks lived in 1964, remain stagnant. A smaller percentage of blacks graduate from high school than in 1964, and home ownership among blacks is actually less than it was in 1964. As one commentator offered, the same three issues that plagued the community and led to the violence in 1964 were still the three major concerns in 2005, when Eison filmed that segment of his documentary. Those concerns are "health, education, jobs."

It is indeed a small historical circle that transforms seeming gains into losses, seeming advances into steps backward. The situation in Rochester, therefore, is emblematic of what I see as the consequences of attempted desegregation. I emphasize "attempted" because the reality never measured up to expectation, and I emphasize "desegregation" because this country has never been, nor do I ever expect it will be, truly, fully, irrevocably integrated. The circle that looped Rochester out of its stagnation briefly, gave it hope for a brighter future, and then dropped it back into the problems of 1964 is the same circle that controls just about every other city in America that tried, in the height of integrationist zeal, to transform itself into something beyond the color of black and white skins.

And there is no doubt that some progress was made. After all, we can tout statistics about African American CEOs and other business people, about blacks in government, science, education, and a host of other fields. However, black communities around the country are still teetering on the brink of destruction as a result of so-called integration. Sociologists have documented the pattern of the best and the brightest taking advantage of educational opportunities proffered by predominantly white colleges and universities eager to claim their space at the integrationist table, and they have similarly documented what the moving on of a select few has meant in terms of leaving black communities where kids no longer have intellectual and professional role models, where black businesses have been forced to shut down because black folks could now shop at the clean, well-lit stores in predominantly white neighborhoods. Then, of course, came Wal-Mart, and any hope of independent black business ventures pretty much went down the tubes, except for the traditional beauty and barber shops, funeral homes, greasy spoons, and an occasional print or garden shop.

Over time, schools have become re-segregated—with the full approval of many boards of education. Indeed, in my hometown of Tuscaloosa, Alabama, the chairperson of the Board of Education recommended early in 2007 that schools return to a "community-based" mode of operation. "Community-based" is now the catch phrase for re-segregation. In other words, the powers that be are saying, "We got tired of bussing black kids into white communities, especially when the white parents took their kids and put them into private academies. So-called integration of public schools has failed, so let's just go back to being the way we were before 1954." Of course, we must now surround "community-based" with the positive aura that "segregation" could never exude. We must think of "community-based" in the same way that we think of "urban villages," and my goodness, who could object to "urban villages"?

One of the most offensive consequences of desegregation, therefore, is that thousands of black schools throughout the South and elsewhere were made into middle schools or turned into administrative offices for their school districts, and some were even destroyed. The high school I attended in Tuscaloosa, and which was large enough to hold 1600 students when I attended, was literally demolished in late 2006 and early 2007. Institutions that meant so much to African Americans and that were sacrificed in the name of so-called integra- tion are now lost. In the short time it took for so-called integration to be seen as the faulty concept Zora Neale Hurston suggested that it was, almost three generations of black public school children have been damaged or lost. A part of that loss is the substantially reduced quality of teaching that has abounded over the past forty years. Teachers frightened of students or unable to maintain discipline in desegregated classrooms seem to have given up teaching more frequently than they have sought creative ways of reaching those whose minds they have held in their teaching plans—or lack thereof. In other instances, students taught during the so-called integrated years were oftentimes educated out of empathy with other blacks. Still others, who found so-called integration troubling at very personal levels, simply left school and swelled the ranks of those most mired in poverty and ignorance.

If, as Ralph Ellison suggested in *Invisible Man*, history is indeed a boomerang, merely keeping a helmet ready has not been sufficient to blunt the inevitable blow of a return to some of the most degraded forms of living in America. We all wanted, like Rita Dove's Beulah, "to taste change." We all wanted opportunity. However, we never imagined that our dreams, founded in such pristine expectations, would result in such unending nightmares.

Works Cited

Dove, Rita. "Sunday Greens." *Thomas and Beulah*. Pittsburgh: Carnegie Mellon UP, 1986. 69.

Eison, Carvin. *July '64*. DVD. ImageWordSound, 2006.

In the Crowd series, Untitled #2 (Florida, 1935). Archival ink print, 14 × 11 inches. Image courtesy of the artist, Shawn Michelle Smith.

Section II

Imagining and Subverting Jim Crow in Charles Chesnutt's Segregation Fiction

Charles Chesnutt, whose career spans the promises of Reconstruction to *de jure* segregation, stands as a key stem in a literary tradition associated with U.S. practices of segregation as he grapples with how to represent the arbitrary and newly bright line of Jim Crow segregation. To that end, this section offers an extended study of Chesnutt as a key figure, perhaps even a case study, in the creation of a segregation narrative tradition. The section comprises a trio of articles that together pose Chesnutt and his work as formative to a literary tradition associated with U.S. race segregation, especially as his artistic projects evolve to meet changing attitudes toward race relations in the transition from Reconstruction to Jim Crow.

These articles approach Chesnutt from three different angles: legal marriage and its legal ability to tie slavery to Reconstruction; racially motivated violence and its effects across the color line; and the creation of a culture of segregation in concert with the new legal realities of race relations in a post-Reconstruction era. Tess Chakkalakal examines the role of marriage in stories from Chesnutt's *The Wife of His Youth and Other Stories of the Color Line* (1899) in the context of scholarly conversations about slavery's legacy, domestic fiction, and historical understandings of marital legal arrangements. She finds that the relation between quasi-legal slave marriages and legal marriages during Reconstruction creates a conflict between post-Emancipation desires to break from the past and abolitionist desires to endow slaves—and now former slaves—with rights and dignity. Lori Robison and Eric Wolfe counter some scholarly assumptions about Chesnutt's creative arc by tracing aesthetic connection between Chesnutt's "The Dumb Witness" and that story's relation to some of his other key work in *The Conjure Tales* and *The Marrow of Tradition,* especially in the context of historical scholarship on Southern cultures of segregation. Birgit Brander Rasmussen follows with another reading of the same novel that delivers an original analysis of Chesnutt's relation to segregationist ideologies and the threat of racially motivated violence. Whereas lynching and other forms of racial terror are primarily directed at African Americans in a post-Reconstruction era, Rasmussen finds that in his fiction Chesnutt pushes against assumptions of *white* safety to show the moral consequences of white complicity in anti-black violence and disenfranchisement. Although these three articles each approach Chesnutt differently, they each tease out how Chesnutt rose to the new challenge of representing social and legal systems of segregation while depicting an African American culture worthy of literary attention.

Wedded to the Color Line

Charles Chesnutt's Stories of Segregation

TESS CHAKKALAKAL

Uncle Wellington, the title character of Charles Chesnutt's 1899 short story, "Uncle Wellington's Wives," must grapple with an unusual marital problem. It is a problem that is absent from most nineteenth-century fictions about marriage; and yet it was one that thousands belonging to, what Chesnutt calls, "the newly emancipated race" were forced to confront. Uncle Wellington learns from his local "colored lawyer" that Aunt Milly, the woman he had married " 'fo de wah" is not his "lawful wife." Although Aunt Milly may, as the lawyer explains to Uncle Wellington, be his wife in one sense of the word, she is not his wife from a legal standpoint. Without any legal ties binding him to Aunt Milly, Uncle Wellington is free to leave her and the relations he formed during slavery.

Along with the load of legal jargon the lawyer freely dispenses, he also advises Uncle Wellington not "to do anything of the kind, for you have a very good wife now." But Uncle Wellington does not heed the lawyer's advice. When Uncle Wellington learns that he is not bound legally to Aunt Milly he experiences "a feeling of unaccustomed lightness and freedom. He had not felt so free since the memorable day when he had first heard of the Emancipation Proclamation." But that feeling of freedom is soon curtailed by his efforts to cross the color line by marrying a white woman in the North. Uncle Wellington ultimately learns that although he is not legally married to Aunt Milly he is bound to her by a force more powerful than the legal rites of marriage. Their relationship is based on who they were *before* that memorable day of the Emancipation Proclamation.

"Uncle Wellington's Wives" is one of the nine stories in Chesnutt's *The Wife of His Youth and Other Stories of the Color Line*, all preoccupied with the role of marriage in the transition from slavery to freedom. For Chesnutt, the slave's investment in marriage becomes a substitute for the economic and political rights—wage labor, property ownership, and suffrage—typically associated with freedom. Unlike economic and political institutions, marriage promises the former slave an absolute and immediate entry into freedom. Of all the rights

slaves were denied, the inability to marry marked more than any other the
slave's experience.[1] By granting former slaves the privileges and protection of
marriage, they would be able to integrate and adapt fully into American civil
society. Former slaves, as the narrator of "Uncle Wellington's Wives" informs
us, had the choice to register marriages formed during slavery or leave them
behind in order to form new relations in freedom. Chesnutt's stories reveal
how this choice was limited by the commitment to race in the post-slavery
era. Chesnutt's stories narrate the ways in which marriage was used to preserve
relations formed in slavery thereby undermining the freedom promised by the
Emancipation Proclamation. Marriage, Chesnutt observed, was not just about
a commitment between a man and woman, it also signified the ongoing commitment to race after slavery, a commitment that we now understand as Jim
Crow segregation.

   The complex role marriage plays in Chesnutt's stories of the color line
confounds its readers. Engaged in the literary conventions of the marriage plot,
Chesnutt's characters find themselves trapped within a fiction of race that prevents them from achieving the happy endings typical of the marriage plot. The
tension between the conventions of race and marriage central to Chesnutt's plots
make his stories difficult to categorize. Read as "a fiction of manners" in which
characters are forced to confront color prejudices in their efforts to comply with
the rituals of courtship and marriage, Chesnutt's fiction dramatizes, as Nancy
Bentley recently explained, "the stakes of civil marriage in a post-slavery era"
(463). The didactic element found in much of Chesnutt's fiction sets it apart,
according to recent critics, from the school of American literary realism that
marks Chesnutt's contemporary era. Emphasizing the importance of the historical
conditions informing much of Chesnutt's fiction, critics have tended to focus
on his novel *The Marrow of Tradition,* which provides a fictional account of the
organized violence against black citizens living in Wilmington, North Carolina
in 1898. The romantic elements of Chesnutt's stories of the color line and his
first novel, *The House Behind the Cedars* (1900), have become mere sidebars to
the critique of race Chesnutt provides in his historical fiction. Critics in search
of historical truth have little interest in his fictional romances aimed at dissolving
the color line that prevents his characters from attaining the happily-ever-after
ending of the marriage plot. In Chesnutt's stories of the color line, a character's
belief in race conflicts with romantic conventions making it impossible for them
to end happily, with marriage. The narrative disruptions that marriage causes
breaks the unity conventionally associated with marriage revealing the principles
of the segregation plot that constitutes the most enduring aspect of Chesnutt's
oeuvre. In Chesnutt's segregation plot, marriage is regulated by racial principles
and prejudices that result in two separate but equal definitions of marriage.
Marriage is based on love and consent if you are white but on a commitment
to race if you are not. For this reason, Chesnutt's stories of the color line end

tragically, the happy endings associated with the conventional marriage plot always elude Chesnutt's protagonists.

The first, and most famous, of Chesnutt's stories of the color line is the title story, "The Wife of His Youth," which relates the effects of a slave marriage on the life of an individual committed to erasing his past slave experiences in order to make a future for himself in freedom. As a young man Mr. Ryder had fled North to escape slavery. After the Civil War, he rose to a position of eminence and leadership among the "light-colored" community and devoted himself to elevating the status of the community to which he so proudly belonged (*Wife* 2). In the course of the story, marriage becomes essential to Mr. Ryder's program for social elevation. His plan to "marry up" is interrupted by the appearance of a former slave who has spent twenty-five years in search of a man she had married during slavery. The slave's commitment to the marriage she formed within the bonds of slavery, Chesnutt's story suggests, is just as, if not more, powerful than the advancement promised by a legally sanctioned marriage in the midst of freedom.

The story's success lies in the tension surrounding the marital decision Mr. Ryder is forced to make. Mr. Ryder must choose between his past marriage with a former slave, Liza Jane, a woman who risked her own life to save his and a future marriage to the fair Mrs. Dixon, who embodies the qualities of the "Ideal Wife." The tension surrounding Mr. Ryder's decision has most often been read in terms of racial identity. The story's "central character," Charles Duncan explains, "must confront his own past in determining whether he can reconcile his urge to 'advance' his race with his family duty" (282). Like Uncle Wellington, Mr. Ryder's marital decision is thus read as an allegory for the "mulatto" subject who must choose between a black or white racial identity, realizing in the end that choosing to be black, by maintaining his commitment to his "slave-wife," is the right thing to do, even though it involves personal and economic sacrifice.

The foregoing allegorical reading of "The Wife of His Youth" is complicated, as Henry Wonham recently explains, by the "anti-race" position Chesnutt articulates elsewhere. Well-known nonfiction essays, such as "What is a White Man?" and the three-part series on "The Future American," evinces Chesnutt's belief that "amalgamation" of the races will bring an inevitable and desirable end to racial identification (831). Departing from the anti-amalgamationist or black separatist positions represented in the works of contemporary African American novels—those by Frank Webb, Frances Harper, and Sutton Griggs—Chesnutt understands amalgamation not just as a mixture of the races but as an end to the very idea of racial difference. Mr. Ryder's decision is nevertheless valorized by Chesnutt's readers today for maintaining the commitment to race.[2] Although Mr. Ryder does choose race over amalgamation, Chesnutt makes clear that it is a choice he is not free to make alone, and one with potentially disastrous consequences. Before deciding between Liza Jane and Mrs. Dixon, Mr. Ryder first asks members of the community what he should do: "And now, ladies and gentlemen, friends and companions, I ask you, what should he have done?" (*Wife* 23) Mr. Ryder's marital choice is presented in the form of a racial dilemma. To do what is right in the eyes of the community, he must choose Liza Jane, setting aside his personal desire to make a new life with Mrs. Dixon. Although the slave marriage lacks legal recognition it nonetheless is deemed preferable to the much-anticipated civil union between Mr. Ryder and Mrs. Dixon. The important role the community plays in determining Mr. Ryder's marital decision is, of course, inherent to the institution of marriage itself. "To *be* marriage," Nancy Cott explains, "the institution requires public affirmation" (1). But in this case, public affirmation is not just about silently witnessing a union. This community is granted the power of speech and, as a result, plays an active role in determining the outcome of Mr. Ryder's choice.

Mr. Ryder chooses Liza Jane out a sense of duty and honor, that is to say, he chooses to marry a woman he no longer loves because of his commitment to race. It is only after the community concedes that "he should have acknowledged her" that Mr. Ryder introduces Liza Jane as his wife (23). Although still lacking legal sanction the slave marriage is deemed to be the proper one because it has received the required public affirmation. The symbolic power of marriage, even for this color-conscious community committed to social advancement and integration, lies in its commitment to protecting the rights of the slave. "Exercising the civil right to marry," Claudia Tate writes, "was as important to the newly freed black population as exercising another civil right. . . . Negro suffrage" (103). But in "The Wife of His Youth," the parallel Tate draws between marriage and the slave's "rights" is presented as an obstacle to both individual freedom and social progress. In the end, Mr. Ryder has no choice but to sacrifice his future in order to give meaning to promises made "in de old days befo'de wah" (*Wife* 14).

Why did former slaves and government officials go to the trouble of registering marriages if, as Liza Jane tells Mr. Ryder, such legal recognition "would n make no diff'ence" to her bond "wid Sam" (15)? As historian Amy Dru Stanley explains, marriage was integral to, "the passage from slavery to contract." According to this view, marriage is no different from labor contracts that made slaves into free subjects; registering slave marriages thus protected the "sanctity of contract" (35). But here I would displace, or at least add to, the findings of historical analysis in order to address the sentiments and desires of the newly freed that Chesnutt's stories represent. Marriage in Chesnutt's fiction constitutes a distinct personal dilemma, one in which the future of race is at stake. Although historians typically view marriage as key to the transition from slavery to freedom, Chesnutt reveals it to be a technology of segregation, an aspect of segregation that goes well beyond designating racial divisions between public spaces; marriage, in Chesnutt's postslavery fiction, maintains the bonds of slavery.

When "The Wife of His Youth" was first published in the July 1898 issue of the *Atlantic Monthly*, it met with rave reviews from critics and readers alike. One reviewer summed up the story's virtues by exclaiming that it is "marvelously simple, touching and fascinating" (qtd. in Helen Chesnutt 98). After having experienced a series of blows to his efforts to publish literary fiction, the affirmative response to "The Wife of His Youth" came at a critical moment in Chesnutt's literary career. In a letter to his editor, Walter Hines Page, Chesnutt expressed the importance of the story in helping him to establish his credentials as an author: "I have been hearing from my story every day since its publication . . . I have had letters from my friends and notices in all the local papers . . . and taking it all in all, I have had a slight glimpse of what it means, I imagine, to be a successful author" (qtd. in Helen Chesnutt 98). Being a "successful author" was, for Chesnutt, a priority. "The Wife of His Youth" was published without any mention of Chesnutt's racial identity and so, for the first time in his life, he experienced the psychic and intellectual freedom of being a man without racial qualification.

But that freedom, as Chesnutt would soon realize, came with a cost. Without grasping the force of racial identity, the narrative logic of the story falls apart. For all the accolades heaped upon "The Wife of His Youth," Chesnutt was troubled by misreadings of it that undermined its message. "It is surprising," Chesnutt later writes to Page, "what a number of people do not seem to imagine that the old woman was entitled to any consideration whatever and yet I don't know that it is so astonishing either, in the light of history" (qtd. in Helen Chesnutt 102). Although Chesnutt's contemporary readers were surprised by Mr. Ryder's choice, more recent interpretations suggest the opposite response. Liza Jane has thus emerged as the story's heroine "for her *womanly* 'fidelity and devotion to those she loves' " (DuCille 16). In celebrating Liza Jane's fidelity, however, readers have opted to sentimentalize a story that goes to considerable lengths to remove such conventions from the form of its narrative.

"The Wife of His Youth," as in much of Chesnutt's fiction, presents history not just as a chronology of past events, but also as an unconscious desire to preserve the past by reproducing it in the present. In Chesnutt's terms, the affective dimension of history is more powerful than most of us imagine; it has the capacity to threaten progress and stifle growth. Based on Chesnutt's sense of history, his fiction is devoted to exposing the effects of history on determining, even limiting, the individual's future prospects. Ultimately, Chesnutt's stories narrate the ways in which the commitment to history makes it impossible to imagine a future without race.

It is perhaps not surprising that Chesnutt expressed his vision of the future in the form of nonfiction rather than fiction. In this mode, Chesnutt could

plainly present a program for the future without having to account for the effects
of history and the sentiments of characters susceptible to its pressures. Although
the majority of black Americans advocated marriage for its capacity to protect
and unite former slaves, Chesnutt presents marriage as a way of reorganizing
American society as a whole. In a series of essays published in 1900 for the
Boston Transcript, Chesnutt provides a "mechanical" (the opposite of sentimental)
solution to the race problem, one that radically revises the conventions of love
and consent that distinguish the institution of marriage (Chesnutt, *Stories* 849)
The revolution that Chesnutt's "Future American" essays outline is based upon
doing away with racial divisions by creating a single "American race" through
the reproductive potential of marriage:

> Taking the population as one-eighth Negro, this eighth, married
> to an equal number of whites, would give in the next generation
> a population of which one-fourth would be mulattoes. Mating
> these in turn with white persons, the next generation would be
> composed one-half of quadroons, or persons one-fourth Negro. In
> the third generation, applying the same rule, the entire population
> would be composed of octoroons, or persons only one-eighth Negro,
> who would probably call themselves white, if by this time there
> remained any particular advantage in being so considered. Thus in
> three generations the pure whites would be entirely eliminated and
> there would be no perceptible trace of the blacks left. (849)

What does this belief in numbers, in an arithmetic solution to the race problem,
signify? How will arithmetic present a viable alternative to "the vulgar theory of
race" (*Stories* 846)? By making marriage a matter of adding a certain number
of "Negroes" with an equal number of "whites," marriage constitutes a method
of dissolving racial distinction. By privileging numbers in his discussion of
marriage, Chesnutt systematically removes any mention of sentiment or affect.
Thus, one does not choose a martial partner based on mutual love, affection
or, most importantly, racial affiliation. Instead, the sole purpose of marriage is
to progress toward the future, a future in which race does not exist. Chesnutt
employs the word *race* in his theory of the future only in its "popular sense,"
conceding that the term holds no scientific meaning or truth-value. For Chesnutt, race is merely genealogical (a matter of who one's ancestors are) and it
can be made not to count by giving everyone the same ancestry. It is precisely
because race lacks any "real" meaning that Chesnutt believes it can "disappear"
through a series of marital arrangements. However desirable a future without
race may be, Chesnutt concedes that his theory "will never happen" (850).
Changing the hearts and minds of individuals who believe in racial difference,
and who believe, furthermore, that marriage should maintain such differences,

is ultimately easier said than done. "So ferocious is this sentiment against inter-marriage," Chesnutt laments, "that in a recent Missouri case, where a colored man ran away with and married a young white woman, the man was pursued by a 'posse' . . . and shot to death" (*Stories* 859). The laws restricting marriage to men and women of the same race are backed not only by courts, but also by a vigilante justice system that pays little attention to the logical solution to the race problem that Chesnutt's theory outlines.

Whether Chesnutt's readers denounce his vision of the future as a "theory [that] implicitly celebrates white skin" (Ferguson 109) or extol it "as a kind of utopian solution to a problem that seemed otherwise intractable" (Wilson 11), they all foreground "race" as the key component of the essay. But race is secondary to Chesnutt's theory; its first priority is imagining a future in which racial divisions have disappeared. To imagine this disappearance, Chesnutt's fiction demands that we first rethink the meaning of marriage. Marriage is about making a promise to the future, a promise that should affect a break with the past.

ಶ

The anti-racial act *par excellence* that emblematizes, in Chesnutt's fiction, both a future without race and the commitment to a racial past is the repetitive violation of the institution of marriage. Nowhere is this violation made more apparent than in the climax of what critics have called Chesnutt's major novel of segregation, *The Marrow of Tradition* (1901).[3] Detailing the events leading up to a violent race riot, Chesnutt's novel occupies a central position in the African American literary canon. The novel's importance for current concep-tions of the canon lies in its retelling of an infamous race riot that broke out in Wilmington, North Carolina in 1898.[4] The violence the novel represents is the consequence of the racial logic underlying the enactment of the "separate but equal" principle articulated by the Supreme Court in *Plessy v. Ferguson*. The novel depicts the progress of two families—the Cartarets and the Millers—one white, one black, who would be a single family if not for the "arbitrary" color line that divides them. *The Marrow of Tradition* imagines the color line as a fiction cooked up by a cabal of Southern white men, led by Major Cartaret, who find common cause in their perceived threat of "negro domination" (*Stories* 535). In stark contrast to the "fiction" of the color line is the "reality" of the marriage certificate. Interestingly, the fiction of the color line is associated with the novel's white male characters, whereas marriage is presented as the purview of women. It is through Cartaret's wife, Olivia, that the novel articulates its position on marriage and how the terms it establishes for intimacy are a vital supplement to the rhetoric of the color line.

The color line appears in full force in the novel's opening chapters, and helps to frame the introduction of the novel's chief black character and hero,

Dr. William Miller. Miller is distinguished not by the color of his skin, which happens to be "a light brown," but by the "health and prosperity" he embodies. We meet Miller on a south-bound train from Philadelphia where he notices the presence of a former friend and colleague, Dr. Burns, who is headed to North Carolina to perform an operation on Major Cartaret's only son. The chance meeting between the two doctors on the train leads to one of the most memorable scenes of racial segregation in literary fiction. The conversation between them is interrupted by the train's conductor who insists that they separate to comply with "the law of Virginia [that] does not permit colored passengers to ride in the white cars" (506). This scene dramatizes the circumstances that led to the Supreme Court's decision in *Plessy v. Ferguson*. As is well known, the plaintiff in the case, Homer Adolph Plessy, argued that the segregation laws prohibiting him from sitting in the "Whites Only" car of the train denied him his constitutional rights guaranteed by the thirteenth and fourteenth amendments. But the argument Miller makes against segregation is a slightly different one. When approached by the conductor, Miller insists that he has paid his fare on the sleeping car "where the separate-car law does not apply" (506). His ability to pay the proper fare, in other words, gives him the right to sit in the white car. But Miller's economic logic is easily refuted by the conductor's racial logic. "But this is a day coach," he responds, "and is distinctly marked 'White,' as you must have seen before you sat down here" (506). Of course Miller had seen the sign, but he "had hoped, on account of his friend's presence" that such an altercation "might be avoided" (506). Miller soon learns that a friendship between a white and black doctor is not enough to undo the laws of segregation: "It is the law, and we are powerless to resist it" (507).

In his failed attempts to continue his conversation with Miller, Dr. Burns repeatedly cites Miller's "rights" to remain in the white car. "You shall stay right here," he instructs Miller, then, turning to the conductor explains, "And my friend has his rights to maintain. . . . There is a vital principle at stake in the matter." Seeing that his invocation of rights and principles are no match for the law when the conductor dispassionately informs him that "the law gives me the right to remove him by force," Dr. Burns loses not just the argument but also his self-control. "This is a d___d outrage! You are curtailing the rights, not only of colored people, but of white men as well. I shall sit where I please!" (507) But Burns's blustery rhetoric of rights has little effect. The scene concludes without violence and a passive acceptance of the laws of segregation which prove too powerful for even a man of Burns's racial and class status to overcome: "Dr. Burns, finding resistance futile, at length acquiesced and made for Miller to pass him" (508). Segregation is a legal matter and yet has little to do with what is right. The language of rights Burns employs to persuade the conductor only frustrates him, leaving both men entirely at the mercy of the law. But this is only the beginning of the story. At the heart of the novel lies a secret history of a family romance that, when finally revealed through Cartaret's wife, Olivia, has the power to change the hearts and minds of those who believe that segregation is right.

Olivia finds herself in possession of her father's marriage certificate to a former slave whom he married after the death of her mother. This certificate renders the ideology of white supremacy that structures not only her life but also the lives of all those around her to be absolutely false. To deal with the shock of her discovery, Olivia destroys the marriage certificate. But the flames that consume the document do not diminish its meaning:

> As the day wore on, Mrs. Cartaret grew still less at ease. To herself marriage was a serious thing—to a right-thinking woman the most serious concern of life. A marriage certificate, rightfully procured, was scarcely less solemn, so far as it went, than the Bible itself. Her own she cherished as the apple of her eye. It was the evidence of her wifehood, the seal of her child's legitimacy, her patent of nobility—the token of her own and her child's claim to social place and consideration. (669)

Just as Dr. Burns invokes the rhetoric of rights to argue against Virginia law, Olivia sees herself as a "right-thinking woman" who understands marriage as a right that protects her white privilege. But the marriage between her white father and a former slave by the name of Julia Brown and their child, Janet Miller, undermines that privilege. To protect her "rights," she has no choice but to destroy the marriage certificate. While considering herself to be a "right-thinking woman," Olivia's actions reveal something about marriage that those who view it as essential to the slave's freedom consistently neglect to mention. Marriage sanctifies some couples at the expense of others and is selective legitimacy. "This," as Michael Warner reminds us, "is a necessary implication of the institution" (18).

The marriage certificate is like the Bible insofar as it is a document that has the power to convert or change the status of those it engages. But this marriage certificate has no legal effect. By destroying the certificate Olivia believes she has not only "removed all traces of her dead father's folly" but also protected him from being implicated in a crime. "The marriage of white and colored persons was forbidden by law. Only recently she had read of a case where both the parties to such a crime, a colored man and a white woman, had been sentenced to long terms in the penitentiary" (*Stories* 669). Olivia finds herself torn between legal and filial duties. The law, as her husband explains to her, would not recognize the union between her father and a former slave, even if the certificate had been preserved. Like the will he leaves behind recognizing the daughter of his union with a former slave as his legitimate heir, the certificate legally as well as morally has "no effect." Although the public meaning of marriage is foreclosed by Olivia's actions she has no control, Chesnutt makes clear, over its private meaning. "She had destroyed the marriage certificate," Chesnutt writes, "but its ghost still haunted her" (669).

Olivia's efforts to destroy or erase her father's marriage and the existence of her half-sister, Janet Miller, backfire terribly. The novel concludes with a confrontation between the sisters. Olivia begs forgiveness for her past sins and, finally, acknowledges her father's daughter as her sister. "Listen, sister!" she said, "I have a confession to make. You *are* my lawful sister. My father was married to your mother. You are entitled to his name, and to half his estate" (717). Although Olivia has no evidence but her word, Janet accepts "the recognition for which, all her life, she had longed in secret" (717). But that recognition does not change the meaning of Janet's life: "You imagined that the shame of being a negro swallowed up every other ignominy—and in your eyes, I am a negro (718). Olivia's words cannot undo her past actions for Janet's life has been formed entirely by her racial status to which she clings, finally, "imperiously" (718). In the end, Olivia and Janet both find themselves wedded to the color line by marriage. "Now, when an honest man has given me a name of which I can be proud, you offer me the one which you robbed me, and of which I can make no use" (718). In other words, the laws of segregation and marriage appear to be one and the same. Olivia initially refuses to recognize the union between her father and Janet's mother because she believes such a union to be against the law; she thus destroys their marriage certificate to protect her inheritance as her father's only legitimate heir. Acknowledging Janet as her sister would result in "a division of her father's estate" and "a scandal Mrs. Cartaret could not have endured" (671). Olivia only acknowledges her sister in order to "save her child [for that] she would shrink at no sacrifice" (717). By the time Olivia is forced to recognize Janet, however, the damage has already been done. The belief in the sanctity of marriage has ultimately bound both women, even more tightly than the laws of segregation separating men on trains, to their race.

The equality promised by the laws of segregation is, as Chesnutt demonstrates throughout his literary career, a promise that is repeatedly broken. That broken promise is the structuring principle of Chesnutt's "Stories of the Color Line." The difference between these stories and Chesnutt's first book of stories, *The Conjure Woman*, is often read as "an emblem of Chesnutt's divided sensibilities."[5] But such criticism fails to see that these stories present the "wrongs and sufferings of this past generation" as the subject of history rather than fiction. Fiction allows the author to invent a story, a way of presenting the world as it should be, rather than merely as it is.

Through fiction, Chesnutt reveals the terms by which racial intimacies develop between the teller and listener of a story. By revealing the structures of racial intimacy, Chesnutt's fiction wavers between maintaining the bonds of those intimacies and leaving them behind to pursue an uncertain future. In "The Wife of His Youth" the relation between Mr. Ryder and Liza Jane develops when he invites her to tell him her story. As she tells her story, Chesnutt provides bits of information about how it is being received by her listener. Liza Jane relates her story in a distinct vernacular voice that departs from the story by Tennyson Mr. Ryder "had just been reading." The formal differences between the two love stories affect Mr. Ryder in kind. While he experiences "an appreciative thrill" (9) reading Tennyson, he merely looks "curiously [at Liza Jane] when she finished" (14). Mr. Ryder seems not to know how to respond to her story, so far removed is he from the experiences she relates. As a result, he questions both the teller's authority and the facts she relates. "Do you really expect to find your husband? He may be dead long ago" (14). To which Liza Jane "shook her head emphatically" (15). Liza Jane's unequivocal responses to Mr. Ryder's questions and the hard evidence she provides to justify the claims she makes eventually diminish his disbelief and forces him to admire "such devotion and confidence [which] are rare even among women (20). Liza Jane's story produces a change in her listener that forces him to see himself in the image of the man Liza Jane has devoted her life to finding.

But Mr. Ryder does not become that man until he retells Liza Jane's story "in the same soft dialect" himself. Interestingly, when Mr. Ryder tells the story, "the company listened attentively and sympathetically," producing in his listeners an aesthetic response previously associated with Mr. Ryder's reading of Tennyson's poem:

> For the story awakened a responsive thrill in many hearts. There were some present who had seen, and others who had heard their father and grandfather tell the wrongs and suffering of this past generation, and all of them still felt, in their darker moments, the shadow hanging over them. (20)

The story Mr. Ryder tells is not exactly a love story, it is something deeper and "darker" that does not conclude with the happy marriage of the story's central male and female characters. This story is as much about the listeners as it is about the characters involved in the action, it is a story about how slavery makes them feel, how slavery experienced by their fathers and grandfathers controls the most intimate aspects of their lives.

In the ethical relation between teller and listener that the story develops, Mr. Ryder has no choice but to choose, in the useful formulation of Werner

Sollers, descent (acceptance of inherited categories based on race) over consent (choice of culture defined outside inherited ethnic or racial boundaries). "The Wife of His Youth" ends with Mr. Ryder's sense of honor intact but leaves readers wondering whether or not he has done the right thing. Was the old woman *really* entitled to such consideration, as the story's first readers complained? Or should Mr. Ryder have chosen Mrs. Dixon in order to affect his break with a past that he had long left behind? Should he be responsible for Liza Jane's deluded belief that the reunion of the former slaves will enable them to "be as happy in freedom as we wuz in de old days befo' de wah"? Or might it be impossible to be as happy in freedom as Liza Jane claims they were in slavery? In order to keep a promise he made during slavery, Mr. Ryder has no choice but to abandon his mission to dissolve the difference between black and white.

Just as in "The Wife of His Youth," the other stories of the color line dealing explicitly with marriage—"Her Virginia Mammy," "A Matter of Principle," "Cicely's Dream," "The Passing of Grandison" and "Uncle Wellington's Wives"— the commitment to the past forecloses the possibility of a future without race. "Her Virginia Mammy" introduces Clara Hohlfelder, the adopted daughter of German immigrants who withholds her response to a marriage proposal until she can determine her racial origins. Clara reasons that marrying without such knowledge has the potential to cause future harm to her lover. But John remains unconvinced by Clara's "tragic view of life" (*Wife* 32) John wants to marry Clara because she is "[t]he best and sweetest woman on earth, who [he] love[s] unspeakably" (32). But John's reason does not satisfy Clara. According to her, "the consciousness that [her origins were] not true would be always with me, poisoning my mind, and darkening my life and yours" (32). Playing with literal and figural meanings, Chesnutt suggests that the mere idea of origins, whether they are known or unknown, are tied to racial thinking, a way of thinking that is linked here to Clara's "tragic view of life."

Clara's resistance to marrying John is presented as a side effect of her sentimental nature, whereas John's desire to marry her is deemed rational and right. Their different natures are reflected in their chosen professions. Clara works as a dance instructor and John is a doctor. The views John presents are difficult to dispute not only because they are backed by science and reason but also because they undoubtedly represent those held by the author. "For the past we can claim no credit," John explains to Clara, "for those who made it die with it. Our destiny lies in the future." Clara cannot refute John's declaration. Instead, she merely sighs and agrees: "I know all that. But I am not like you. A woman is not like a man; she cannot lose herself in theories and generalizations" (33). And that is precisely Clara's problem. Clara cannot commit to a marriage based on love alone because of the force of a feminine nature that clings to the past. But when she tells her story to a particularly attentive listener, Clara finds herself released from her obsession with her unknown past by the power of fiction.

The sacrifice Mr. Ryder makes in "The Wife of His Youth," is reversed by the circumstances of "Her Virginia Mammy." Clara tells her story to a quiet old woman who, unknown to her, happens to be her birth mother. After hearing Clara's story, a resemblance between the two women becomes apparent. Clara misses not only the resemblance but even more obvious signs that establish a bond between the two women: "Mrs. Harper following her movements with a suppressed intensity of interest which Clara, had she not been absorbed in her own thoughts, could not have failed to observe" (50). Clara's failure to recognize Mrs. Harper as her mother turns out to save her marriage. Clara's self-absorption coupled with Mrs. Harper's rhetorical suppressions allows Clara to be happy. But Clara's happiness comes with a tremendous cost, to marry the right man she must forsake the mother who loves her.

Unlike Clara who is granted a fiction that will enable her to marry the man she loves, the female characters in "A Matter of Principle" and "Cicely's Dream" do not share her good fortune. In both cases, "the truth of origins" interrupts their marriage plots. "A Matter of Principle" introduces Mr. Cicero Clayton who sees himself as a man of principle, a man who believes—against all evidence to the contrary—"that he himself was not a negro" (94). Although Mr. Clayton is the story's main character, the story is not about him. The story is actually about his daughter, Alice, and the effect of her father's racial principle on her marital prospects. Although Alice affirms her father's class and race values, she learns that upholding such principles only diminishes her prospects as well as her potential for happiness.

This story, like "Uncle Wellington's Wives," provides a good deal of "historical" information about marriage practices among the newly freed black population. But the historical information the stories provide is placed within the context of stories of failed marriages, marriages that are not legal, marriages that end in divorce, and those, like Alice's and Cicely's, that never happen at all. When placed in such a fictional context, the freedom promised by marriage turns out to replace the literal bonds of slavery with a figural double-bind. Marriage, as Chesnutt presents it, promises freedom, but it is a promise that can only be kept by making an unequivocal break with the past. Chesnutt's stories of the color line designate the Civil War as a site of rupture, but a rupture that does not break the bonds of slavery entirely. Instead, the bonds that tie master to slave are displaced onto marital forms of sociality. The insistence on legalizing slave marriages after the war forced the newly freed to preserve relationships formed in slavery foreclosing the experience of falling in love. In doing so, Chesnutt's fictional portrayal of marriages predicated upon a commitment to slavery, rather than personal choice, narrates the private dimension of segregation as it became public policy for future generations.

Notes

1. See Cott, 33.
2. See DuCille, 16.
3. See Kawash, 88.
4. See Bentley and Gunning, 4.
5. See Sundquist, 301.

Works Cited

Bentley, Nancy. "The Strange Career of Love and Slavery: Chesnutt, Engels, Masoch." *American Literary History* 17.3 (2005): 460–85.

Bentley, Nancy and Sandra Gunning. Introduction. *The Marrow of Tradition*, by Charles W. Chesnutt. New York: Bedford/St. Martin's, 2002. 3–26.

Chesnutt, Charles W. *The Wife of His Youth and Other Stories of the Color Line*. Ridgewood, NJ: The Gregg Press, 1967.

———. *Stories, Novels and Essays*. New York: Library Classics of the United States, Inc., 2002.

Chesnutt, Helen M. *Charles Waddell Chesnutt: Pioneer of the Color Line*. Chapel Hill: U of North Carolina P, 1952.

Cott, Nancy F. *Public Vows: A History of Marriage and the Nation*. Cambridge, MA: Harvard UP, 2000.

DuCille, Ann. *The Coupling Convention: Sex, Text, and Tradition in Black Women's Fiction*. New York: Oxford UP, 1993.

Duncan, Charles. "Telling Genealogy: Notions of Family in *The Wife of His Youth*." *Critical Essays on Charles Chesnutt*. Ed. Joseph R. McElrath Jr. New York: G.K. Hall, 1999. 281–96.

Ferguson, SallyAnn. "Chesnutt's Genuine Blacks and Future Americans." *MELUS* 15.3 (1988): 109–19.

Kawash, Samira. *Dislocating the Color Line: Identity, Hybridity, and Singularity in African-American Narrative*. Stanford, CA: Stanford UP, 1997.

Stanley, Amy Dru. *From Bondage to Contract*. Cambridge, UK: Cambridge UP, 1998.

Sundquist, Eric J. *To Wake the Nations: Race in the Making of American Literature*. Cambridge, MA: Harvard UP, 1993.

Tate, Claudia. "Allegories of Black Female Desire; or, Rereading Nineteenth Century Sentimental Narratives of Black Female Authority." *Changing Our Own Words: Essays on Criticism, Theory, and Writing by Black Women*. Ed. Cheryl A. Wall. New Brunswick, NJ: Rutgers UP, 1989. 98–126.

Warner, Michael. *The Trouble with Normal: Sex, Politics, and the Ethics of Queer Life*. New York: The Free Press, 1999.

Wilson, Matthew. *Whiteness in the Novels of Charles W. Chesnutt*. Jackson: U of Mississippi P, 2004.

Wonham, Henry. "What is a Black Author?: A Review of Recent Charles Chesnutt Studies." *American Literary History* 18.4 (2006): 829–35.

Charles Chesnutt's "The Dumb Witness" and the Culture of Segregation

LORI ROBISON AND ERIC WOLFE

In 1897, when Charles Chesnutt composed "The Dumb Witness," he was returning to the literary form—his "conjure tales"—that had won him his earliest successes. That literary return was likely bittersweet for Chesnutt, because although it led directly to the publication of his first book—*The Conjure Woman*—it also meant working again in a genre about which Chesnutt was ambivalent. In 1889, after publishing the first four conjure tales, he was already expressing his impatience with this form: "I think I have about used up the old Negro who serves as mouthpiece, and I shall drop him in future stories, as well as much of the dialect" ("To Be an Author" 44–45). Chesnutt's discomfort came, no doubt, from the support that the dialect story gave, in Richard Brodhead's succinct phrasing, to the "preferred fictions of racial life" operating in the postbellum United States (*Cultures* 210).[1] Most closely associated with the tremendously popular work of Joel Chandler Harris and Thomas Nelson Page, this genre depended on the representation of a seemingly "authentic" African American voice. Speaking a stylized literary form of black dialect, characters like Harris's Uncle Remus and Page's Sam were ex-slaves who ventriloquized a sense of nostalgic longing for the antebellum south. Chesnutt's conjure tales resisted these cultural implications, even as they worked within the same conventions. Nonetheless, he was concerned with a growing tendency to limit representations of African American identities to this single image: he complained to George Washington Cable in 1890 that the "chief virtues" of all the African American characters appearing in recent popular fiction was their "dog-like fidelity and devotion to their old masters" (*"To Be an Author"* 65). Indeed, the two elements of his conjure tales that Chesnutt seemed most eager to abandon—the "old Negro who serves as mouthpiece" and the "dialect" in which he speaks—were those perhaps most closely associated with this growing plantation mythology, which worked to fix notions of African American identity in the stereotypical figure of the ex-slave.

In the ten years between the publication of "The Goophered Grapevine," Chesnutt's first conjure tale, and the composition of "The Dumb Witness," the development of segregation culture had even more firmly cemented the popular notions of black and white identities in the United States. Yet if Chesnutt returned, in the late 1890s, to the type of tale written by Harris and Page, he did so in a way that continued to resist the essentialization of racialized identities in which the stories of Harris and Page participated. Chesnutt was, as Henry B. Wonham has recently remarked, a "writer suspicious of race consciousness in any form" (830). Arguing that "race integrity" was "a modern invention of the white people to perpetuate the color line" ("Race Prejudice" 91), Chesnutt demonstrates a skepticism about categories of racial classification that makes him a precursor of contemporary thinkers, like Henry Louis Gates Jr., who understand the concept of race as a "fiction," a "dangerous trope" ("Writing Race" 4, 5).[2] The logic of segregation rests on the belief that the social world can be neatly divided into separate identities, and with the writing of "The Dumb Witness," we want to argue, Chesnutt finds a literary strategy for undermining this logic. Recognizing that what underpins segregation culture is a desire to construct clearly demarcated identities, the story, with its incessant interrogation of the witnessing of vision and the dumbness of speech, subverts the notion that identity can be fixed.

The segregation period was a crucial moment in the construction of modern American conceptions of racial "difference." The last decades of the nineteenth century saw an increased emphasis on stereotypical representations of African Americans in literature and popular culture and on scientific, biological theories of race. These cultural attempts to fix blackness were aided by the codification of public spaces in segregation culture. *Plessy v. Ferguson* (1896) confirmed the legality of designating schools, railroad cars, hotels, and public buildings for "white" or for "colored." These practices served to severely limit Reconstruction's promises of social and economic mobility, citizenship, and political enfranchisement for all Americans. Although modern-day Americans are often aware of the horrifying toll that segregation took on the rights of African Americans, we may not see other legacies of segregation culture that remain with us. If we understand segregation to be not only about racial discrimination, but also, perhaps even more fundamentally, about the fixing and anchoring of racial meanings that had been exposed—as slavery ended—to be arbitrary and socially constructed, then we can see that segregation participated in the very construction of what we now understand blackness and whiteness to mean.

In *Making Whiteness: The Culture of Segregation in the South, 1890–1940*, historian Grace Elizabeth Hale effectively challenges common assumptions about this period by arguing that southern segregation culture was not the final product of deep racial antagonisms but instead itself participated, through an active negotiation of racial meanings, in the production of racial identities. Understanding race as the invention of social needs and economic practices, Hale argues that the end of the Civil War raised the possibility that the social meanings of whiteness and blackness could be disconnected from their historical associations with the categories of citizen and slave and that African Americans would therefore "no longer connote for whites the antithesis of agency" (21). Race thus would not necessarily have become the primary category through which Americans identified themselves. Despite the promise Reconstruction held, Hale demonstrates that cultural changes in the last decades of the century created anxieties that led to an increased insistence on the fixing of racial identities. New definitions of national citizenship, the advent of a mass consumer culture, the rise of a black middle class, and increased national mobility disrupted the markers of identity that Americans had once used to understand themselves. Hale argues that an increased investment in the categories of white and black served to supply anxious white Americans with a renewed sense of stable national identity. Segregation became the fundamental tool in this process. With segregation's insistence that people of various classes and of possibly unknowable racial backgrounds understand themselves as embodying one of two possible identities, with its attempt to firmly identify individuals by linking them to labeled geographic spaces, and with its creation of inferior spaces for those who seemed to embody blackness, segregation maintained social hierarchies by anchoring identities that had threatened, at least temporarily, to become chaotically unknowable. Whiteness thus could resist narrow, racialized definitions, and remain invisible while asserting a normative definition of national identity.

Hale's challenge to traditional ways of thinking about segregation generates new paradigms for understanding the literature of this period. What Hale helps us recognize is that literary protests against the politics of segregation would not necessarily need to take the culture of segregation as their overt theme. Textual challenges to segregation might instead embrace the fluidity of identity opened up by the shifting social relations of the postbellum period. Acknowledging that there is a political value to moving between identities, between cultural positions, such texts would resist the reification of race as a legible sign of an underlying, knowable identity. Of course, writing against dominant cultural values, particularly values as entrenched as the investment in transparent identity, provides a significant rhetorical challenge.[3] With "The Dumb Witness," we would like to suggest, Charles Chesnutt finds a way of meeting this challenge and of disrupting the narrow essentialization of racial identity that this historical period demanded.

Reframing Identity

"The Dumb Witness" was not originally published in Chesnutt's *The Conjure Woman,* probably because, as Brodhead has suggested, it did not fit the aesthetic criteria imposed by Walter Hines Page, the collection's editor.[4] The story is, as

Eric Sundquist has cleverly remarked, "a conjure tale without conjure and a Julius tale without Julius" (389). Like many of Chesnutt's conjure tales, "The Dumb Witness" opens with John, the transplanted white northerner, finding yet another profitable way to use the resources of the rural North Carolina county in which he and his wife now live. This story, like the others, opens with John in the role of the first-person narrator, and yet, in a break with Chesnutt's other conjure tales, this story never moves from John's framing of the story into one of Julius's inner tales. In "The Dumb Witness," then, Chesnutt has dropped, as he had hoped to do, both the "old Negro who serves as mouthpiece . . . as well as much of the dialect." John remains the narrator throughout the frame and the inner tale, and, though the story begins as Julius's, it is John himself who finally constructs the narrative: "Some of the facts of this strange story—circumstances of which Julius was ignorant, though he had the main facts correct—I learned afterwards from other sources, but I have woven them all together here in orderly sequence" (162).

John's framing narrative begins as he travels to buy timber from the Murchison plantation. As Julius and John approach the deteriorating property, John becomes aware of "a curious drama" being enacted on the piazza (161). An old white man and a woman, who looks something like the man—although John guesses her to be black—are speaking in an agitated manner. (159). Seemingly unaware that he is being observed, the man demands information, threatens the woman with violence, and then, seconds later, pleads for forgiveness. Viney, the woman, responds with silence, then more silence, and finally with incomprehensible, "discordant jargon" (168). John asks Julius to explain, and Julius replies, "Dey's be'n dat-a-way fer yeahs an' yeahs" (161).

What happened in the past to precipitate this endlessly recurring scene becomes the inner narrative that John constructs. We learn that Viney, a slave, housekeeper, relation to, and—perhaps—mistress of Murchison, tells Murchison's intended wife something that causes her to call off the wedding. When he discovers Viney's actions, Murchison responds violently and the story implies that he mutilates her tongue. Soon after, however, Murchison's wealthy uncle dies, revealing in a deathbed letter the terrible irony that only Viney knows the hiding place where the will and inheritance can be found. Murchison then begins a lifelong, unrealized effort to coax the information from Viney. As a desperate Murchison, with his debts growing, begs her to help recover the inheritance, Viney watches him with "inscrutable eyes" and responds only with "meaningless inarticulate mutterings" (170). The inner tale ends with the sense that both characters have gone insane through the constant rehearsing of this never-ending conflict.

In the final paragraphs of Chesnutt's story, John closes the framing narrative by returning to Murchison's place to discover that the conflict has ended. Malcolm Murchison has died and the house and grounds show new "signs of prosperity" (170). The biggest surprise is that when John asks Viney to see Murchison's nephew, Viney responds with clear words, " 'Yas, suh,' she answered, 'I'll call 'im' " (171). Once Malcolm dies her silence ends; she reveals to the nephew where the papers and money are and she begins to speak.

Like many of Chesnutt's "conjure" tales, this story relies on the tensions between frame and inner tale to question the racist assumptions that the white narrator John—and, by implication, a white reader of the story—brings to the representation and interpretation of African American characters. And yet "The Dumb Witness" introduces perhaps an even more complex layering of narration by making John the narrator of an inner tale that was once Julius's story. What this structure helps Chesnutt to produce is a story with an even greater emphasis on John's perceptions and misperceptions. Calling attention to the fact that it has been filtered through the incomplete perspectives of many spectators, this story avoids implying what is common with traditional, omniscient narration: that meanings—and identities—can be fully understood. The story that the reader gets from John is suggestive and at times even incomplete. We never learn, for example, the nature of Malcolm and Viney's familial relationship; nor can we be sure that they were lovers before Malcolm's thwarted engagement; nor do we know what Viney tells Malcolm's intended. Such omissions raise questions that can never fully be answered. What is Viney's racial and familial background? Is it the knowledge that Murchison has had an affair that causes the woman to break off their engagement, or is it that she was aware of the incestuous nature of the relationship, or is it that she was angered that Murchison would be involved with a black woman? Charles Crowe wonders at Murchison's own racial background: if Viney is "of our blood," as the dying uncle writes to Murchison (166), then isn't it possible that Murchison himself has black ancestors?

That the answers to some of these questions are never supplied could be explained by a desire not to offend the sensibilities of late nineteenth-century readers. It is worth noting, however, that much of what is not said would more carefully define who these people authentically "are" under the terms of late-century segregation culture. With this narrative structure, Chesnutt avoids giving us family and racial lineages, or even a precise notion of the relationships and connections between characters. Crowe has argued that Julius, and therefore others in the African American community, must have known all along that Viney could speak and that she was manipulating Murchison. This is another intriguing speculation that the story invites but never fully confirms, and that it remains unknown demonstrates that the reader knows nothing about to whom, outside the drama on the piazza, Viney speaks; without a sense of the larger community with whom Viney identifies, the story denies the reader yet another traditional marker of who she is. John, as narrator, does attempt, at two points in the story, to understand Viney by linking her identity to race, and yet, because Chesnutt has written John into the role of a narrator whose knowledge of Viney is limited, the validity of this linkage is checked. In both instances John himself is quick to undercut his own assertion by recognizing that an appeal to Viney's racial identity is not needed to understand her behavior. He attributes her initial anger when she hears of Murchison's engagement to "some passionate strain of the mixed blood in her veins" but quickly renames it "a very human blood" (164). In the other passage he says, "she had too a dash of Indian blood, which perhaps gave her straighter and blacker hair than she would otherwise have had, and perhaps endowed her with some other qualities that found their natural expression in the course of subsequent events" (164). Here he adds: "if indeed her actions needed anything more than common human nature to account for them" (164). Chesnutt makes Viney hard to read and he resists, through the narrative structure, the cultural impulse to make her more legible by inscribing her connection to family, community, or race.

It is this difficulty reading Viney on which the story's surprise ending—and thus its narrative power—rests. First Murchison, then the story's narrator John, and perhaps too the story's reader cannot imagine that Viney has the ability to play someone other than she appears to be. Like Melville's *Benito Cereno*, to which Brodhead compares it (Introduction 18), the social critique offered by "The Dumb Witness" rests on white misreadings of a black character. Despite the willingness she shows, before Murchison's violent attack, to stand up to him and to take action against him, the Viney portrayed by John's story is a passive, even somewhat addled, victim who apparently lacks the agency to take Murchison to the hiding place or the intelligence to find a way of representing the hiding place to him. Neither Murchison nor John ever question this apparent change in Viney, ever suspect what she is up to, presumably because the new Viney fits their expectations of black identity better than does the old Viney. This ability to make sense of Viney's actions by reading her through white expectations of black character is illustrated again when John discusses her decision to stay on the estate, despite Murchison's attack, once slavery ends. By the end of story, of course, readers recognize that Viney has stayed in order to undo Murchison, but when attempting to explain what, at face value, seems a very odd choice, John supplies the following: "There was some gruesome attraction in the scene of her suffering, or perhaps it was the home instinct" (170). Surely it would not be that difficult to understand why Viney might stay, and yet such an understanding would have to assume her agency. What gets in the way of John guessing at Viney's motives is his willingness to read her actions through his assumption that she would embrace the position of victim or to read her through the stereotype of the slave who confuses the "scene of her suffering" with "home." Like the African American characters in popular fiction about which Chesnutt complained, that is, Viney is understood by John to exhibit a version, albeit perverse, of that "dog-like fidelity" to her old master. These misreadings, committed by Murchison and John, ultimately demonstrate how definitions of blackness limit the vision of white Americans. In its very narrative structure, then, the story indicts the cultural investment in codifying blackness; these white readers of Viney simply cannot see, until it is explicitly revealed to them, the complexity of her identity.

The Witnessing Gaze

With its highly visible ordering and categorizing of people, segregation culture attempted, as Hale argues, to address cultural anxieties about shifting identities. Using visual markers, such as signs and public space, to enforce definitions of race, segregation might have worked much like Foucault's panopticon—by using surveillance to cause African Americans to internalize a racialized identity. Chesnutt, in contrast, represents Viney as having the ability to dissemble, to play with various subjectivities, and as having, therefore, the ability to resist the white gaze. For these reasons, she is not like the heroines of much of the antiracist literature of this period, in which racism is attacked through a senti-mental appeal to readers' morality and humanity.

The sentimental, which works by eliciting the emotions of the reader as it engages the reader in a sympathetic response, was well suited to the task of educating nineteenth-century Americans about the oppressions suffered by others. Karen Sánchez-Eppler explains how the sympathy generated by the sentimental text worked in the battle for the abolition of slavery:

> as a sentimental tale elicits tears and sighs, it enrolls the reader's bodily responses in the act of overcoming difference. The sobs of character and reader work to blur the distinction between them. This literary strategy thus proves particularly pertinent for the political project of claiming personhood for the racially different body of the slave. (134–5)

Although sentimental texts undoubtedly contributed to the end of slavery by insisting on the humanity of African Americans, the use of this discursive strategy was not without its political risks. As Sánchez-Eppler points out, the rhetorical move of depicting African Americans as the objects of white sympathy also is a move toward objectification. As politically powerful as the creation of sympathy between reader and character can be, this strategy can efface—by making the black character the object of the white gaze—the subjectivity and agency of those for whom it attempts to "claim personhood."

This troubling dynamic is further aggravated by the implicit assumption that the sentimental object of sympathy is necessarily a transparent character who cannot dissemble. To elicit the reader's emotions and engagement, the reader must immediately see the sympathetic object's worthiness and goodness, which serves to further fix the object's identity. Simultaneously, the move to objectify makes the representation of interiority quite difficult, stripping from these characters a potentially politically powerful illegibility. Like the culture of segregation itself, then, strategies of literary sympathy could work to secure African American identities by presenting them as transparently legible.[5]

The scene in *Uncle Tom's Cabin* in which Eliza arrives at the Bird's house provides a brief example of how white discursive sympathy can humanize while simultaneously objectifying. With its emphasis on Eliza's maternal feelings, her beauty, and the pathos she inspires in the Bird family, the scene insists on her humanity. The family becomes a representative of the sympathizing reader that is placed in the text, instructing the reader in the appropriate response to her suffering. And yet, as Eliza is made the object of white sympathy, she is stripped of much of the agency that characterized her in earlier scenes of the novel. The Eliza who actively plots her escape plays different parts, preventing her owners and the slave catchers from transparently reading her intentions. But once in the position of object, in the position of the one who makes the Birds cry, Eliza cannot retain any illegibility—and thus her control over her interiority is compromised. As she leaves the Birds, she is an open book to which they respond:

> Eliza leaned out of the carriage, and put out her hand—a hand as soft and beautiful was given in return. She fixed her large, dark eyes, full of earnest meaning, on Mrs. Bird's face, and seemed going to speak. Her lips moved—she tried once or twice, but there was no sound—and pointing upward, with a look never to be forgotten, she fell back in the seat and covered her face. (155)

Although she does not act here and although she does not speak, Eliza conveys "earnest meaning." Her body—her hand, her eyes, her "look"—speaks for her. Even as she "covers" her face, thereby occluding the subjectivity signaled by her gaze, she is objectified, her gratitude and sadness made transparently visible to the Birds.

This example helps to throw into relief the many ways that Chesnutt was working, with his representation of Viney, against cultural discourses that would essentialize her. Like Eliza in this passage, Viney does not speak, and yet, unlike Eliza, she remains "inscrutable" to Murchison, to John, and to the reader as well. By the end of the story, readers recognize that even the "meanings" that she seemed to convey were not at all "earnest." Viney is not like the sentimental object of sympathy, then, because her ability to dissemble remains unchecked and her interiority remains undisturbed:

A closer observer than Malcolm Murchison might have detected at his moment another change in the woman's expression. Perhaps it was in her eyes more than elsewhere: for into their black depths there sprang a sudden fire. Beyond this, however, and a slight quickening of her pulse, of which there was no visible manifestation, she gave no sign of special feeling; and even if these had been noticed they might have been attributed to the natural interest felt at hearing of her old master's death. (167)

Chesnutt's language in this passage echoes sentimental language—language like that Stowe uses to highlight Eliza's transparency: there is a "sudden fire" in her eyes and "a slight quickening of her pulse." And yet the emphasis here is on what cannot be understood by Murchison, and, by extension, other white spectators: there is "no visible manifestation" and "no sign of special feeling" that one can apprehend by looking at Viney.

What is striking about Chesnutt's construction of this story is that he writes a heroine who gains the sympathy of John and the reader, without writing Viney into the position of legible object. What happens to Viney is horrifying and the story John tells registers that; even Murchison, the first time he sees her after his attack, feels "remorseful as he looked at her" (166). And yet the story's political power does not come from the sympathy it generates for Viney. Instead, the story's power comes from its dramatization of the act of mis-see-ing. In the text, John seems to be positioned much like the Birds in the above scene: he is the spectator—or "witness"—who is positioned within the text to gaze upon Viney and to educate the reader in the appropriate response to her. But Chesnutt disrupts this common discursive dynamic by undercutting the validity of John's vision in the final paragraphs of the story. By demonstrating that John, much like Murchison, has gotten Viney wrong, Chesnutt checks John's role (and by implication, the reader's role) as gazing subject. The story thus resists the objectification of Viney by showing John that he simply does not see what he thinks he sees. In fact, the power of the final disclosure is that it reveals that Viney has been the active subject who has possessed the gaze all along. Early in the story she turns that gaze on Murchison: "She looked at him with an inscrutable face as he came in, and he felt uncomfortable under the look" (166), and by the end of the inner tale she is still "watching him from the porch, with the same inscrutable eyes" (170).

The story's final revelation that Viney had never been transparent, that she had indeed been "inscrutable," also reveals her to have never been the object that Murchison and John imagine her to be. Although we do not want to make too strong a case for the agency Viney holds (clearly, she endured horrific violence and gave over her adult life to exacting revenge), we do think it worth noting that Viney, who was understood—at least by white "witnesses"—to be capable only of reacting to Murchison, was the subject who actively created the terms of the drama that ultimately drove him to madness. She wrote Murchison's role by giving herself multiple parts to play: the injured but forgiving victim; the willing servant who wanted to help but simply could not; the stupid slave who, despite her best efforts, could not learn to read and write. These roles endlessly and predictably elicit from Murchison demands he cannot enforce, threats he will never carry out, and displays of sympathy that he immediately undercuts with reprisals of his demands and threats. Viney, it seems, has carefully scripted this drama to underscore for Murchison his lack of any real power over her, himself, or the situation. By creating a heroine who is willing to play with identity and to manipulate the assumptions others make about her, Chesnutt writes a character unlike the traditional sentimental heroine: Viney can ultimately destroy Murchison because she recognizes the power of dissembling.

The Dumb Voice

Speech and identity have long been linked through a belief in the transparency of voice. For this reason, the voice became another likely site for addressing cultural anxieties about the loss of firm markers of identity amidst shifting social relationships in the late nineteenth-century United States. The Western cultural understanding of speech as the fullest and most accurate expression of self is the historical outcome of the Western philosophical tradition Derrida called the "logocentrism which is also a phonocentrism" (11). An idealized conception of speech has been constructed by this philosophical tradition, Derrida explains, in which the voice is posited as being "heard and understood immediately by whoever emits it" (166). The cultural belief, then, is that signifier and signified collapse into each other in a moment of instantaneous "living" speech. As the voice utters a word, that word seems immediately recouped by the ear (and consciousness), and thus speaking appears to be subject to no loss or delay of meaning. Vocal conversation seems to double but does not alter this experience: the voice is heard/understood by the other at the same time as it is heard/understood by the self. Even in conversation, then, the *identity* of the voice appears to remain intact; the voice is transmitted without loss to the other, and the voice also seems to immediately communicate the identity—the interiority—of the speaker. Because the workings of language are effaced, speech is therefore reduced to voice and understood to convey an authentic bodily essence.

As the culture of segregation hardened in the mid-1890s, a number of essays appeared in prominent American periodicals as part of a cultural conversation about, to cite the shared title of three of these essays, "The American Voice."[6] The concern of these essays is not with the secondary manifestations of speech, but with the physical voice. Coupled to the body, the voice, in the logic of all of these essays, provides a stable marker of identity; functioning as an "index to the soul," the voice becomes a manifestation of inner essence (Cocke 251). In one of these essays, an anonymous contributor to the *Atlantic Monthly* is quick to diagnose the defects of the American voice as originating in "some moral shortcoming or distortion; for men of science tell us that a moral perversion or infirmity is quickly reflected in the eyes and the voice" ("American Voice" 853). That essay also demonstrates that the central concept undergirding the late-nineteenth-century discussion of voice is nature. The writer laments the nasal quality of the typical American voice by citing two contrasting examples: the first is "an ordinary Russian Jew" whose baritone voice is "so full, so strong, so melodious that the music of it echoes still the caves that lie somewhere between my tympanum and my heart . . ."; the second is an Irishman, "newly arrived in the country," with a tenor voice "as clear as a linnet's" (852). Suggesting that these foreign, ethnicized voices are more sonorous because they are closer to nature, the essay concludes that Americans' voices would improve if they "loved nature a good deal more trustfully" (854). With this insistence on the voice as a reflection of nature, the bodily voice could function as a clear marker of a transparent identity. Just as segregation posted skin color as a natural, visible sign of essential identity, so did voice stand as that identity's authentic, audible sign.

Understood to immediately communicate identity, the voice could therefore be situated as perhaps the last bulwark against the dissolution of social markers in the rapidly changing social landscape:

> The revelation by the voice of the nature, training, and social posi-
> tion is acknowledged. Dress no longer reveals the distinctions of
> the social scale. The manners cannot always put the person where
> he belongs; but the voice at once gives the gauge, not altogether
> accurately, but approximately. (Thompson 867)

The cultural anxieties that Hale details are in clear evidence here. Where the subject "belongs" is no longer clear, but voice can be an instrument that more clearly marks "the distinctions of the social scale." If, as Hale argues, the cultural response to such anxiety is to stabilize racial meanings to consolidate a national collectivity, we see that dynamic at work in these essays. The "American" voice is expressive of essential American identity. Yet constructed as it is against markers of ethnicity ("a Russian Jew" or "an Irishman"), this essence is figured as normatively "white."

In contrast to the fantasy of a voice that would reveal inner essence and, perhaps more importantly, testify to the fixed and natural hierarchies of the "social scale," Chesnutt's "The Dumb Witness" disrupts the usual equation of voice with authentic identity. To put it simply, the story demonstrates that there is nothing "natural" about the voice. The story's opening scene, in which John and Julius witness one of the endless replayings of Viney and Murchison's failed conversation, shows the limits of John's attempts to fix her identity in terms of her voice (or voicelessness). When Murchison's threats finally force Viney to break her silence, John struggles at first to place her voice within recognizable linguistic structures—he thinks "at first" she is speaking "some foreign tongue."[7] Yet as the scene continues, Viney's voice exceeds John's understanding. He can overhear only a "discordant jargon," a "meaningless cacophony" (160). Viney's voice sounds, yet she is "inarticulate" (161). She mimics the forms of language without content, "pouring out a flood of sounds that were not words and which yet seemed now and then vaguely to suggest words . . ." (160). Severed from any immediate meaning, Viney's voice can—at least in John's hearing—represent no inner self. When Julius answers John's query—"What the matter with them?"—he represents Viney and Murchison through the figure of absence: they are "out'n dey min' " (161). Without vocal meaning, Viney's interiority appears empty.

Like John, Murchison also attempts to fix Viney's identity through the voice. If John focuses on the lack of meaning in the external voice, Murchison focuses on the identity that presumably lies behind the voice. For Murchison, Viney's voice always represents the potential communication of the essential secret that she hides. This explains why, despite the absence of recognizable linguistic meanings in Viney's vocalizations during the opening scene, Murchison responds as though he has understood her. Her first burst of sound brings forth an apology, and throughout the scene we see Murchison carry out half of an imagined conversation. This conversation only ends when Murchison believes that Viney has answered his pleas: he "seemed to comprehend," walked to a spot in the yard and "began digging furiously" in an attempt to find the hidden papers (161). If voice appears to be the carrier of essential truth, Chesnutt inverts that figure in his description of Murchison's violent desires to penetrate Viney's interiority: "in her lay the secret he longed for and which he hoped at some time in some miraculous way to extract from her" (169). The fluidity of Viney's voice disrupts any simple communication of stable identity. John and Murchison demonstrate differing responses to this disruption, yet both continue to believe in the authenticity of the voice, constructing their understandings of Viney in order to make voice and self coincident. John believes that Viney is speaking nonsense because her interiority is absent; Murchison believes that Viney's speech still carries her secret. In both cases, voice remains expressive of inner essence.

Yet the eventual revelation of the story that, as Julius puts it, "Ole Viney could 'a' talked all de time, ef she'd had a min' ter" undercuts any notions of authentic voice (171). With the understanding that Viney has strategically withheld her voice, we can understand voicelessness as a trope rather than a representation of Viney's essential identity. And what this shift in perspective makes visible is the culturally coded character of the vocal roles—including silence—that Viney has occupied throughout the story. Just as she subverts the drama that would position her as an object, so she takes advantage of the ways in which the culture of slavery—and later of segregation—has already written African Americans as voiceless.[8] Initially, by sharing her secret knowledge about Murchison with his fiancée, and thus preventing his marriage, Viney has refused to be the "quiet and obedient" slave (165). Yet once her secret knowledge of the location of the papers is the key to securing Murchison's inheritance, she *plays* the "quiet and obedient" slave, occupying that role with (literally) a vengeance. Viney also uses the associations between African Americans and illiteracy to shield that secret. Murchison's attempts to substitute for her voice by teaching her writing fail. Viney "manifested a remarkable stupidity while seemingly anxious to learn," yet John (as he retells her story) does not have to look far for explanations; he imagines that she cannot learn to read and write because she had "begun too old" or because "her mind was too busily occupied with other thoughts" (168).

Once again, we do not wish to romanticize the conditions that give rise to Viney's agency; the story never minimizes the profound violence enacted by Murchison. What is important is that Chesnutt gives Viney some agency—no matter how truncated—by having her manipulate the strictures of identity operating in her culture. In this sense, Viney performs a version of "subaltern agency," which Homi Bhabha describes as "the power to reinscribe and relocate the given symbols of authority and victimage" (212–3). Viney's voicelessness does not define her. Placed into the context of the binarized segregation culture within which Chesnutt was writing, "The Dumb Witness" works to resist fixed, racialized categories of identity, instead reinscribing dominant "symbols of authority and victimage" in order to make them signify in new ways.

The moment when Viney speaks is the hinge around which "The Dumb Witness" pivots. At hearing her "intelligible" voice, John remarks that he "was never more surprised in my life" (171), and that moment in which John's readings of Viney's identity are shown to be inadequate is, as we have argued here, the key element in Chesnutt's critique of segregation culture. *What* she says is perhaps unimportant, yet Chesnutt's revision of the story suggests that *how* she says it might be. Two versions of the manuscript exist: in the earlier version, Viney speaks "standard" English ("Yes, sir, I'll call him"); in the later revision, she speaks in dialect ("Yas, suh, I'll call 'im") (171). For our purposes, we are less concerned with speculating about why Chesnutt chose one version and rejected the other. That he could imagine both demonstrates again that he did not understand his character to have a "natural" voice. Nor, as Michael A. Elliott has argued, did he understand the very form of dialect fiction to accurately represent African American voices. As he wrote to Walter Hines Page, the Houghton Mifflin editor who helped assemble *The Conjure Woman*, "The fact is, of course, that there is no such thing as Negro dialect" (qtd. in Elliot 78–79); rather, Chesnutt understood dialect as a literary construction that was inextricably connected with the discourses of race and identity circulating in segregation culture.

It is tempting to see Chesnutt using the character of Viney as a representation of himself as author. He seems at times in his literary career "voiceless," unable to publish anything but the dialect tales that white readers expected of him; he even referred to the period in the 1890s, when he unsuccessfully worked to publish nondialect stories, as his "years of silence" (qtd. in Brodhead, Introduction 15). If Chesnutt cannot escape the constraints of his culture, he does demonstrate the agency, through his writing, to "reinscribe and relocate" the cultural discourses that attempted to define him: "The Dumb Witness," as we have argued here, studiously avoids the replication of the cultural discourses of transparent identity upon which segregation culture's essentialization of black and white rested. Perhaps Chesnutt imagined himself, like Viney, as one who is perceived as a "dumb witness" and yet is actually neither voiceless nor passive.

In this sense, we can read "The Dumb Witness" as a thematization of Chesnutt's concerns about the possibility of using fiction in the service of a radical cultural critique.[9] Would contemporary readers only have understood Chesnutt—as Murchison and John understand Viney—through a lens tinted by segregation's desire for transparent identity? Would Chesnutt too have been "inscrutable" for a reader who might be, as Chesnutt represents John, another kind of uncomprehending "dumb witness"? That the story went unpublished in Chesnutt's lifetime might serve as an ironic confirmation of these fears. And yet to recognize the limits of Chesnutt's attempt, in "The Dumb Witness," to disrupt the growing consolidation of fixed racial meanings under segregation is not to suggest that the story can have no political impact. There is a continuing political value to examining how this nation has made race, because retracing how we have arrived at our contemporary understandings of blackness and whiteness is an important part of forging "a twenty-first century American collectivity outside whiteness's denial that will actually include us all" (Hale xii). A scholarly engagement with segregation, in terms similar to those we have laid out here, is therefore necessary to lead us beyond merely lamenting the past and into a more careful examination of how the cultural discourses of the past have shaped our continued ways of understanding race. With this kind of reading, Chesnutt's story, we would suggest, still has the potential to change how we live race in the present. If we begin with the premise that what we now understand to be black and white has been constructed through cultural negotiations, like those surrounding slavery and segregation, we question what has seemed to become "natural": the essentialization of race as a primary category of identity and the metonymy of whiteness with agency and American national identity.

Notes

1. Our reading is influenced by Richard Brodhead's compelling interpretation of Chesnutt's conjure tales in *Cultures of Letters* and in his introduction to *The Conjure Woman and Other Conjure Tales*. While Brodhead focuses primarily on the constraints of authorship, we focus here on Chesnutt's literary challenge to the culture of segregation.

2. In "What is a Black Author?: A Review of Recent Charles Chesnutt Studies," Wonham points out that literary critics increasingly understand Chesnutt to resist limiting racial categories.

3. See Karen Halttunen on the investments in transparent character operating in sentimental middle-class (white) United States culture in the mid-century (xvi).

4. See Brodhead's introduction for more on the publication history of *The Conjure Woman* (14–18). A revised version of the story is included as one of the plotlines in Chesnutt's late novel *The Colonel's Dream* (1905). See Sundquist (390) on the two versions.

5. See Robison for further analysis of this dynamic.

6. See "The American Voice," Bissell, Cocke, Osgood, Parsons, and Thompson.

7. Eric Sundquist argues that the "intimation of an African language (or perhaps American Indian, given her 'dash of Indian blood') hidden within Viney's array of sounds suggests, moreover, that Chesnutt intended the tale to operate as a critique of American culture's exclusion of the folkloric oral world of black culture" (390). Still, we are concerned that the connections between language and race in Sundquist's reading come perilously close to repeating the logic of segregation against which we think Chesnutt is working.

8. Gates points out that the trope of blacks as silent or voiceless has a long history in Western thought (*Figures in Black* 104).

9. Brodhead notes that the conjure tales thematize Chesnutt's own "negotiation with a dominant literary culture" (*Cultures* 204).

Works Cited

"The American Voice." *Atlantic Monthly* 78 (1896): 852–54.

Bhabha, Homi. "Anxious Nations, Nervous States." *Supposing the Subject*. Ed. Joan Copjec. New York: Verso, 1994.

Bissell, Kathryn Leavitt. "The American Voice." *The Outlook* 57 (1897): 376–78.

Brodhead, Richard H. *Cultures of Letters: Scenes of Reading and Writing in Nineteenth-Century America*. Chicago: U of Chicago P, 1993.

———. Introduction. Chesnutt, *The Conjure Woman* 1–21.

Chesnutt, Charles W. "The Dumb Witness." *The Conjure Woman and Other Conjure Tales*. Ed. Richard H. Brodhead. Durham, NC: Duke UP, 1995.

———. "Race Prejudice: Its Causes and Its Cure." *Selected Writings*. Ed. SallyAnn H. Ferguson. Boston: Houghton Mifflin, 2001. 85–94.

———. *"To Be an Author": Letters of Charles W. Chesnutt, 1889–1905*. Ed. Joseph R. McElrath, Jr. and Robert C. Leitz, III. Princeton, NJ: Princeton UP, 1997.

Cocke, James R. "The Voice as an Index to the Soul." *The Arena* 9 (1894): 239–52.

Crow, Charles. "Under the Upas Tree: Charles Chesnutt's Gothic." *Critical Essays on Charles W. Chesnutt*. Ed. Joseph R. McElrath Jr. New York: G. K. Hall, 1999. 261–70.

Derrida, Jacques. *Of Grammatology*. Trans. Gayatri Chakravorty Spivak. Baltimore: Johns Hopkins UP, 1976.

Elliot, Michael A. *The Culture Concept: Writing and Difference in the Age of Realism*. Minneapolis: U of Minnesota P, 2002.

Foucault, Michel. *Discipline and Punish: The Birth of the Prison*. Trans. Alan Sheridan. New York: Vintage, 1979.

Gates, Henry Louis, Jr. *Figures in Black: Words, Signs, and the 'Racial' Self*. New York: Oxford UP, 1987.

———. "Writing 'Race' and the Difference It Makes." *"Race," Writing, and Difference*. Ed. Henry Louis Gates Jr. Chicago: U of Chicago P, 1986.

Hale, Grace Elizabeth. *Making Whiteness: The Culture of Segregation in the South, 1890–1940*. New York: Vintage, 1999.

Halttunen, Karen. *Confidence Men and Painted Women: A Study of Middle-Class Culture in America, 1830–1870*. New Haven, CT: Yale UP, 1982.

Osgood, Fletcher. "Why The American Conversational Voice is Bad." *Forum* 19 (1895): 501–7.

Parsons, Louise B. "The American Voice." *The Outlook* 54 (1896): 867–68.

Robison, Lori. "An 'imperceptible infusion' of Blood: *Iola Leroy*, Racial Identity, and Sentimental Discourse." *Genre: Forms of Discourse and Culture* 37 (2004): 433–60.

Sánchez-Eppler, Karen. *Touching Liberty: Abolition, Feminism, and the Politics of the Body*. Berkeley: U of California P, 1993.

Stowe, Harriet Beecher. *Uncle Tom's Cabin or, Life Among the Lowly*. Ed. Ann Douglas. New York: Penguin, 1981.

Sundquist, Eric J. *To Wake the Nations: Race in the Making of American Literature*. Cambridge, MA: Harvard UP, 1993.

Thompson, Grace. "The Defects of the American Voice." *The Outlook* 52 (1895): 867.

Wonham, Henry B. "What is a Black Author?: A Review of Recent Charles Chesnutt Studies." *American Literary History* 18 (2006): 829–35.

"Those that do violence must expect to suffer"

Disrupting Segregationist Fictions of Safety in Charles W. Chesnutt's *The Marrow of Tradition*

BIRGIT BRANDER RASMUSSEN

Despite Charles W. Chesnutt's often noted internalized racism, a passionate rebuke of racial logic and narratives energizes his work.[1] In his short stories and novels, Chesnutt challenges the logic of segregation and racial terrorism that organized U.S. society at the close of the nineteenth century. The often veiled and coded nature of Chesnutt's critique reflects the violence that circumscribed African American protest at this time. This narrative strategy enabled Chesnutt to break into the segregated publishing sphere as white readers could enjoy his fiction without confronting its antiracist critique. Although Chesnutt's early short stories often focus on the inhumanity of slavery, they were delivered in the disarming narrative style of "local color" fiction, as stories of the South that could amuse Northern readers without raising their hackles.[2] *The Marrow of Tradition*, on the other hand, is overtly political. In this, his third and final novel, Chesnutt uses the space and license of imaginative literature to present a scathing indictment of white supremacy.

Chesnutt wrote to and for white audiences, who made up most of the literate readership.[3] Inspired by writers like Harriet Beecher Stowe and Albion Tourgée, he considered imaginative literature a uniquely powerful vehicle for addressing a white audience about racial injustice.[4] Chesnutt hoped to seduce his readers, "while amusing them to lead them on imperceptibly, unconsciously step by step to the desired state of feeling" that white supremacy should be dismantled.[5] However, in *The Marrow of Tradition* Chesnutt is anything but subtle and he appeals to self-interest rather than sympathy by constructing a plot where racial violence crosses the lines of segregation to affect all members of society. Chesnutt not only condemns the racial terror that underpins a segregated state, but also warns his readers that such violence will backfire against white Americans for "[s]ins, like chickens, come home to roost" (*Marrow* 241). Many of the white characters in the novel are killed, injured, or otherwise threatened as a direct consequence of racial violence that affects not only its intended victims but also its perpetrators. The unfortunate fates of Chesnutt's white characters convey a central message of the novel: "those that do violence must expect to suffer violence" (*Marrow* 309).

"Those that do violence must expect to suffer"

Published in 1901, *The Marrow of Tradition* is a revisionist portrayal of the 1898 Wilmington Race Riot, in which Reconstruction efforts to de-segregate the city and its institutions were subverted by a political coup that restored white supremacy in both the political and the written spheres.[6] Before this coup, Wilmington, North Carolina, was one of the most economically and geographically integrated cities in the South. A thriving black middle class had emerged to hold important civic positions including justice of the peace.[7] However, a corrupt election in 1898 replaced a racially integrated government with a white supremacist regime. A few days later, the city erupted in violence causing many black families to flee the city, and leaving school and newspaper buildings burned to the ground.

The coup was organized by white Democrats who had lost political control of the city a few years earlier to an interracial alliance of Fusionists and Republicans.[8] Outraged by national press reports characterizing the riot as a justified "revolution" against "Negro domination," Chesnutt set out to tell a different version of the events that had transpired in Wilmington and to create a critical portrait of national racial politics in the post-Reconstruction United States. Set in fictional Wellington, *The Marrow of Tradition* centers around the intertwined destinies of two families. The light-skinned Dr. William Miller is married to Janet, who is the unacknowledged half-sister of Olivia, a member of an old and established family in the city. Olivia is married to Major Carteret, a newspaper publisher. Along with two other men, he leads efforts to reinstate white supremacy in the city. When Olivia's aunt Polly Ochiltree is murdered during a robbery, the blame is placed on Sandy, the African American servant of Mr. Delamere, an elderly white gentleman. The real culprit turns out to be Mr. Delamere's grandson, Tom. Although Sandy is found to be innocent, he only narrowly escapes lynching as Carteret and his group publishes an editorial that conjures up the specter of rape and encourages violent retribution. A full-scale riot follows in which dozens of African American citizens of the town are killed, and Dr. Miller's hospital is burned. One of the victims is Dr. Miller's only son. At the end of the novel, the Carterets' son is also near death, and, since all other doctors have left town, the Carterets must beg the Millers for help.[9]

Chesnutt's use of light-skinned characters like Dr. Miller and the phenotypically identical "black" and "white" sisters, Janet Miller and Olivia Carteret, explicitly critiques essentialist notions of race as biological difference that underwrote segregation. However, Chesnutt goes further in this novel by representing the destinies of white and black characters as intimately intertwined and violence as a destructive force that segregation cannot contain. Chesnutt thus advocates for the dismantling of white supremacy by constructing a storyline in which no one is safe from the violence that organizes and maintains a racially segregated state. Indeed, a central message of the novel is that white characters are also imperiled by the violence they instigate against black people.

Numerous white characters die or fall ill in the novel and their injuries are often linked to racial violence and the institution of white supremacy. The list of dead white characters includes Polly Ochiltree, whose death provides a key motor for the plot, Mr. Delamere, and Captain McBane. Olivia and Dodie also find themselves repeatedly in grave danger. Polly Ochiltree, Olivia's aunt, is a member of an old slave-holding family and plans to leave her possessions to Olivia's son, Dodie. Olivia discovers that when her father died, Polly personally secured Olivia's status as sole heir to her father's fortune by stealing his will and certificate of marriage to his housekeeper, Janet's mother. The reader learns about Olivia's kinship with Janet in the very first chapter, but only during the course of the novel does it become clear how the social disavowal of Janet is linked to her legal dispossession and conversely how Janet has a legitimate claim to Olivia's family name and fortune. Polly is not only a symbolic representative of the Old South, but has played an active role in the present to secure the social order for future generations, represented by her niece, Olivia, and Olivia's son, Dodie. Her fate embodies Chesnutt's warning that such injustice will incur punishment by a higher power because she dies a violent death.

Half-way through the novel, Polly is murdered by a burglar who turns out to be Tom Delamere disguised as Sandy, his grandfather's black servant. Tom's social status has been secured by his slaveholding forefathers and he represents the most degenerate of the aristocratic class.[10] Not only is he directly responsible for Polly's death, he is also indirectly responsible for his grandfather's death as Old Mr. Delamere dies of a heart attack shortly after he learns that Tom murdered Polly. These deaths are symbolically significant. Polly is guilty of racial crimes within the moral universe of the novel and her death represents a kind of cosmic punishment.[11] Mr. Delamere is morally superior to Polly, but like her he embodies the Old South. The fact that both of their deaths are associated with Tom Delamere suggests a kind of implosion of white supremacy, a turning against itself of the forces created by racial violence because Tom is heir to the wages and crimes of slavery.

Tom, Mr. Delamere, and Polly Ochiltree all represent the slave-holding class. Captain McBane, on the other hand, is the son of an overseer with aspirations to move up Wellington's social ladder. He is working with Major Carteret and Captain Belmont to foment racial violence and reinstate white supremacy in the city. These men, called the "Big Three," are the major players orchestrating the near-lynching of Sandy and the subsequent riot. Captain McBane dies as a direct consequence of the violence he has helped instigate when he is stabbed to death by the heroic black dockworker Josh Green. Common to all these injuries is their narrative relationship to the legacy and institution of white supremacy, which either directly or indirectly causes the death of Polly Ochiltree, Mr. Delamere, and Captain McBane.

Olivia and Dodie Carteret represent the bridge between the past and future of white supremacy. They do not die, but they find themselves seriously ill or near death multiple times in the novel. Their peril is consistently linked to the crimes of slavery and segregation. Olivia's health is threatened twice in the novel, and each time the physical distress is triggered by nervous strain following meetings with her disavowed, "black" half-sister, Janet Miller. Janet's mother Julia was a black housekeeper who worked for and conceived a child with Mr. Merkell, Olivia's father. Although Olivia has denied her biological ties to Janet, she is forced to confront them whenever she sees her, because the two look exactly alike. This narrative device enables Chesnutt to critique notions of biological difference that organize racial segregation and to suggest that the crimes that undergird a segregated society will not only haunt its perpetrators but also threaten their own happiness and safety.

Olivia and Dodie become key narrative devices for this message. The novel opens at Olivia's sick bed, where she is in danger of losing her first child to premature labor brought on by the nervous shock of encountering Janet (*Marrow* 2–9). Olivia's second illness comes after she learns that her father actually married Julia, and that Janet has a legal claim to her kinship and, even more troubling, to her estate (*Marrow* 254–67). This time her illness is brought on by nervous tension over her own decision, in the present, to burn her father's marriage certificate and will. This action mirrors and extends Polly Ochiltree's interception of these legal papers decades earlier. In this way, Chesnutt shows the agency of contemporary white Southerners (women as well as men) in actively maintaining the injustices of racialized inequality. Polly and Olivia's actions secure the fortune with which Major Carteret founds his paper and fans the flames of racial violence in the city. Chesnutt thus reveals how control of and privileged access to the sphere of writing—represented by the legal papers Olivia destroys and by Carteret's editorials—enables racial injustice. However, he also warns that white Southerners may pay a personal and "fearful price" for their collective sins.

This warning is realized most dramatically in the final chapters of the novel as racial violence spills over to the white side of the social color line where the Carterets thought themselves safe from the repercussions of their actions. This "fearful price" is forecast in a dream sequence earlier in the novel when Olivia's trespasses against Janet are directly linked to Dodie's endangered destiny. Immediately following the chapter in which Olivia burns her father's will and marriage certificate, she has a dream. Along with her son Dodie, Olivia is in a boat on the sea when a sudden gale and a huge wave capsize the boat. Olivia struggles to hold up herself and her son. Janet comes by in a boat, but after a moment of recognition refuses to help Olivia. Although she can float in the sea "as though sustained by some unseen force" and "as if it was her native element," Olivia cannot hold up her son, who becomes heavy as lead (*Marrow* 268–73). Although white supremacy has indeed sustained Olivia's social position, and is "her native element," it is a lethal environment for her son who is sinking and drowning just before she wakes up. This dream sequence repeats with a difference an earlier scene in the book, where Olivia recognizes and then ignores Janet. Significantly, Olivia's refusal to acknowledge Janet is narratively tied to another threat to Dodie's life when he nearly falls out the window to a certain death (*Marrow* 106). It also foreshadows the ending of the novel, where Dodie's life is threatened once again, and Olivia must plead with Janet for help. This thematic repetition suggests both the price Olivia might pay for robbing Janet of financial and social capital, and the causal relation between these misdeeds and the distress of herself and her son.

The novel begins and ends with moments of crisis organized around the life and impending death of Dodie. The first threat to his life comes before he is even born, as his mother goes into premature labor after seeing Janet. After his birth, Dodie nearly dies again from choking on a piece of a rattle given to him by Polly Ochiltree. The rattle represents the material and cultural inheritance bestowed upon Dodie by the old South, embodied by his aunt. This legacy nearly kills the infant in symbolic terms when a piece of the rattle lodges in his throat and impairs his ability to breathe. Significantly, this incident immediately follows in narrative time the first meeting of the Big Three, which concludes with a unified toast to white supremacy (*Marrow* 28–47). In both instances, threats to Dodie's health are linked narratively to the social order of the old South and contemporary efforts to reinstate it.

The final time Dodie's life is threatened, the indirect cause is the riot fomented by his father and his co-conspirators. Afraid for their lives, black servants flee and leave Dodie by the window where he develops membranous croup. The croup is potentially deadly, and Dodie needs an operation or else he will suffocate. Dodie's bout with the croup represents the third time in the novel where he nearly dies because he cannot breathe. The first time is during Olivia's dream sequence, when he nearly drowns. The second time is when he nearly chokes on Polly Ochiltree's rattle. These allusions to suffocation have a particular symbolic significance. Shortly after Dodie's birth, Mammy discovers a small mole under his left ear, "just where the hangman's knot would strike" (*Marrow* 46). On a "black, or yellow, or poor-white" child, such a mark would suggest the child was destined for "judicial strangulation." Although Mammy considers it "manifestly impossible that a child of such high quality" should suffer such a fate, she nonetheless regards this mole as a bad omen (*Marrow* 10). The mole is mentioned each time Dodie's life is in danger, and as the mark of a criminal it suggests that Dodie's health problems are connected to the historical sins that have made him heir to a racist state.

Chesnutt thus warns his white readers that racial violence may backfire, and that "those that do violence must expect to suffer violence" (*Marrow* 309). However, he is careful to make this point without advocating black militancy. That is why all threats to Dodie's life are biological, accidental, and only indirectly linked to white racist practice. After all, Chesnutt hopes to seduce his readers to his point of view, "while amusing them to lead them on imperceptibly, unconsciously step by step to the desired state of feeling" that white supremacy should be dismantled.[12] This represents not only his political strategy, but probably also his personal convictions, as Chesnutt never advocated violent resistance. Thus, each instance of Dodie's life being threatened represents a "fatality for which no one could be held responsible," although there is always in narrative terms a connection to white racist practices (*Marrow* 47).

In *The Marrow of Tradition*, violence does not respect the boundaries of segregation. In the final scenes of the novel, grief and loss caused by the riot reach across lines of race and class into the Carteret home. Chesnutt devotes the final pages of the novel to an exploration of the ways in which the private and public actions of both Olivia and Major Carteret have finally "come home to roost." This is the moment when Dodie is near death from the croup, which he caught during and as a direct result of the riot. As Dodie struggles for his life, Olivia sits alone with the sick child:

> She was wiping the child's face, which was red and swollen and covered with moisture, the nostrils working rapidly, and the little patient vainly endeavored at intervals to cough up the obstruction to his breathing. . . . The little lips had become livid, the little nails, lying against the white sheet, were blue. The child's efforts to breathe were most distressing and the gasp cut the father like a knife. Mrs. Carteret was weeping hysterically. (*Marrow* 313–16)

Chesnutt's move from realism to a sentimental narrative mode emphasizes the helplessness and fragility of the child. Although protest fiction such as Stowe's had used sentimental representations of racial violence, such as Uncle Tom's whipping, to generate sympathy for black characters, Chesnutt takes a different route. When he represents suffering in sentimental terms, it is the suffering of white characters with whom white readers might identify. For example, we are simply notified after the fact that Miller's son was struck by a stray bullet during the riot (*Marrow* 320). Thus Chesnutt appeals to the self-interest, rather than sympathy, of his readers by constructing a plot that reveals the lives of black and white people to be intimately connected. Because of the riot, all doctors are unavailable, apart from Dr. Miller. Only Miller can save Dodie, and Olivia must ask Janet for her permission while there is "time enough, but none to spare" (*Marrow* 329). In this way, Chesnutt asks his white readers to recognize how the lives and destinies of black and white citizens are inextricably intertwined. Not only are they dependent on each other, but also the violence unleashed against the Millers and other African American people comes home to roost and threaten the life of Dodie Carteret. In *The Marrow of Tradition*, the shared blood, past, and society of the Carterets and the Millers bind their fates together. They are each other's damnation and only hope.

Race, Violence, and the Fiction of Safety

Elizabeth Alexander has argued that African American people's relationship to their racial group is formed in part during moments of physical and psychic violence which constructs that identity as abject.[13] Confronted with the public violation of black bodies, African Americans are forced into a particular understanding of their own identities. Alexander's analysis and Chesnutt's novel suggest the ways in which a white racial consciousness is co-constructed in those same moments. If the black body is defined by its lack of legal protection, the white body is defined dialectically as the legally protected body. One can be violated with impunity, the other cannot: "From time immemorial it had been bred in the Southern white consciousness, and in the Negro consciousness also, for that matter, that the person of a white man was sacred from the touch of a Negro, no matter what the provocation" (*Marrow* 303). The most important difference between white and black experiences of racial violence is the belief among white people that they are relatively safe from the violence of racism. Thus, Ellis can be against lynch law, and yet remain divested from (if "vaguely uncomfortable" with) the controversy over Sandy in a way that Miller and Weston cannot. For although Ellis "could not approve the acts of his own people; neither could he, to a Negro, condemn them. Hence he was silent" (*Marrow* 291). In *Marrow*, Chesnutt reveals the fallacy of this racially segregated sense of destiny and responsibility. Ellis's silence makes him complicit in Sandy's near-lynching and for that matter in Tom's crimes. Ellis's sense of social obligation makes him cover for Tom, permitting the latter to act with impunity and to remain a rival for Clara's affections longer than otherwise possible. This romantic triangle enables Chesnutt to suggest how self-interest should disrupt the sense of loyalty between whites, which makes Ellis silent in the novel and the North complicit with the South in turn-of-the-century America. The conclusion of the novel, where Dodie's life hangs in the balance, extends that point to all white Americans as Carteret, the mastermind behind the violence, faces the loss of his own son as a direct consequence of the riot.

In *The Marrow of Tradition*, Chesnutt reveals whiteness and blackness to be interdependent constructions underpinned by performances of racial violence in which black Americans are forced to become unwilling participants. Chesnutt also suggests that the significance of racial violence goes beyond the need to discipline the newly emancipated African American population, for it is the glue that holds together otherwise tenuous white coalitions. In the meetings of the Big Three, Chesnutt shows how the practice of racism enables strategic unity across class and regional divisions among white Americans. In the tensions between McBane on one side and Major Carteret and General Belmont on the other, Chesnutt foregrounds the conflicts between whites of different classes and backgrounds. Each time the three men meet, Carteret must control his displeasure with McBane: "McBane had always grated upon his aristocratic sensibilities. The captain was an upstart, the product of the democratic idea operating upon the poor white man, the descendant of the indentured bond-servant and the socially unfit" (*Marrow* 86–87). As the son of an overseer, McBane represents more than just a member of a "lower" social class. He also is a reminder of the dirty work that underpinned the Southern slave economy. McBane, in turn, knows Carteret's feelings and has his own hostilities:

> The captain flushed at the allusion to his father's calling, at which he took more offense than at the mention of his own. He knew perfectly well that these old aristocrats, while reaping the profits of slavery, had despised the instruments by which they were attained—the poor-white overseer only less than the black slave . . . he had never been invited to the home of either General Belmont or Major Carteret. . . . He would help these fellows carry the state for white supremacy, and then he would have his innings—he would have more to say than they dreamed, as to who should fill the offices under the new deal. (*Marrow* 82, emphasis added)

Chesnutt reveals that such conflicts run deep and are tied to histories of uneven class privilege and tensions among white Americans. What ultimately unites McBane and Carteret—the only thing that can unite them—is the practice of white supremacy. Each time their underlying tensions flare up, Chesnutt shows how their "shared sentiments" of white supremacy enable them to overcome their differences and toast to a common political cause (*Marrow* 87–88). The illusion of a white "we" organized around race animosity consolidates an otherwise fractured "white America." However, it is a dangerous illusion that is purchased at great cost as evident in the many injuries to white bodies throughout the novel including, of course, McBane's demise at the conclusion of the novel.

The promise of a whiteness unified around anti-black violence posits the possibility of displacing conflicting class interests among white Southerners and putting in its place the pseudodemocratic moment of the public lynching. Here everybody (white) can participate in the illusion of plantation power over and access to black bodies: "We couldn't afford [killing African Americans] before the war," said McBane, "but the niggers don't belong to anybody now, and there's nothing to prevent our doing as we please with them. A dead nigger is no loss to any white man" (*Marrow* 183). McBane's assertion that "*We* couldn't afford that before the war" suggests a sense of belonging to a slave holding "we," enabled by post-emancipation equal access to black bodies. In *The Marrow of Tradition,* the near-lynching of Sandy is represented as a staged production, complete with the construction of bleacher seating, where white folks from all walks of life can participate in and even profit from the public spectacle of black bodies being compelled to act out the nature and meaning of racial domination and subordination.[14]

The moment of public violation constructs the social space in between, and the lived experience of, racially differentiated bodies. As a black "we" is constructed through identification with the violated victim's fate—so a white "we" must be constructed at that same moment through an absolute dis-identification with such a fate, an understanding that one's body ensures membership among the untouchable executioners regardless of whether one actively participates in the violence. It is this dis-identification, this sense of racialized safety, which Chesnutt sets out to disrupt by revealing it to be a dangerous fiction. Indeed, the many white bodies in danger throughout the novel testify to the fallacy of segregation as a system in which racial terror impacts only one segment of society. Although the victims of violence in Wilmington in 1898 were overwhelmingly African American, white Fusionists were also threatened and of course they lost their positions in government. Wilmington was so significant not only because it exemplified the best hopes of Reconstruction, but also because it illustrated what could be gained through interracial cooperation and how the reassertion of white supremacy ran counter to the interests of many white Americans.

Chesnutt's many endangered and injured white bodies is historically revisionist, but narratively necessary to bear out the central claim of the novel that white Americans risk paying a terrible price for tolerating and participating in racial violence. Because the fiction of racialized safety, which he wants to disrupt, is written on black bodies, it must be "unwritten" on white bodies. The constant danger to Dodie's life is emblematic of a plot filled with white bodies in danger. What makes Dodie particularly significant as a character is his function as a hieroglyph in the racial grammar book of the novel: he is the heir to and future of white supremacy. His birth reinvigorates the major's sense of purpose in shoring up white supremacist rule. Dodie represents the future of the South, but unlike Tom Delamere he is not yet corrupted and not yet an active participant in the social order. It is the simultaneous innocence and guilt of this child, tied to the past he inherits, to the present in which he has no agency, and to the future he will help to shape, that make him such a crucial character in Chesnutt's story. And it is through the precarious life of Dodie, and the sign that marks him, that Chesnutt suggests the "fearful price" the South will pay if it does not abandon its racist practices. However, Dodie's body also signifies the possibilities of healing suggested by the end of the novel, where his life can still be saved if the Millers and the Carterets can reconcile and together rewrite the terms of their relationship.

Protest and Literary Ventriloquism in *The Marrow of Tradition*

Dodie's injuries are directly tied to the legacy and reassertion of white supremacy in the novel. The representation of these injuries as biological and accidental enables Chesnutt to issue his warning that "those that do violence must expect to suffer" without advocating black militancy for they are injuries "for which no one can be held responsible" (*Marrow* 47). This narrative choice is an important aspect of Chesnutt's strategy. At the turn of the century, the United States was a dangerous place for black activists and writers critiquing white supremacy. Ida B. Wells had been run out of Memphis for writing and publishing her 1892 anti-lynching editorials in the *Memphis Free Speech*, and her offices had been burned to the ground. The same fate was suffered by black newspaper editor Alexander Manly in Wilmington during the riot. Manly had published his own anti-lynching editorial in the city's black newspaper, the *Wilmington Record*, in 1898. The editorial claimed the white paternity of many African American people and defended the right of white women and black men to be intimate. It created an uproar in the South, where it was widely reprinted and excerpted in newspapers. Journalists nationwide later held the editorial responsible for the Wilmington riot and coup.[15] Manly's editorial provides one important intertextual referent for *Marrow* and exemplifies Chesnutt's narrative strategy of speaking indirectly, through his characters, in order to circumvent censorship and escape racial terrorism. Rather than openly espousing similar views, Chesnutt presents the very same arguments in his summary of an article written by a fictional black editor, named Barber, without explicitly authoring it (*Marrow* 85). This narrative strategy provides the author a "safety cover" and enables Chesnutt to recirculate what is substantially Manly's infamous editorial in a novel distributed by a national publishing house.

The use of fiction, a form that accommodates a variety of rhetorical and analytical modes, was a crucial aspect of his strategy.[16] Chesnutt himself described *The Marrow of Tradition* as the blending of a "novel and a political and sociological tract," which he considered "a tremendous sort of combination if the author can but find the formula for mixing them."[17] His approach to the Wilmington Riot testifies to the ability of fiction to represent forbidden and subversive knowledges.[18] His deft deployment of heteroglossia allows Chesnutt to present multiple and contradictory voices within his narrative.[19] Speaking through both white and African American characters, Chesnutt performs acts of literary ventriloquism that allow him to express opinions and critiques that would otherwise be censored in a racially repressive written sphere. This literary device provides a cover for the author and enables him to circulate a subversive critique of white supremacy and racial segregation to a national audience.[20]

The displacement and disavowal enabled by the use of fictional characters permits Chesnutt to reveal the repressive nature of the national written sphere, particularly through the dialogue and thoughts of white characters with whom the writer would not be directly identified:

> "Gentlemen," said the general soothingly, after the first burst of indignation had subsided, "I believe we can find a more effective use for this article, which, by the way will not bear too close analy-sis—*there's some truth in it*, at least there's an argument."
>
> "That is not the point," interrupted Carteret.
>
> "No," interjected McBane with an oath, "that ain't at all the point. Truth or not, no damn nigger has any right to say it." (*Marrow* 86–86, emphasis added)

Here Chesnutt validates the substance of Manly's editorial at the same time that he reveals the political climate with which his own writing must contend. The use of literary ventriloquism thus enables Chesnutt simultaneously to inscribe his own voice onto the "white text" of national memory, while using the thoughts and dialogue of white characters to affirm and recirculate black protest writing. In this way, Chesnutt appropriates the racialized protection afforded white bodies even as he posits it to be a dangerous fallacy.

After the death of Polly Ochiltree has permitted Chesnutt to underscore his point that there is "some truth" to the controversial editorial and its claims, the narrator emerges without the cover of a fictional character to validate the editorial:

The article was read aloud with emphasis and discussed phrase by phrase. Of its wording there could be little criticism—it was temperately and even cautiously phrased. As suggested by the general, the Ochiltree affair had proved that is was not devoid of truth. Its great offensiveness lay in its boldness: that a Negro should publish in a newspaper what white people would scarcely acknowledge to themselves in secret. (*Marrow* 242–43)

Here Chesnutt explicitly vindicates the editorial while indicting the press for its hypocrisy and its role in manipulating racialist sentiment.[21] More often, however, he uses white characters such as Carteret, Belmont, and McBane to make that point. This group postpones the use of the Manly editorial twice, publishing it at the precise moment when it is most likely to generate a violent response. In this way, Chesnutt represents racial violence as a calculated rather than a spontaneous, social event and reveals as a lie the notion that lynching is the result of "intense and righteous anger of the moment . . . rough but still substantial justice; for no Negro was ever lynched without incontestable proof of his guilt" (*Marrow* 114–15). Like Ida B. Wells and others, Chesnutt argues that lynching is a form of violence used specifically to terrorize and discipline African Americans, because if Sandy "were white he would not be lynched" (*Marrow* 191). However, Chesnutt escapes the violent censure aimed at Wells, and for that matter Alexander Manly in Wilmington, by ventriloquizing this assertion through a fictional character.

Because Chesnutt makes this claim in a work of fiction he can "prove" it in his storyline. When the murderer turns out to be white, there is, indeed, no lynching or any other punishment. In fact, there is barely a crime at all, as the murder of Polly Ochiltree becomes a "mere vulgar robbery," the extent of which cannot be determined. The charge finally appears absurd, and the case is abandoned (*Marrow* 233). Chesnutt thus reveals the threadbare notions of justice that underlie a system of separate but unequal legal systems for black and white, and exposes the way political considerations undermine just treatment of African Americans who are known to be innocent. However, he also proposes that white Americans may end up paying a "fearful price" for fomenting or tolerating such a system of segregated violence by representing racial injustice as a practice with disastrous and unforeseen consequences for all members of society.

After Sandy is exonerated, Carteret determines that the "truth of this ghastly story must not see the light," and his social and political power enables him to repress it. Radical journalists such as Wells and Manly were trying to bring that "ghastly story" to light, and were to varying degrees censured by violence. Chesnutt's success lies in the way in which he chooses to bring the same "ghastly story" to light: ventriloquized through the mouths of those who held the power to determine whether it would be told. And he appeals to his white readers to recognize that their own destinies are linked to those of African Americans and that racial violence poses an unacceptable danger to all of society. Furthermore, he proposes that the very logic of racial violence is itself flawed because racial violence once unleashed cannot be easily contained and it can backfire in unexpected ways. Thus, the novel is not simply a revisionist portrayal of what happened in Wilmington in 1898, but an appeal to the nation to recast the terms of national unity and to reject racial violence as a means of social discipline.

Representing racial violence as a performance, "scripted" by the press to shore up the fiction of race written on black bodies, Chesnutt reveals the ways in which white bodies can function as counternarratives. If black bodies become the slate on which the "New South Creed" will be written, Chesnutt in turn uses the bodies of white characters such as Dodie as the media on which he unwrites the fiction that racial identity can shield anyone against the consequences of racial violence.[22] Thus, the carefully orchestrated script of white supremacy spins out of control as Chesnutt compels his white characters to act out its costs and contradictions.

"Time enough, but none to spare"

Chesnutt's novel remains compelling and his warning to America relevant even though legal segregation and the lynch law have long been outlawed. Ninety-one years after *The Marrow of Tradition* was published, another destructive and deadly riot erupted across the continent in the city of Los Angeles. This time, violence broke out in response to the acquittal of four police officers accused of excessive use of violence in the videotaped beating of Rodney King.[23] The grainy recording of this beating circulated around the world and functioned, perhaps, as a textbook example of Elizabeth Alexander's thesis of the relationship between racial identity and the spectacle of violence. In the days that followed, this recording was joined by many others which affirmed Chesnutt's warning of the destructive and indiscriminate consequences of racial violence.[24] One clip was shown repeatedly. Television cameras in news helicopters hovering above south central Los Angeles filmed the beating of a truck driver named Reginald Denny. A slight man who happened to be in the wrong place at the wrong time, Denny was pulled from his truck and beaten senseless. The battered and bruised bodies of Rodney King and Reginald Denny testify to the cost of racial violence and confirm Chesnutt's warning that such violence may spill across the boundaries of segregation, be they formal or *de facto*.[25] The conjoined bodies of Rodney King and Reginald Denny, like those of Olivia and Janet, Josh Green and Captain McBane in *Marrow of Tradition*, stand as a testament to the shared destinies which belie mythologies of racial difference and social segregation. There is still "time enough, but none to spare."

Acknowledgments

I thank Brian Norman and Piper Kendrix Williams for their excellent suggestions on a draft of this chapter. I am also grateful to Saidiya Hartman for helpful comments on an earlier version of this material.

Notes

1. See for example Ferguson and Yarborough on Chesnutt's ambivalent relationship to poor African Americans and his strategic accommodationism.

2. In his short stories, Chesnutt opened up the regional fiction genre to a subversive critique of slavery and colonialism and its late-nineteenth-century aftermath, but he did so in careful and subtle ways. See Goldner for an anti-imperialist reading of Chesnutt's short stories.

3. The black illiteracy rate was at approximately 75 percent in North Carolina in 1880 (Broadhead 27).

4. As Wilson argues, Chesnutt's work was received differently because, unlike Stowe and Tourgée, he was black. Furthermore, he contended with a very different historical context.

5. Chesnutt 1993b, 140.

6. For accounts of the Wilmington Riots, see Prather, Edmonds, Cecelski, and Tyson. For a broader discussion of post-Reconstruction violence, see Shapiro. North Carolina's Historical Society has published an extensive report on the Wilmington Race Riot on the society's website, http://www.ah.dcr.state.nc.us/1898-wrrc/

7. Wagner, 311–37. For an overview of government posts held by African Americans in Wilmington at this time, see Prather, 22–29.

8. Prior to the 1898 elections, the campaign to restore white supremacy was waged through the press. The *Raleigh News and Observer*, along with the *Wilmington Messenger*, ran numerous articles that vilified African American figures in offices of public authority. The burning of the African American newspaper offices stands as a potent symbol of the reinstatement of a white monopoly on the written public sphere. See also Wagner on the re-establishment of white supremacy in the city's economic and political realms, as well as in everyday social life.

9. The case of Homer Plessy also provided a crucial impetus for Chesnutt's protest novel. This test case, which involved a light-skinned man not unlike Dr. Miller or Chesnutt himself, wound its way through the legal system during the 1890s before culminating in the infamous 1896 Supreme Court ruling that formalized segregation.

10. Chesnutt links slavery and aristocracy by defining the latter as the "prerogative . . . to live upon others" (*Marrow* 97).

11. Chesnutt calls this "God, or Fate, or whatever one may choose to call the Power that holds the destinies of man in the hollow of his hand" (*Marrow* 253).

12. Chesnutt Journals, 140.

13. Alexander, 81–98.

14. Knadler notes the performative aspect of racial identity, white as well as black, citing Judith Butler's work on gender and performativity to get at the forced performance of abjection at work in lynchings and other moments of racial violence (428).

15. See Eric Sundquist's introduction to *Marrow*, xvi–xix.

16. John Reilly argues that Chesnutt helped establish "the practice of grounding racial protest in fictionalized versions of actual historical events." See Reilly, 31.

17. Personal letter, Charles W. Chesnutt to Isaiah B. Scott. Chesnutt 1997, 167.

18. See Gordon.

19. According to M. M. Bahktin, multiple and contradictory voices within a single narrative, which he calls heteroglossia, is a basic feature of the novel's stylistics (263). Chesnutt stands out for his self-conscious engagement with and strategic use of voices. See also Finseth, 1–20.

20. See also Delmar, who focuses on Chesnutt's use of the mask as a thematic and structural device in two of Chesnutt's short stories.

21. Pettis argues Carteret's newspaper "leads the way in creating the climate for the riot" (37–48).

22. The New South Creed was famously articulated by Henry Grady in 1887: "This is the declaration of no new truth. It has abided forever in the marrow of our bones, and shall run forever in the blood that feeds Anglo-Saxon hearts." He added, "the supremacy of the white race of the South must be maintained forever" (53). Chesnutt's title picks up on Grady's use of the term "marrow" although he is not explicitly cited as is Charles Lamb.

23. See Gooding-Williams for a range of analytic perspectives on this event. I draw, as well, on my own observations as a resident of Los Angeles in 1992.

24. Although Chesnutt represents a black and white world, the victims and perpetrators of violence in Los Angeles in 1992 represented a fuller spectrum of the diversity of American society.

25. The distribution of such violence remains highly inequitable and often correlates with race.

Works Cited

Alexander, Elizabeth. " 'Can you be BLACK and Look at This?': Reading the Rodney King Video(s)." *The Black Public Sphere*. Ed. The Black Public Sphere Collective. Chicago: U of Chicago P, 1995. 81–98.

Bakhtin, M. M. *The Dialogic Imagination: Four Essays by M. M. Bakhtin*. Ed. Michael Holquist. Austin: U of Texas P, 1981.

Broadhead, Richard H. "Introduction." *The Conjure Woman and Other Tales: Charles W. Chesnutt*. Durham, NC: Duke UP, 1993. 1–22

Cecelski, David S., and Timothy B. Tyson, eds. *Democracy Betrayed: The Wilmington Race Riot of 1898 and Its Legacy*. Chapel Hill: U of North Carolina P, 1998.

Chesnutt, Charles Waddell. *The Conjure Woman and Other Tales: Charles W. Chesnutt*. Ed. Richard H. Brodhead. Durham, NC: Duke UP, 1993.

————. *The Journals of Charles W. Chesnutt.* Durham, NC: Duke UP, 1993.

————. *The Marrow of Tradition.* New York: Penguin, 1993.

————. *To Be an Author: Letters of Charles W. Chesnutt, 1889—1905.* Ed. Joseph R. McElrath Jr. and Robert Z. Leitz III. Princeton, NJ: Princeton UP, 1997.

Delmar, P. Jay. "The Mask as Theme and Structure: Charles W. Chesnutt's 'The Sheriff's Children' and 'The Passing of Grandison.'" *American Literature* 51.3 (1979): 364–75.

Duncan, Charles. *The Absent Man: The Narrative Craft of Charles W. Chesnutt,* Athens: Ohio UP, 1998.

Edmonds, Helen G. *The Negro and Fusion Politics in North Carolina, 1894–1901.* Chapel Hill: U of North Carolina P, 1951.

Ferguson, SallyAnn H. "Book Reviews" *Resources for American Literary Study* 23.1 (1997): 133–35.

Finseth, Ian. "How Shall the Truth Be Told? Language and Race in *The Marrow of Tradition.*" *American Literary Realism* 31.3 (1999): 1–20.

Goldner, Ellen J. "(Re)Staging Colonial Encounters: Chesnutt's Critique of Imperialism in *The Conjure Woman.*" *Studies in American Fiction* 28 (2000): 39–64.

Goodell, William. *The American Slave Code in Theory and Practice: Its Distinctive Features Shown by Its Statutes, Judicial Decisions, and Illustrative Facts.* New York: American and Foreign Anti-Slavery Society, 1853.

Gooding-Williams, Robert, ed. *Reading Rodney King, Reading Urban Uprising.* New York: Routledge, 1993.

Gordon, Avery. *Ghostly Matters: Haunting and the Sociological Imagination.* Minneapolis: U of Minnesota P, 1995.

Grady, Henry Woodfin. "The South and Her Problems." *The New South and Other Addresses.* New York: Haskell, 1969.

Knadler, Stephen P. "Untragic Mulatto: Charles Chesnutt and the Discourse of Whiteness." *American Literary History* 8 (1996): 426–48.

McElrath Jr., Joseph R. *Critical Essays on Charles W. Chesnutt.* New York: G.K. Hall & Co., 1999.

Miller, Ruth, ed. *Blackamerican Literature: 1760–Present.* Beverly Hills: Glencoe Press, 1971.

Pettis, Joyce. "The Literary Imagination and the Historical Event: Chesnutt's Use of History in *The Marrow of Tradition.*" *South Atlantic Review* 55 (1990): 37–48.

Prather Sr., H. Leon. *We Have Taken a City: The Wilmington Racial Massacre and Coup of 1898.* Rutherford, NJ: Fairleigh Dickinson UP, 1984.

Reilly, John M. "The Dilemma in Chesnutt's *The Marrow of Tradition.*" *Phylon* 32.1 (1971): 31–38.

Shapiro, Herbert. *White Violence and Black Response: From Reconstruction to Montgomery.* Amherst: U of Massachusetts P, 1988.

Sundquist, Eric J. *To Wake the Nations: Race and the Making of American Literature.* Cambridge, MA: Harvard UP, 1993.

Wagner, Bryan. "Charles Chesnutt and the Epistemology of Racial Violence." *American Literature* 73.2 (2001): 311–37.

Wilson, Matthew. "Who Has the Right to Say? Charles W. Chesnutt, Whiteness and the Public Sphere." *College Literature* 26.2 (1999): 18–35.

Yarborough, Richard. "The Wilmington Riot in Two Turn-of-the-century African American Novels" in *Democracy Betrayed: The Wilmington Race Riot of 1898 and Its Legacy.* Chapel Hill: U of North Carolina P, 1998.

In the Crowd series, Untitled #3 (Florida, 1935). Archival ink print, 14 × 11 inches. Image courtesy of the artist, Shawn Michelle Smith.

Section III

Inside Jim Crow and His Doubles

Because the last section posed Chesnutt and the post-Reconstruction movement as formative to a literary tradition associated with segregation, the essays
in this section work outward, geographically and chronologically, to see how
later writers addressed Jim Crow segregation and its doubles, such as *de facto*
urban segregation in the North. Anne Rice is interested in some of the more
extreme forms of racially motivated violence in the South as she identifies
"white islands of safety and engulfing blackness" in Angelina Weld Grimké's
story "Blackness" and its reprinted version "Goldie" in the context of lynching
in Valdosta, Georgia. Moving North, Michelle Gordon turns to *A Raisin in the
Sun* to identify a segregation aesthetic in Hansberry's famed play. For Gordon,
this segregation aesthetic helps to explain some of the historical misreadings
of the play and the playwright as not radical enough or naively committed to
American promises and the integration ideal.

Like Gordon's study of Hansberry, GerShun Avilez is interested in literary
responses to the notorious racially restrictive housing covenants in the urban
North. He argues for the importance of domestic space in our understanding
of segregation's effect on African American experience in *Trumbull Park* by
Frank London Brown and *Maud Martha* by Gwendolyn Brooks, especially the
way the effects of segregation were not limited to the color line but penetrate
seemingly safe black domestic spaces. Finally, Elizabeth Boyle Machlan also
looks at domestic space in the segregated urban North, but this time by attending to architectural histories of the setting of Ann Petry's *The Street* in order
to pose segregation's effect on the disintegration of American dreams of black
homeownership and strong families.

White Islands of Safety and Engulfing Blackness

Remapping Segregation in Angelina Weld Grimké's "Blackness" and "Goldie"

ANNE P. RICE

We with our blood have watered these fields
And they belong to us.

—Margaret Walker, "Delta" (1942)

Loss and the Literary Landscape

Jim Crow apartheid and Northern segregation alike operated through the racialization of space, in which geography and the built environment produced and expressed "the inequitable power relations between races" (Mohanram 3). Memory turns space into place, and a sense of place is "central to the formation of racial identity. The category of 'black body' can only come into being when the body is perceived as being out of place, either from its natural environment or its national boundaries" (ix). Segregation was all about place, the ownership of physical space conferred by memory, tradition, and the law, but also the elaborate social and symbolic code that signified such ownership. Knowing one's "place" for African Americans required giving up rights to physical space, including freedom of movement within and inscription of one's presence upon the landscape. Particularly prohibited, in the North as well as the South, were public monuments commemorating and celebrating the African American experience. The spatial environment thus normalized the silences and erasures of racial apartheid (as well as visual spectacles such as public lynching), making them seem indigenous to the land.[1]

What does it mean to commemorate and to mourn your losses on a landscape designed to erase all traces of your presence? After catastrophe, memorials provide the "foci of the rituals, rhetoric, and ceremonies of bereavement," underlining the crucial importance of returning to the place of loss, or at least having a place that "embodies that loss and allows collective mourning" (Winter 78). In the case of those displaced or traumatized by lynchings and race riots, what forms of commemoration are possible when there is no place to return to? Craig Barton explains that the intersection of space and race produced "separate, though sometimes parallel, overlapping or even superimposed cultural landscapes for black and white Americans," resulting in a "complex social and cultural geography in which black Americans occupied and often continue to occupy distinct and frequently marginalized cultural landscapes" (xv). Barton insists, moreover, that the presence of "larger cultural landscapes, defined by custom and events as much as by specific buildings, and represented in text, image, and music" provides "invaluable insights into the memory of a place" (xvi). When the physical landscape remains mute, stories, images, and songs carry the burden of memory.

In this article, I examine mourning and memory, motherhood and citizenship, body and land in Angelina Weld Grimké's 1920 short story, "Goldie," and an earlier unpublished version "Blackness." These stories were based on Mary Turner, who at eight months pregnant, was lynched in Valdosta, Georgia, in 1918—an event that I suggest constituted a primal trauma for the African American community. I place Grimké's text in the context of other African American women writing at the end of the World War I, particularly in reaction to the violence against women and children epitomized by the East Saint Louis Riot of 1917, and continuing on into the "Red Summer" of 1919. At the crest of this wave of violence, the killing of Mary Turner and her child because she protested her husband's lynching raised profound questions about how it could be possible to live in an America that had become a "sorrow home."[2] For Grimké, witnessing and mourning demanded breaking through violently maintained boundaries of "blackness" and "whiteness," those lines of force constructing the U.S. landscape as always raced white and gendered male. I argue that Grimké uses landscape images—the lynching tree, "white islands of safety" on segregation's road, and an unguarded house in the clearing—to mourn the violence done to Turner, her husband, and her child, to protest racial oppression, and to highlight white vulnerability in the face of certain retribution.

The Lynching of Mary Turner and the Landscape of Terror

While African American soldiers were off fighting for democracy in France, urban labor struggles and rural racial tensions flared at home, placing families under siege as never before. Scholars have scrutinized the violent backlash against returning veterans for demanding their rights, yet critical work remains to be done on the effect of home-front violence against African American women and children. Two wartime atrocities on the U.S. home front in particular drew expressions of maternal grief and outrage from female African American writers: the July 1917 race riots in East Saint Louis, Illinois, and the May 1918 lynching of Mary Turner and her unborn child. During the war, U.S. cities erupted into racial violence against African Americans, but East Saint Louis was by far the worst. In a carefully planned rampage, mobs of white workers, incensed about black employment in factories holding government contracts, roved the streets attacking and murdering African Americans, including women and children. They set entire residential areas alight, leaving residents the choice of being burned in their homes or risking death outside. Witnesses described police and soldiers helping these uncontrolled gangs, which included among them white women and children. In a special report in the September 1917 *Crisis*, twenty-four-year-old Lula Suggs recalls hiding in a cellar with "about one hundred women and children" while "the School for Negroes on Winstanly Avenue was burned to the ground. When there was a big fire the rioters would stop to amuse themselves, and at such time I would peep out and actually saw children thrown into the fire" (Du Bois 231). Beatrice Deshong, age 26, reported seeing "men, small boys, and women and little girls all . . . trying to do something to injure the Negroes. . . . I saw the mob chasing a colored man who had a baby in his arms" (231). Newspapers put the death toll at 200, but Congress gave a low estimate of forty blacks and eight whites killed, with six thousand people displaced at least temporarily. On July 28, when the National Association for the Advancement of Colored People (NAACP) staged a silent parade down Fifth Avenue to protest the riots, marchers pointedly did not carry the U.S. flag. The silent men, women, and children streaming down the center of Manhattan instead carried signs reading: "Mother, Do Lynchers Go to Heaven?"; "Pray for the Lady Macbeths of East St. Louis"; "Mr. President, Why Not Make America Safe for Democracy?"; and "Give Us a Chance to Live."

In May 1918, less than a year after the East Saint Louis riots, a convict laborer in Valdosta, Georgia named Sidney Johnson shot and killed Hampton Smith after the white landlord refused to pay him for hours worked in excess of his debt. Although Johnson made it known that he had acted alone, rumors quickly circulated of a conspiracy mastermind by Hayes Turner, who also had labored for Smith, and whose wife had been beaten by Smith on several occasions. With the apparent complicity of law enforcement, Turner was arrested, and then seized by a mob while being transported to a new jail. The mob hung him from a crossroads tree, allowing his body to remain on display where it was viewed by hundreds of people who came by automobile, wagon, buggy, and on foot. His wife, Mary, spoke out against the mob, only to be hunted and brutally murdered. The Turner lynching deeply traumatized the African American community, drawing an immediate and anguished response from black politicians, artists, and journalists.[3] In a letter accompanying her submission to the *Atlantic Monthly* of "Blackness," a short story based on the lynching, Angelina Weld Grimké wrote:

> I am sending enclosed a story. It is not a pleasant one, but it is based on fact. Several years ago, in Georgia, a colored woman quite naturally it would seem became wrought up, because her husband had been lynched. She threatened to bring some of the leaders to justice. The mob, made up of "Christians" and brave white men determined to teach her a lesson. She was dragged out by them to a desolate part of the woods and the lesson began. First she was strung up by her feet to the limbs of a tree, next her clothes were saturated with kerosene oil, and then she was set afire. While the woman shrieked and writhed in agony, a man, who had brought with him a knife used in the butchering of animals, ripped her abdomen wide open. Her unborn child fell to the ground at her feet. It emitted one or two little cries but was soon silenced by brutal boots that crushed out the head. Death came at last to the poor woman. The lesson ended.[4]

Grimké's description of the incident makes clear that this lesson was "learned" not just by Turner, but by Grimké and others who witnessed its aftermath, especially as mediated through news reports and heightened by a horrified identification with the victim that produced an outpouring of words and art. Many connected the assault against Turner with the earlier riots.[5] For instance, Meta Warrick Fuller's 1919 statue of a woman clutching her stomach protectively as figures swirl around her lower limbs bore the title: "Mary Turner: A Silent Protest Against Lynching." Like the marchers in Harlem's Silent Protest Parade, Fuller's statue restores speech to the silenced, abjected black body through a physical presence that communicates dignity, anguish, and rage exceeding words.

Anne Spencer's poem "White Things," on the other hand, written in outrage over Turner's lynching and published in the *Crisis* in 1923, seeks to make visible the unnatural and destructive power of white supremacy. Noting that "most men are black men, but the white are free," Spencer describes a race of mutants who steal onto the earth and in a nihilistic rampage bleach everything of beauty they find. Her invocation of landscape recalls how this culture of violence displaced the native populations and destroyed the natural resources of the country to fuel its imperialistic industrial expansion. Reversing traditional Western associations of white and black as good and evil, Spencer shows that the white things consume people as well, burning "a race of black, black men" to "ashes white." The white skull of the black man, "a glistening awful thing" and a "trophy for a young one," becomes in Spencer's poem a prophetic symbol of the accelerating degeneration of white civilization (204).

The fact that Spencer, like Grimké, drew on nature imagery in much of her poetry provides one explanation for why she chose to express her anger and sadness over the murder of Mary Turner through a landscape ravaged by white supremacy. This devastated landscape was not simply a poetic device, however, but also is a faithful depiction of the landscape in which African Americans lived and moved in the years during and after the war. Twenty-six race riots took place during the summer of 1919, a period so bloody James Weldon Johnson christened it "The Red Summer." White riots broke out in cities across the country, including Washington, DC, Chicago, Omaha, Charleston, and Knoxville. Violence swept rural areas as well, most infamously in the massacre of black sharecroppers who had dared to form a union in Elaine, Arkansas.[6] In all, seventy-six lynchings were officially recorded for the year.

Perhaps Grimké drew on her own experience of five days of white veterans rampaging and killing near where she lived in Washington when she imagined Mary Turner's feelings of panic and fear during the invasion of her home. Inspired by Turner's lynching and published in 1920 in Margaret Sanger's *Birth Control Review*, "Goldie" has enjoyed renewed attention as a critique of the racist underpinnings of the eugenics movement. Although scholars have examined in detail the space in which "Goldie" appeared (a magazine promoting birth control and catering to white women), a more detailed examination of the spaces appearing within the story itself can tell us a great deal about the lived experience of Jim Crow segregation. Lynching produced terror that disoriented people, changing their experience of space itself by dramatizing their vulnerability and lack of both public and private protection. Daylanne English has observed that African American women protested lynching "by stretching the literary form—to and beyond—its limits" (119). In both versions of the Turner story examined here, Grimké stretches the literary form to repair terror's disorientation by externalizing it, while also creating new possibilities for recovery through the remapping of psychic spaces.

The Revolutionary Space of "Blackness"

Grimké's papers contain three different stories, each with numerous draft versions, written in response to the murder of Mary Turner and her child.[7] Claudia Tate maintains that Turner's lynching "so severely affected Grimké that not only did she rewrite that story over and over again, but the activity of rewriting it seems to have been more important than her desire to see it in print or performed" (217). Yet Grimké's letter to the *Atlantic Monthly*, in which she argues for the story's inclusion in a magazine devoted to exposing atrocities abroad, such as the Armenian genocide, suggests that the working through of her own wounding by this ongoing event demanded public as well as private expression. Close attention, moreover, to the evolution of her narrative from a nearly literal retelling of the lynching to the story of a home invasion that is avenged by a man who returns from the North reveals Grimké's desire to portray the lynching as part of a national assault against African American lives, in which denial of full citizenship and opportunity for advancement among even the most educated blacks is part of the same system of oppression as the brutal murder of a sharecropper's family in the deep South.

In Grimké's first retelling, entitled "The Waitin'," Mary Greene, "a little ignorant black woman with wool for hair and indeterminate large features" is murdered along with her unborn child by the same mob who killed her husband after he intervened to protect her from sexual assault. Mary's "crime" consists of her explosion of speech against her husband's murderers, whom she vows to bring to justice. The third-person narrative closely follows Mary Greene as she is escorted by the mob to her death, "shut in by a wall of horrible eyes and horrible breathing," only to pause and draw the veil as the lynching party advances toward the tree and the bushes close behind them. Except for a blaze of light "so vivid it could be seen even through the underbrush," the killing remains screened and available only through the shrieks of the burning woman and—after an excruciating two or three minutes—the "birth" by vivisection of her baby. Grimké obsessively reworked this scene in each of her stories, perhaps trying to find the right distance from which to witness an event at once beyond description and at the same time occupying a psychic space so overwhelming it demanded release through witnessing. Clearly, she found it difficult to imagine the scene without the possibility of redress. In one draft of "The Waitin'," the leader of the mob enters Mary's home—lovingly built by her husband John—and threatens to rape her. Although she is trembling with fear, Mary shows him a crack in the floor and warns him not to step over it. When he does, she nearly strangles him to death. It is interesting to note that Grimké abandoned this draft, along with several others, perhaps, in part, because of her difficulty rendering Mary's speech convincingly in dialect.

In "Blackness," Grimké reworks the narrative to include the possibility of revenge in a number of important ways. First, "Blackness" is a first-person attack on segregation by a member of the Northern black bourgeoisie, a lawyer who inverts the logic of white lynch mobs to argue that the bankruptcy of the system justifies extra-legal violence by blacks. The lawyer, a Southerner who came North after a disappointment in love to make his fortune, delivers his confession in a darkened house to his friend and law partner, Reed, while outside a white detective, unaware that the lawyer has entered the house, awaits his return. The lawyer (whose name we never learn) has murdered the man behind the lynching of his former lover, her husband, and unborn child in retaliation for the husband's "crime" of defending his wife against rape. The lawyer expresses no remorse of his own: "In the most lawless part of the country that is itself steadily growing lawless, I have broken a man-made law, but if there is a God, and He is just . . . I shall not be afraid . . . to stand before Him and look in his eyes" (249).

The movement of the story's opening sentence—"I stepped from the warm and wettest blackness I remember into the chilling blackness of the cellar"—from uterine imagery into death-like suspension describes Reed's journey from false consciousness into immersion in the cold reality of "blackness" in the United States (218). The men communicate strictly through sound and touch as they traverse a house in the dark. This fugitive underground status recalls the fugitive slave narratives and brings to mind later revolutionaries such as the protagonists of Ellison's *Invisible Man* and Wright's "The Man who Lived Underground," who also mine the creative possibilities afforded by such blackness. As in Wright's text, Reed's entrance into the cellar requires him to "dissolv[e] the meaning of conventional cultural and sensory images to reconstruct them on his own terms" (Young 70). As his name suggests, Reed—and along with him the reader of the text—must learn a new way to interpret reality beyond the visual logic of the segregated order.

Domestic space in "Blackness" critiques white terrorism and Jim Crow segregation north as well as south of the Mason-Dixon Line. Reed describes his friend as "rather radical," "unconventional," and perhaps "embittered. But then, were we not all of us as colored men, even though living in a northern city, more or less that? Certainly we had cause enough to be" (223). Reed recalls that the lawyer purchased the house in which they hide as a business venture, but it soon turned into a "very white and heavy elephant on his hands," as he refused to renovate it until he had the capital "to carry out his plans for remodeling." This failure to remake the house to his liking underlines the inability of the black bourgeoisie ever to assimilate into a segregationist society, North or South, lacking money, but also less tangible assets such as cultural capital and the full rights of citizenship. The item that stands out most clearly in the lawyer's darkened study—Reed sees it as a "huge blur of white"—is a bust of Wendell Phillips, the fiery orator who attained prominence in the antislavery movement after an 1837 speech at Boston's former slave market, Fanieul Hall, condemning the mob murder of Elijah P. Lovejoy, a minister whose own persecution began when he denounced the lynching of a black man. By making the bust of Phillips the only whiteness admissible in this space, Grimké establishes the lawyer as the intellectual and moral heir of the abolitionist tradition and links his fugitive status in the North to that of famous runaways such as Frederick Douglass who also felt compelled to "confess" the conditions of their oppression and rebellion.

Grimké's enactment of revenge for the silencing and annihilation of Turner and her child depends on regaining control of speech even at the risk of death. The lawyer tells Reed when he begins his confession: "I am going to do a thing I never remember doing before and, after tonight, I shall never do it again. I am going to talk about myself" (231). The revelation that takes place in hushed tones, circumscribed by the watchful presence of the white man outside, takes on a conspiratorial as well as testimonial charge. Several times during the confession, the two communicate through a silence in which the blackness flows between them, and when he does speak, Reed's voice seems "strange" in his own ears.

The lawyer's lengthy, nearly four-page description of journeying down South in the "pig pen" of the Jim Crow car—a humiliating experience exactly the reverse of Reed's sojourn into emancipatory "blackness"—makes the link between slavery and current conditions even more explicit. He stresses the bankruptcy of a legal system that construes the abject circumstances he witheringly describes as "equal accommodation" (232–236). To his description of the car's "unspeakable" filth into which were herded, "body wedged against body," Reed replies that such tight packing of the cars, with their stifling heat and body odor, might actually be "evidence of [the white man's] long sighted policy. In case of an epidemic, for instance" (234). This passage not only connects such herding and deprivation to the Middle Passage, but also highlights white supremacy's genocidal impulses in the twentieth century.

This drawn-out description of bodies degraded by the Jim Crow car is matched by an equally lengthy and excruciating focus on the bodies of the lynching victims, who have been murdered together.[8] Nearly reproducing the scene Grimké conjured in her letter to the *Atlantic Monthly* (itself a close retelling of accounts in the Negro press), the lawyer's description of this sight comes in bursts that are punctuated by the pounding of his fist on his knee and are so tortured Reed begs him to stop. In "Blackness," sound both precedes and exceeds sight, first in the communication in the invisibility of the lawyer's home and then in nearly four pages describing the "creaking voices" and "the duet"—the sound of the ropes holding bodies of different weight swinging from the tree limb in the breeze, moving first one, then the other, and then together—that the lawyer hears as he waits for dawn outside his lover's home. In a passage of agonizing deferral, the lawyer puts off seeing what he—and we—know is already there in the midst of a new morning "breathtaking" and "poignant" in its beauty. He goes slowly toward the trees, using extraordinary effort to keep his feet moving toward the sound: "I knew that between me and whatever *it* was, was now only this thin screen of delicate and beautiful green leaves. I put up my hands to them and then I noticed an inchworm making his awkward, energetic and seemingly important journey along the leaves and twigs. I watched him a long time, and just beyond were the creaking and the stillness" (243). The lawyer describes closing his eyes and pulling the branches aside, hearing the ominous creaking as he finally opens his eyes to behold his lover and her husband naked and mutilated with their child lying crushed beneath them on the ground.

After discovering the bodies, the lawyer visits the home of the woman's cousin, demands the names of her attackers, then vomits. Earlier on his journey, the Jim Crow car had made him sick to his stomach, and his vigil on the steps of his lover's house during the night produces in him "a most horrible nausea" (240). This abject, nauseous condition is thus portrayed as systemic to segregation. It is significant that the would-be rapist and leader of the lynch mob is a stationmaster, in charge of controlling movement within the territory and ensuring that the Jim Crow system runs smoothly. Asked to name the culprit, the cousin reacts in a "frenzy of fear," imploring his questioner to "be quiet," then finally stammering, "yes," his assent interrupting the linguistic underpinnings and demand for silence in Jim Crow segregation. The revenge scenario also demands the disruption of the stationmaster's ability to speak. After carefully selecting a place—"a little patch of woods. It seemed fitting we should meet where the trees were" (247)—the lawyer takes his time verbally tormenting his victim, who begins to stammer with fear before the lawyer strangles him and leaves him "hidden away—among the trees" (248).

As important as this act of speech is to Reed's witnessing role, when he has unburdened himself, the lawyer tells Reed that he can't imagine what he has done for him by listening to his story. Reed reassures his friend that he has acted in accordance with a higher law: "To have done less would have to have been less than a man." The ending of the story suggests, moreover, the presence of a larger resistance effort, like the Underground Railroad, assisting fugitives and conveying vital messages and information: "He held out his hand and mine gripped it. Neither of us said a word and then abruptly he turned away and went down the alley. . . . He would have to pass under the gas light at the corner. He came to it, passed through and was lost in the blackness beyond. I have reason to believe he escaped. But I have never heard from him or seen him since" (250–51). This story of an African American man who murders a white attacker and seems to operate as part of a group perhaps exceeded what the *Atlantic Monthly*—or any magazine with a predominantly white readership—would be willing to publish in an anti-lynching story authored by an African American woman.

"Goldie" and the Psychological Landscape of Oppression

In contrast to the detailed confession and protest narrative of "Blackness," in "Goldie," the version of the story eventually published, Grimké critiques segregation primarily through a symbolic and allegorical evocation of the southern landscape. Through detailed exploration of this gendered and racialized space Grimké conveys the sensory experience of the besieged female body in a narrative ostensibly told from the viewpoint of the avenging male. The story begins in *medias res* and is told through the third-person perspective of a man newly embarked from the train who battles survivor's guilt on the road toward his sister's home, trying not to think about her frantic telegram summoning him. The slow pace and sheer length of "Goldie" enact a post-traumatic deferral of knowledge. The woods he must pass through seem a "boundless, deep, horrible waiting sea," in which he wrestles to avoid the truth he already knows (that his sister has been lynched) and to deny the dread of a future he can already guess (his own death by lynching). The first sentence makes clear the change in focus from revolutionary blackness to a world divided into black and white: "He had never thought of the night, before, as so sharply black and white; but then he had never walked before, three long miles, after midnight, over a country road" (282). The going is difficult, and he has to pause step by step—much as Reed does when entering the house in "Blackness"—to reorient himself as he draws closer to the violent center of segregation.

The name of Grimké's protagonist, Victor Forrest, marks him as a kind of African American Everyman struggling on an arduous journey toward redemption. The darkness is "palpable" and the landscape seems alive and breathing. Indeed it seems to Victor, that the "woods . . . were not really woods at all but an ocean that had flowed down in a great rolling black wave of flood to the very lips of the road itself and paused there as though suddenly arrested and held poised in some kind of strange and sinister spell" (282). Although he tells himself not to worry and chides himself for his fanciful imagination, he feels as if he's in "actual danger," that "at any second the spell might snap and with that snapping, this boundless, deep upon deep of horrible waiting sea, would move, rush, hurl itself heavily and swiftly together from two sides, thus engulfing, grinding, crushing, blotting out all in its path" (283).

He is kept going only by the "bright spots" that he calls "white islands of safety," where the woods seem to "draw back . . . in order to get a good deep breath before plunging forward" (283). He feels the air in the woods as "dank, black oppressiveness," and he stops in one of the clearings to "fill his lungs anew with God's night air." As he gazes upward, however, he sees millions of stars above him, "each one hardly brilliant stabbing its way whitely through the black heavens." Sometimes "if the islands were large enough," Victor catches sight of "a very pallid, slightly crumpled moon sliding furtively down to the west" (283). The image of violent penetration and furtive criminality suggests that what he takes to be islands of safety have been carved out of a landscape "sharply black and sharply white . . . but mostly black." Danger comes not from the woods, but from his exposed position of vulnerability on the road.

In *Passed On*, Karla Holloway argues that the way many African Americans die—in riots and rebellions, through executions, lynchings, police brutality, suicides, and undertreated illness—produces an association between blackness and mortality that does great harm to the "culture's collective sense of itself" (59). Victor's misidentification of the life-giving and death-dealing values of whiteness and blackness signals the distance he must travel toward racial self-awareness. Victor discovers that "a dark road . . . could make it possible for you to see yourself quite plainly—almost too plainly" (286). The nauseous condition of "Blackness" arises with his memory of why he left: "Certainly a colored man couldn't do the things that counted in the South. To live here, just to *live* here, he had to swallow his self-respect. . . . The trouble was he couldn't keep it swallowed—it nauseated him" (285).

Part of the terror of white violence required that it remain unacknowledged as such. Without courtroom depositions or official inquiry, violent spectacles and mass crimes rarely entered the public archive, or entered through white supremacist manipulations of the language of innocence and victimization, goodness and evil, suffering and moral responsibility. Although African Americans always had to perform their knowledge of white violence through submissive actions, to speak this knowledge in the South amounted to suicide; in the North such speech provoked an immediate silencing and censorship. Creating images of whiteness as concentrated evil and bringer of death became an important aesthetic strategy for African Americans to turn their "grief to grievance" and to move "from suffering injury to speaking out against that injury" (Cheng 5).

The "dank, blank oppressiveness" of Grimké's living forest, therefore, describes not an intrinsic property of blackness, but the emotional and psychological condition described in Grimké's January 1920 *Competitor* article: "From morning to night, week in week out, year in year out, until death ends all, [African Americans] never know what it means to draw one clean, deep breath free from the contamination of the poison of that enveloping force which we call race prejudice. Of necessity they react to it." Although some "are made hopeless, indifferent, submissive, lacking in initiative," and others pursue "temporary pleasures to drown their memory," still others are "embittered, made resentful, belligerent, even dangerous" (413). It is the presence of this last group that Victor feels all around while journeying down segregation's road. In defiance of racism's toxicity, the woods remain alive, palpable, and threatening, pushing ever more insistently at the artificial margins of whiteness.

Trees and Roots: African American Embodiment and Memory

In Grimké's fiction and poetry, trees operate as complex and often occult figures of African American embodiment and experience. At times, as in her poem, "At April," such embodiment is an expression of joy: "Toss your gay heads,/Brown girl trees;/Shake your downy russet curls/ . . . Who knows better than we,/With the dark, dark bodies/What it means/When April comes . . . ?" (65). At others, as in "The Black Finger," Grimké uses the tree to express racial uplift and pride: "I have just seen a most beautiful thing/ . . . A straight black cypress,/ Sensitive,/

Exquisite,/ A black finger/Pointing upwards" (101–2). More often, however, her use of the tree recalls violent oppression, lynching in particular. Her undated poem, "Trees," begins with a conventional salute to trees as special symbols of God's providence that is canceled out by the uncanny eruption of evil in the tranquil landscape: amid the "wistful sounds of leaves," a "gruesome black hued something . . . swings and swings." The traumatic rupture of the everyday in "Trees" is answered in her poem, "Tenebris" (1927), by an indeterminacy of dread: "There is a tree, by day,/That at night,/ Has a shadow." Falling like huge black hand moving against the white man's house, the shadow's "fingers long and black" pluck at bricks which are "the color of blood and very small." The title, Latin for "in darkness," refers to the moral state of the South and to the blindness of whites to the coming threat against their power structure. Retribution and guilt, fingers on the hand, relentlessly work to destroy the house of pain built on the bodies of the tortured and enslaved.

The lynching tree held great symbolic importance for many white communities, with mobs ritually returning with new victims to a favored spot, usually a tree near the center of the community. Orlando Patterson explains that the "religion of the lost cause" that emerged in the South after the Civil War fused the secular and sacred, with political symbols and rituals assuming a religious aura and Christian symbols and rituals taking on "political-cultural meaning. Southern culture, society, and landscape became a sacred space, the home of a 'chosen people' " (205). In Christianity, the cross "is usually symbolically conflated with a tree," and Patterson sees a "substantial minority of lynchings" as partaking of a "cult of human sacrifice," in which the destruction of the African American body consecrated white supremacist ownership of Southern space.

Many African American writers also saw lynching as a ritual of human sacrifice, but they connected the victims with the martyrdom of Jesus Christ. In their poetry and fiction they therefore identified the tree as a memorial site and a place of transcendence. Countée Cullen, for example, in his long poem, "The Black Christ," refers to the lynching site as a "Second Calvary," with the tree becoming "the cross, the rood" and the ground becoming sanctified space for African Americans. By the time of the 1935, NAACP-sponsored "Art Commentary on Lynching," the representation of Christlike lynching victim merging into the tree had become commonplace. Grimké herself explicitly connects the tree with the cross when she asks at the end of "Trees": "Was Christ Himself not nailed to a tree?" Yet she tempers this reminder with an observation of how "slowly God weaves" (109). Grimké's diaries, poetry, and stories often struggle to reconcile the image of a merciful god with the daily onslaught of violence. In "The Puppet-Player," for example, a sadistic puppeteer, "clenched claw cupping a craggy chin," controls the universe, sitting "just beyond the border of our seeing,/Twitching the strings with slow, sardonic grin" (94).

Even Goldie, whom Grimké portrays as a paragon of true womanhood, worries that she must bargain with God for any chance at happiness. Her highest aspiration is to have a "little home" all her own filled with children and pets. Worried that she may be asking too much from God, she speculates that God might grant her wish if she gives up her pets, then panics at the idea of also having to give up the children, hoping that if she were good "always—from now on," God might relent and allow her the happiness of motherhood. The newly wed Goldie's prayers seem to have been answered. She writes that she lives in a house so beautiful "the very trees came right down to the very edges of the clearing on all four sides just to look at it. If he could only see how proudly they stood there and nodded their entire approval to each other" (290). Her husband, Cy, has the habit of "mooning" among the trees, as if communicating with the ancestors: "Talk to me—they do—sometimes. Tell me big, quiet things, nice things." Cy builds his home in a clearing just beyond a great live oak that Victor remembers playing in as a child and carving "his initials all over," inscribing African American memory and belonging onto the landscape (289).[9]

Endangered Families and the Landscape of Apocalypse

"How happy it all had sounded," Victor remembers, yet "once or twice—he had had the feeling that something wasn't quite right" (291). Noting the difference in literary style between "Goldie" and "Blackness," Ericka Miller maintains that the "highly sentimentalized dialogue of the latter," particularly evident in Goldie's childhood prattle and her letters to Vic, should not be dismissed as evidence of Grimké's "difficulty with convincing dialogue," but as a deliberately "genteel mannerism rendered parodic by the ultimate barbarity of the crime against Goldie and her family" (92). To read Goldie's sentimentalized dialogue as simply parodic would be, however, to miss its evocation of the vulnerability of African American female embodiment, expressed through spatial metaphor, which makes this idealized space a sorrow home. In her letters to Vic, Goldie describes her house as having "a hall that had the most absurd way of trying to get out both the front and rear doors at the same time. Would he believe it, they had to keep both the doors shut tight in order to hold that ridiculous hall in. . . . Why the unbearable thing might rise up, break down the front and back doors and escape" (290). Embedded in her coy description of domesticity is panic verging on hysteria, filled with images of flight and pursuit: "it wasn't safe, if you had any kind of heart trouble at all, to stand in the road in front of the little home all her own, because it had a way of calling you that before you knew it, you were running to it and running fast" (291).

Goldie's letters move from such manic descriptions of domestic "bliss," to her frightened confession of longstanding and intensifying harassment by Lafe

Coleman, a sexual predator whose abject and repulsive whiteness starkly contrasts with Goldie's beautiful golden skin and hair. Victor remembers "a stringy, long white man with stringy colorless hair, quite disagreeably under clean; eyes a pale grey and fishlike," whose grin reveals "the dark and rotting remains of tooth stumps" (295). Goldie is afraid to tell her husband about the harassment, fearing that mob retribution for what Cy might do could destroy the entire community, as recently happened in the next county. When he reaches "the little colored settlement," therefore, Victor is immediately relieved, to see the "silent, black little masses "of the houses" (198). Viewing the homes still intact, he realizes "there was something to this home idea, after all." Yet his return to his origins has brought him to a community under a siege that renders the "home idea" virtually impossible. The corpselike imagery of the "black little masses" recalls the "black hued something" of "Trees." Just as white violence turns the black body into a thing, the threat of violence similarly destroys the life of the black home. In the lynching climate he has entered, Victor's musings on the ways of country folk carries a sinister edge: "Bet every window is shut tight too. Turrible, the night air always used to be. Wonder if my people will ever get over these things" (293).

He sees a faint illumination from the home of Aunt Phoebe, a former slave, whom he reckons must be "way over ninety" (294). The "muffled but continuous" sound reaching him from her window strikes him as "remarkably like the keening he had heard in an Irish play" (294).[10] Although he tells himself she is probably dreaming, her moaning communicates with him, releasing his understanding: "Thoughts, conjectures, fears that he had refused, until now, quite resolutely to entertain would no longer be denied." Victor's repression of memory up to this point, although partially post-traumatic deferral, also should be seen as strategy to conserve his anger until the moment to strike: "Way down, inside of him, in the very depths, a dull cold rage began to glow, but he banked it down again, carefully, very carefully, as he had been able to do, so far, each time before that the thoughts of Lafe Coleman and little Goldie's helplessness had threatened anew to stir it" (297).

When he reaches the live oak, illuminated only by the "stabbing white stars above," Victor finds himself advancing only by "an act of sheer will" toward "a dark small mass" in the center of the clearing that is "the little home" (297). Victor ascends the steps, stumbles over a broken chair, and feels his way along the house front. The realization that the house lies penetrated and opened (as he will discover, like his sister's body), leads to traumatic splitting in which he sees his movements as performed by "the other person" who seems to have entered his body (299–300). Victor takes an agonizing tour of the destroyed house, finding on every surface traces of the now-withdrawn invading white bodies, as the gendered space of the home reverberates with accumulating images of rape. He discovers a boot print on the floor and a bloody handprint on the wall. The shards of a bourgeois domestic idyll lie everywhere, torn to pieces by the mob—pictures, knickknacks and vases, a smashed china clock, "frail white curtains," and shattered panes of glass (300). The black notes on the overturned piano with one side caved in evoke nauseating memories of Lafe Coleman's "rotting stumps of teeth" (300). In the bedroom "the stranger" finds "something dark at the foot of the bed. He moved nearer, and understood why the air was not pleasant. The dark object was a little dead dog. . . . A kick in the belly had done for him" (302). These discoveries both displace and multiply the horror of what has happened to the family.

As in "Blackness," Victor waits out the night on the steps of the ruined home. Dawn brings a breeze, and with it, the sound of "two creakings . . . among the trees" (301). As the light grows, the mob's physical imprint, a trampled path from steps to trees, emerges on the landscape. Still in a state of shock, Victor moves toward the terrible discovery: "Quite automatically he arose and followed the path. Quite automatically he drew the branches aside. Underneath those two terribly mutilated swinging bodies lay a tiny unborn child, its head crushed in by a deliberate heel" (301–2). Victor cannot comprehend what he has just seen: "Something went very wrong in his head. He dropped the branches, turned and sat down. A spider, in the sunshine was reweaving the web someone had just destroyed while passing through the grass. He sat slouched far forward watching the spider for hours."

Like the lawyer in "Blackness," Victor sees no other course open to him but to act in a manner guaranteed to bring destruction upon himself, and in all likelihood on the entire community. Grimké highlights the impossible position of African American masculinity in the face of white violence. Victor abdicated his own responsibility as male protector by leaving his sister behind in the South to pursue his fortune in the North. Yet the invasion of Goldie's home and the slaughter of her family comes as a result of Cy's *acting like a man* in response to sexual threats against his wife, a response Goldie tried to prevent with her own silence. This silence is mirrored by the reaction of the men in the community when Victor returns from the woods. Emerging only reluctantly from their homes, they offer "too noisy explanations, excuses, speeches in extenuation of their own actions, pleas, attempted exonerations of themselves," before Victor's "contemptuous eyes" compel them to stop.

Only Aunt Phoebe, who is nearly blind from cataracts—yet gifted with a second sight born partly of her ability to communicate through memory with the children and husband torn from her during slavery—will tell him where Lafe Coleman can be found. It is important to note that whereas in "Blackness" sanction for the revenge plot came from another man who also represents the law, in "Goldie," sanction comes from a woman, a mother who embodies collective memory of enslavement and endurance. It is important, too, that whereas Mary Turner's speech act in "Blackness" had been displaced into the creaking of the trees—the woman's body "speaking" in protest even after death—here Goldie speaks to Victor through memory, her words assuring him that Aunt Phoebe is sanctified and one of "God's elect." As the woods swallow Victor on his search for revenge," Aunt Phoebe begins a low keening, the last voice heard in the text (205). Lafe Coleman is found strangled to death, and we learn that thereafter "Victor Forrest died, as the other two had died, upon another tree" (205).

The lynching rampage that claimed the lives of Hayes and Mary Turner and their unborn child culminated with the death of Sidney Johnson, the person who by all accounts actually shot and killed Hampton Smith. Incensed when Johnson chose to die fighting rather than be captured alive, the mob castrated his dead body, and then dragging it through the streets to a neighboring town, where he was "put on exhibit," before he was finally burned at a local campground until "nothing but ashes remained" (Meyers 222). The killing spree leading to Johnson's death sparked a mass exodus, with "more than five hundred Negroes" fleeing the vicinity and with many more expressing their determination to leave once they could settle their affairs. In his *Crisis* expose, Walter White described a landscape in which "hundreds of acres of unfilled land flourishing with weeds and dozens of deserted farm-houses" offered "their own mute testimony" (221) of the aftermath of terror.

Grimké's story does not end, however, with the death of Victor Forrest, but with the striking image of a forest of thousands of transplanted trees—each of which has once borne a lynching victim—that crowd up against the edges of a country road along which many carefree people travel. Significantly, Grimké's text does not disclose the agent behind this transplantation: "Each tree has been chosen and transplanted here for a reason and the reason is that at some time each has borne upon its boughs a creaking victim" (305). This passive construction may hint, as in "Blackness," at the concealment necessary for revolution, but it also describes the operation of traumatic memory, in which events become implanted in the subconscious. The forest in this view also describes the individual struggle to defend against dangerous memories, which can surface belatedly, threatening to fragment and obliterate personality in their wake. These dangerous memories are not limited to the African American community.

Most people who pass along this road, "even at night," can't hear the "many things" there are to hear, for their souls are deaf to the messages of the creaking and keening in the forest.[11] This refusal to see or to hear corresponds to the silence of both North and South about lynching. At once a living memory of the enormity of African American suffering and loss and the overwhelming nature of their trauma, Grimké's wood ocean also signals the instability of the system of segregation that, like the white road, cuts brutally through the woods, and through African American lives. This foundational illusion that white islands of safety can exist in the middle of others' trauma portends an apocalyptic end to the structure of segregation: "At night the trees become an ocean dark and sinister . . . made up of all the evil in the hearts of all the mobs. . . . It is an ocean arrested at the very edges of the road by a strange spell [that] may snap at any second and . . . this sea of evil will move, rush, hurl itself heavily and swiftly, engulfing, grinding, crushing, blotting out all in its way."

Grimké's complex image of the arrested wood ocean reminds us that the mutilated black body exhibited in public space could never be the last word on the power of the event. Even after the population has fled in terror, even without a marker to signify the scene of the crime, traces and residues remain within the collective memories of both black and white Americans.[12] Intertwined with the African American victimization and protest, the wood ocean also preserves the memory of the depravity and evil of the white mob (306). As the African American women writing in the wake of East Saint Louis, the lynching of Mary Turner, and the Red Summer of 1919 understood so well, mass murder and racial violence bequeath a continuing legacy of moral and psychological damage to its perpetrators that endures for generations and continues to trouble us to this day. As a site of commemoration embodying the loss of Mary Turner and her family, preserving a record of the lived experience of a community under siege, and of the evil committed against them, Grimké's text becomes itself a monument, giving form to African American collective grief and continuing to speak loudly in protest.

Notes

1. See Loewen on the dearth of monuments dedicated to African American achievements and losses. On spectacle lynchings and the white supremacist sacralization of space, see Patterson and Hale.

2. I am borrowing this phrase from Margaret Walker's "Sorrow Home," her 1942 lament over her displacement from her Southern homeland. "O Southland, sorrow home, melody beating in my bone/and blood! How long will the Klan of hate, the hounds and/the chain gangs keep me from my own?" (12).

3. See Meyers, White. For many, Turner's lynching surpassed the worst stories of German depravity. In *Cane*, Jean Toomer makes the details of Mame Lamkins death identical with Mary Turner's—with one notable exception—his story goes that "some white man . . . jabbed his knife into the baby an' stuck it to a tree" (90), echoing wartime propaganda about German bayoneting of Belgian infants.

4. Text is taken from the back of a draft holograph attached to a holograph copy of "Blackness" in the Angelina Weld Grimké Collection, Moorland-Spingarn Research Center, box 38-11, folder 180.

5. A good literary example is Carrie Williams Clifford's *The Widening Light* (1922), which included a sequence of poems documenting her reaction to wartime terrorization at home, including "Little Mother," which memorialized Mary Turner. She thus identifies Turner's death as a primal trauma for African American mothers.

6. See Williams, Pickens.

7. Grimké's papers are housed in the Moorland-Spingarn collection at Howard University. "The Waitin' " can be found in box 38, folder 12. "Blackness" and "Goldie" are both reprinted in Carolivia Herron, *Selected Works of Angelina Weld Grimké,* which is part of the *Schomburg Library of Nineteenth Century Black Women Writers.* All quotations of Grimké within this paper unless otherwise noted are taken from Herron's text.

8. The lynching rampage that took the lives of the Turner family killed at least thirteen and more likely eighteen people. Meyers reports, "hundreds and probably thousands of people from surrounding counties viewed the remains of several victims who were left hanging for days." As in Carrie Clifford's poem, "Little Mother," both "Blackness" and "Goldie" feature the discovery of husband, wife, and child murdered together at their home. As NAACP anti-lynching activists, both authors knew that Turner and her husband died three days apart in different locations. The choice to represent the family murdered together and outside their home would seem therefore to address a psychological truth about the event.

9. Forrest's act of writing on the live oak recalls the trope of the Witnessing Tree in Paul Laurence Dunbar's "The Haunted Oak" in which the memory of the victim's suffering is inscribed on the landscape through the withering of the branch on which the victim hung and spoken by the tree through the poem.

10. David Lloyd sees in the mourning ritual of keening both during and after the Irish famine "both colonial mastery of and loss of control over colonized space" (Eng 21). Noting how "in account after account of the famine, the terrible silence of the land is . . . counterpointed by the sound of wailing or howling," Lloyd maintains that this marks "the historical emergence of a new kind of Irish subject" (360). Fred Moten's essay in that volume, "Black Mo'nin" looks at the similar collective function of the ""moan" in African American culture.

11. Although the published version of "Goldie" reprinted in the Schomburg edition refers to a "Creaking Forrest," this is a typographical error not found in either the manuscript or the typed version in the Grimké papers at the Moorland Spingarn archive.

12. See Abel's and Wall's contributions for analyses of lynching in the contemporary political arena, such as ongoing Affirmative Action struggles, Jim Crow memorabilia, and the 2007 Jena Six incident in Louisiana.

Works Cited

Barton Craig Evan, ed. *Sites of Memory: Perspectives on Architecture and Race.* New York: Princeton Architectural P, 2001.

Bay, Mia. *The White Image in the Black Mind: African American Ideas About White People, 1830–1925.* New York: Oxford UP, 2000.

Cheng, Anne. *The Melancholy of Race.* New York: Oxford UP, 2002.

Gates, Henry Louis Jr., ed. *Writings of Carrie Williams Clifford and Carrie Law Morgan Figgs.* New York: Macmillan, 1996.

Cullen, Countee. *The Black Christ and Other Poems.* New York & London: Harper Bros., 1929.

Du Bois, W.E.B and Martha Gruening. "The Massacre of East Saint Louis." *Crisis* 104 (1917): 219–37.

Dunbar, Paul Laurence. "The Haunted Oak." *Witnessing Lynching: American Writers Respond.* Ed. Anne P. Rice. New Brunswick, NJ: Rutgers UP, 2003. 89–90.

Eng, David L. and David Kazanjian. *Loss: The Politics of Mourning.* Berkeley: U of California P, 2003.

English, Daylanne K. *Unnatural Selections: Eugenics in American Modernism and the Harlem Renaissance.* Chapel Hill: U of North Carolina P, 2004. 117–39.

Grimké, Angelina Weld. *Selected Works of Angelina Weld Grimké.* Ed. Carolivia Herron. New York: Oxford UP, 1991.

Hale, Grace Elizabeth. *Making Whiteness: The Culture of Segregation in the South, 1890–1940.* New York: Vintage, 1999.

Holloway, Karla. *Passed On: African American Mourning Stories.* Durham, NC: Duke UP, 2002

Hull, Gloria. *Color, Sex and Poetry: Three Women Writers of the Harlem Renaissance.* Bloomington: Indiana UP, 1987.

Loewen, James. *Lies Across America: What Our Historic Sites Get Wrong.* New York: Simon & Schuster, 1999.

Meyers, Christopher C. "Killing Them by the Wholesale: A Lynching Rampage in South Georgia." *Georgia Historical Quarterly* 90.2 (2006): 214–35.

Miller, Ericka. "The Fly in the Buttermilk, or the Legacy of Margaret Garner: Despair, Agency, and Retaliation in Angelina Weld Grimké's 'Birth Control' Stories'." *The Other Reconstruction: Where Violence and Womanhood Meet in the Writings of Ida B. Wells-Barnett, Angelina Weld Grimké and Nella Larsen.* New York: Taylor & Francis, 1999. 57–99.

Mohanram, Radhikah. *Black Body: Woman, Colonialism, Space.* Minneapolis: U of Minnesota P, 1999.

Patterson, Orlando. *Rituals of Blood: Consequences of Slavery in Two American Centuries.* New York: Basic Civitas, 1998.

Pickens, William. "Lynching and Debt Slavery." American Civil Liberties Union pamphlet, May 1921.

Power, Samantha. *A Problem from Hell: America and the Age of Genocide.* New York: HarperCollins, 2003.

Soady, Vicky. "Women's Studies 'Where Civil Rights Never Made It.'" *Chronicle of Higher Education.* 22 Nov. 2002: B12–13.

Spencer, Anne. "White Things." *Crisis* Mar. 1923: 204.

Stavney, Anne. " 'Mothers of Tomorrow': The New Negro Renaissance and the Politics of Maternal Representation." *African American Review.* 32.4 (1998): 533–61.

Tate, Claudia. *Domestic Allegories of Political Desire.* New York: Oxford UP, 1992. 209–30.

Toomer, Jean. *Cane.* New York: Liveright, 1923.

Walker, Margaret. *This is My Century: New and Collected Poems.* Athens, GA: U of Georgia P, 1989.

White, Walter. "The Work of a Mob." *Crisis* 16 (1918): 221.

Williams, Lee E., II. *Anatomy of Four Race Riots: Racial Conflict in Knoxville, Elaine (Arkansas), Tulsa and Chicago 1919–1921.* Hattiesburg: UP of Mississippi, 1972.

Winter, Jay and Emmanuel Sivan, eds. *War and Remembrance in the Twentieth Century.* New York: Cambridge UP, 1999.

Young, Joseph A. "Phenomenology and Textual Power in Richard Wright's 'The Man Who Lived Underground' *MELUS* 26.4 (2001): 69–93.

"Somewhat Like War"
The Aesthetics of Segregation, Black Liberation, and *A Raisin in the Sun*

MICHELLE Y. GORDON

We must come out of the ghettoes of America, because the ghettoes are killing us, not only our dreams, as Mama says, but our very bodies. It is not an abstraction that the average American Negro has a life expectancy of five to ten years less than the average white. You see, Miss Oehler, that is murder, and a Negro writer cannot be expected to share the placid view of the situation that might be the case with the white writer.

As for changing "the hearts of individuals"—I am glad that the American nation did not wait for the hearts of individual slave owners to abolish the slave system—for I suspect that I should still be running around on a plantation as a slave. And that really would not do.

Sincerely,

Lorraine Hansberry, *To Be Young, Gifted, and Black*[1]

In early summer 1937, a mob arrived at 6140 Rhodes Avenue to convince the Hansberrys of Chicago to abandon their new home. Instead, the Hansberrys convinced their new white neighbors to disperse, with a shotgun. As expected, the neighborhood "improvement association" sought an injunction against the Hansberrys, on the grounds that blacks legally could not occupy any residence in any neighborhood covered by a "race-restrictive covenant." In their attempt to combat legal segregation in the North, and to open up desperately needed housing around Chicago's Black Belt, the Hansberrys and local NAACP attorneys took their case before the U.S. Supreme Court. Lorraine Hansberry later recalled her "desperate and courageous mother, patrolling [the] house all night with a loaded German luger, doggedly guarding her four children, while [her] father fought the respectable part of the battle in the Washington court" (*Young*

20). In its 1940 decision on *Hansberry v. Lee*, the Supreme Court ruled in Carl Hansberry's favor on a technicality, while declining to address the constitutionality of the covenants themselves. It would not be until 1948, in *Shelley v. Kraemer*, that the North's legal bulwark of racial segregation—the race-restrictive covenant—was declared unconstitutional.[2]

Coming of age amid the tensions and violence surrounding Chicago's "series of Mason-Dixon lines" fundamentally shaped Lorraine Hansberry's self-consciousness, radical politics, and revolutionary art. As a young playwright, Hansberry shaped her aesthetic practices to respond directly to the urban segregation her family had fought for so long, and, in the midst of the cold war, the capitalist systems from which segregation grew. Her first play, *A Raisin in the Sun* (1959), directly engages segregation struggles in Chicago, as a penultimate symbol of black oppression and resistance. In doing so, she brought local, individual struggles of African Americans—against segregation, ghettoization, and capitalist exploitation—to the national stage. "Our Southside," she once wrote, "is a place apart. Each piece of our living is a protest" (*Young* 17).

Set in that South Side "sometime between World War II and the present" (*Raisin* 22), *Raisin* unfolds in a two-bedroom apartment in an overcrowded black ghetto whose borders had shifted little since *Hansberry v. Lee*.[3] In *Raisin*, Hansberry offers an "aesthetics of segregation" to generate public testimony about urban black life, to represent her radically expansive notion of the real, and to provide a prophetic framework for anti-racist, anti-colonialist movements gaining force in America and the world. Within the competing realities of black and white life, she dramatizes Chicago's white supremacist social order, and exposes its connections to the Jim Crow South, capitalist enterprise, and colonialism. Acutely aware of the social organization and violence at the center of Chicago's near-absolute segregation, Hansberry stages a revolutionary intervention into the cyclical systems of ghettoization, proffering *Raisin* as a dramatic prelude and challenge to the racialized rituals of ghettoization, desegregation, and organized white resistance.

Raisin's forthright engagement with Chicago segregation at the grass roots exposes and denaturalizes the workings of mid-century urban segregation and massive white resistance to black self-determination. Like other influential black urban writers—including Richard Wright, James Baldwin, Gwendolyn Brooks, Amiri Baraka, and Langston Hughes—Hansberry deploys her aesthetics of segregation to uncover "not only the results of [segregation], but also the true and inescapable cause of it—which of course is the present organization of American society" ("Scars" 55). Anticipating the limits of traditional freedom-movement emphasis on legal segregation, desegregation is not Hansberry's ultimate answer to segregation, but rather a necessary step toward what she envisioned as "a socialist organization of society as the next great and dearly won universal condition of mankind" ("Tribute" 17). To these ends, *Raisin* insists on local and global black revolution, contests the underpinnings of American segregation, and asserts that civil disobedience, armed struggle, and ideological and economic transformation are imperatives for achieving social justice.

By explicitly confronting segregation in Chicago, Hansberry's anti-racist aesthetic gives shape to a pragmatic social vision and a "genuine realism." Genuine realism, Hansberry explained, imposes on a work "not only what *is*, but what is *possible* . . . because that is part of reality too. So that you get a much larger potential of what man can do" (*Young* 228). Her conception of genuine realism renders human beings as active agents—in their own liberation as well as oppression of others—and opens a cultural space in which to imagine alternatives to a truthfully represented repressive social reality. Equally concerned with present truth and future possibility, Hansberry's genuine realism rejects the deterministic impulses of naturalism; her genuine realism instead relies on what she considered an imperative, but in no way naive, idealism. For instance, Hansberry uses Beneatha's Nigerian suitor, Asagai, to challenge dominant understandings of both realism and idealism: "it is very odd," he muses, "but those who see the changes—who dream, who will not give up—are called idealists . . . and those who see only the circle we call *them* the 'realists'!" (3.1).

"A Negro Play Before It Is Anything Else"[4]

Believing that art possesses the spiritual and intellectual " 'energy that can change things,' " Hansberry's aesthetic is distinctly black, egalitarian, and radical. She places, in the words of Amiri Baraka, "real life under the lights and speaking with the sharp eruptive force of black everyday every where" (Baldwin xx; Baraka "Sweet Lorraine" 526). Her art reflects her own "sense of tactical reality" and her firm belief that "the world is political and that political power, in one form or another, will be the ultimate key to the liberation of American Negroes and, indeed, black folk throughout the world" (*Young* 212, 213). Baraka explains that in

> Hansberry we heard . . . the voice of the people . . . describing, analyzing, recreating the world and demanding change. Demanding Democracy, Self Determination. Even revolution and educating themselves and ourselves as to why and how. . . . with a thrilling language of ideas from the mouths of Black people. . . . Ideology as real life. So that what she said was a thrill of meaning and music. Of explosive revelational image. ("Sweet Lorraine" 525, 527)

Anchored in the traditions of radical black American art, activism, and thought, Hansberry's "explosive revelational" images provide not only instructive social critique but also prophetic inquiry. This prophetic inquiry operates as an integral part of her genuine realism, urging her audience, as *Raisin*'s title suggests, to consider seriously both what happens to millions of dreams deferred, and the trials faced by those who fight for independence.

Locating the Younger family in Chicago's South Side, Hansberry directly engages crises produced by ghetto economies and dehumanizing living conditions, restricted educational access, and explosive encounters along urban color lines. Hansberry understood that residential segregation, and the violence that undergirded it, provided the backbone for racial inequality in the urban North. "This is the ghetto of Chicago," she clarified in the unfilmed screenplay. "Not indolence, not indifference, and certainly not lack of ambition imprisons [the Youngers], but various enormous questions of the social organization around them" (5). By mid-century, Chicago's South Side had become one of the most densely crowded ghettos in the United States, where two generations of Hansberrys had waged, with lawyers and guns, local and national campaigns against racial segregation, terrorism, and injustice. Like the Youngers, sixty-four percent of black women and thirty-four percent of black men in the city worked as domestic servants. Like Mama Younger, some eighty percent of Bronzeville's interwar residents had migrated to Chicago from the South, seeking employment, education, the vote, and freedom from anti-black violence (Drake and Cayton 99, 227). But black unemployment in the city doubled that of whites; the majority of black taxpayers' children, like Hansberry herself, attended overcrowded, underfunded schools on half-day shifts; and black voters found themselves caught within Chicago's far-reaching Democratic Machine.[5]

The most violently and residentially segregated metropolis in the nation, post-World War II Chicago rocked with more bombs in and around black homes and businesses than even Birmingham, Alabama. Hysterical anti-integration mobs of up to ten-thousand whites faced down the National Guard in city streets, and some black families required police escorts of one thousand or more on moving day into all-white blocks or housing projects (Meyer 115–21; Hirsch "Massive Resistance" 529). As Chicago housing historian Arnold Hirsch explains, more "than mere examples of anti-Black animus," these ritualized campaigns of violence and "sophisticated psychological war" around segregated housing reveal the practical, ideological, and political limits of mid-century African American movements for equality ("Massive Resistance" 523).[6]

Most of *Raisin*'s black audiences and critics readily recognized Hansberry's use of Chicago ghettoization as indicative of democracy's national failures. Important Hansberry scholars such as Margaret Wilkerson and Steven Carter have explored the relationships between Hansberry's anti-racist politics and art; this study continues that line of inquiry into her representations of segregation specifically in Chicago. Critics have not yet fully engaged the dynamics of segregation—around which Hansberry structures the entire play—and therefore have not yet fully recognized *Raisin*'s aesthetics of genuine realism as a form of social protest. J. Charles Washington maintains, for example, "Walter's dream remains only that not because of defects in the American system but because of basic flaws in his own character" (120). Similarly, Lee A. Jacobus generalizes the play's social analysis: "This play illustrates the American dream as it is felt not just by African Americans but by all Americans: If you work hard and save your money, if you hold to the proper values and hope, then you can buy your own home and have the kind of space and privacy that permit people to live in dignity" (1214). Although the Youngers have worked hard all their lives, and for two generations in Chicago, they cannot afford suitable housing—until Walter Sr.'s death brings a $10,000 life insurance check. Hansberry turns again to Asagai to confront fundamental questions of the play: "isn't there something wrong in a house—in a world—where all dreams, good or bad, must depend on the death of a man" (3.1)? Here, Asagai brings the local and global together, suggesting that not only should the Youngers question the material aspects of their individual ambitions and values, but that we all should interrogate the capitalist principles upon which modern society is structured.

Like Jacobus, numerous critics have measured the play's "universality" against its racial or cultural specificity, creating what Robin Bernstein describes as an illusory paradox that ultimately divorces the particulars of black life from the realm of "universal"—or human—experience. This willful marginalization of black realities emerged in the enduring and widespread evaluations of *Raisin* as "not really a Negro play . . . . [but] a play about people!"[7] In an interview with Studs Terkel, Hansberry rebutted such critiques: "Well, I hadn't noticed the contradiction because I'd always been under the impression that Negroes *are* people" (*Young* 113). In her work on white supremacist responses to *Raisin*, Bernstein suggests that white critics employed this universality—particularity paradox to neutralize the play's confrontations with America's Jim Crow order, refusing "to engage with—or even recognize—the politics of the play" "in order to stabilize both whiteness and [racial] segregation . . . and thus to produce and enhance white power" (20, 22). James Baldwin speculated on the critical silence surrounding Hansberry's artistic treatment of social protest and black experience, pointing to her "unmistakable power of turning the viewer's judgment in on himself": "*Is all this true or not true?* [Hansberry's] play rudely demands. . . . One cannot quite answer negatively, one risks being caught in a lie. But an affirmative answer imposes a new level of responsibility, both for one's conduct and for the fortunes of the American state, and one risks, therefore, the disagreeable necessity of becoming 'an insurgent again' " (xix–xx).

Both white and black critics misconstrued—or ignored—the play's racialized and gendered class politics. Famously denouncing the play as a "glorified soap opera," for example, Harold Cruse accused Hansberry of reinscribing America's repressive class politics both in Chicago's ghetto and on the stage. Cruse falsely charged that Hansberry and her family owned some thirteen slum properties in the South Side, and deemed "obsequious" and "embarrassing" her "mimicry of the critical standards of white Communists" and her play's "assumption that she knew all about the Negro working class, of which she was not even remotely a member" (268–70). Contrary to Cruse's claims, Hansberry proved acutely aware of her ghetto's class divisions and tensions. Indeed, Bronzeville's working-class youth—particularly their willingness to fight for themselves—profoundly influenced her life and art (*Young* 36, 38, 45–46). Hansberry explained that, in *Raisin*, she created the Youngers as a working-class black family, as opposed to a middle-class family like her own, because she believed the world's coming freedom movements would emerge most forcefully from its laboring classes (*Speaks Out*). In fact, the play treats Chicago's black elite classes—"the only people in the world who are more snobbish than rich white people are rich colored people"—rather unkindly so that wealthy George Murchison's interactions with the Youngers dramatize cross-class tensions, gender conflicts, and relationships between race pride and impulses toward assimilation (1.1). In a 1979 *Freedomways* special issue dedicated to Hansberry, Margaret Taylor Goss Burroughs and Lerone Bennett Jr., evaluate the influence of Chicago's racial geography on Hansberry's art and politics:

> BURROUGHS: How do you account for the fact that a young woman comes out of what's called a black bourgeois background and yet develops a deep understanding of the problems of working people? Is that something that's peculiar to Chicago, or what? A number of people have come out of Chicago: Richard Wright, Margaret Walker, Charlie White, Gwendolyn Brooks. . . . What is it about this town?

> BENNETT: Well, first of all, Chicago is a very brutal city. It's a very raw city. Chicago will destroy anybody, particularly a black person if that person hasn't steeled him- or herself to resist. . . . Another element . . . is that despite, or perhaps because of, the raw, brutal oppression of black people in this city, there has been and still is a sort of *community* here. (227)

In light of his own early dismissal of *Raisin* as a black bourgeois play about integration, Amiri Baraka reconsidered the implications of Hansberry's drama a quarter century after its debut. He acknowledges his previously underdeveloped understanding of Hansberry's class concerns and her emphasis on the social construction of segregation:

We thought Hansberry's play was "middle class," in that its focus seemed to be on "moving into white folks' neighborhoods" when most blacks were just trying to pay their rent in ghetto shacks. . . . The Younger family is part of the black majority, and the concerns I once dismissed as "middle class" . . . are actually reflective of the essence of black people's striving to defeat segregation, discrimination and national oppression. There is no such thing as a "white folks' neighborhood" except to racists and those submitting to racism. ("Wiser Play" 41)

Part of what the younger Baraka failed to understand was the almost absolute system of residential segregation in Chicago. Unlike the New York in which Baraka lived, very few black people lived outside Chicago's ghetto borders—although, until 1948, restrictive covenants had made exceptions for "janitors' or Chauffeurs' quarters in the basement or in a barn or garage in the rear"—and it often cost more to "rent in ghetto shacks" than to reside outside the Black Belt (*Hansberry v. Lee*). Although a white family could rent a five-room apartment for sixty dollars a month in Cicero, for example, a black South Side family of four could pay fifty-six dollars per month to live in *one half* of a two-room flat, infested with rats and roaches, and even well into the 1960s, without electricity or hot water (Meyer 118; "45 ADC Mothers" 1).

In an unpublished 1964 letter to *The New York Times*, Hansberry renders the repeated failures of integration and democracy as deeply personal—and national—tragedies manifest in the segregated, exploitive world of the South Side. Pitting personal experience against public narratives of racial advancement, she describes her family's experiences with residential integration as formative in her developing radical consciousness, class critique, and vision for social change. Hansberry writes:

My father was typical of a generation of Negroes who believed that the "American way" could successfully be made to . . . democratize the United States. Thus, twenty-five years ago, he spent a small personal fortune, his considerable talents, and many years of his life fighting, in association with NAACP attorneys, Chicago's "restrictive covenants" in one of the nation's ugliest ghettoes. (*Young* 20)

The letter demonstrates the "process of representational transformation" at work in Hansberry's cultural politics, which historian Ben Keppel defines as "the processes of public contest and debate by which the members of a culture rearrange and reconstruct the key words, symbols, and icons that constitute its brick and mortar" (2). Throughout the letter, Hansberry employs quotation marks to call into question tools and ideologies of the nation's oppressive social order—"American way," "restrictive covenants," "white neighborhood." She places these contested terms at the heart of America's tremendous racial divide and the highly profitable systems of white supremacy.

Hansberry denaturalizes the coded language of America's social order and suggests that alternative realities and possibilities do exist. As in *Raisin*, Hansberry's letter questions dominant social narratives of reality and "progress":

> The fact that my father and the NAACP "won" a Supreme Court decision . . . is—ironically—the sort of "progress" our satisfied friends allude to when they presume to deride the more radical means of struggle. The cost, in emotional turmoil, time and money, which led to my father's early death as a permanently embittered exile in a foreign country when he saw that after such sacrificial efforts the Negroes of Chicago were as ghetto-locked as ever, does not seem to figure into their calculations.
>
> That is the reality that I am faced with when I now read that some Negroes my own age and younger say that we must now lie down in the streets, tie up traffic, do whatever we can—take to the hills with guns if necessary—and fight back. Fatuous people remark these days on our "bitterness." Why, of course we are bitter. (*Young* 20–21)

Here, Hansberry frames white imperviousness to black rage as a significant obstacle to social change. She then closes the letter by quoting Langston Hughes's "mighty poem," "Harlem." In *Raisin*, she prophetically gives voice to a people's "bitterness" through Walter Lee (described by one critic as "an angry young man who happens to be a Negro"): "Bitter? Man, I'm a volcano" (Bernstein 16; 2.1).

The Aesthetics of Segregation: Realism and Revolution in Chicago, or "A Rat Done Bit My Sister Nell . . . and Whitey's on the Moon"[8]

Hansberry's revolutionary combination of reality and future possibility profoundly shapes her aesthetics of segregation. "Aesthetics of segregation" broadly describes a consciously black artistic approach to black experience under Jim Crow in post-Depression America. This aesthetic appears in myriad forms, from drama to poetry, fiction, essay and spoken word, and in urban texts, such as Richard Wright's *Native Son* (1940), Langston Hughes's *Montage of a Dream Deferred* (1951), from which Hansberry took the title of her play, and Gwendolyn Brooks's *In the Mecca* (1968). Black artists' aesthetics of segregation share four primary attributes: evidence of systemic exploitation and its human costs; prophecy of explosive black rage; demonstration of black resistance to the dehumanizing effects of segregation; and the presence or awareness of the violence that maintains color lines and social inequality.

Hansberry's aesthetic both represents segregation's materiality and depicts various forms of black resistance across space and time. Because individuals cannot fight against that which they do not understand, her art renders visible the compound systems of black oppression in the urban North, which often appears distinctly different from those of the Jim Crow South. What she presents as the *"indestructible contradictions to this state of being"*—the rats, roaches, worn furniture, overcrowded conditions, and anti-integration bombs—therefore not only set the stage for the dramatic action, but also serve as evidence of Chicago's political and economic infrastructures of deliberate segregation (1.1). Rats and roaches, in fact, constitute an important element of the urban aesthetics of segregation for many urban black artists. For instance, in the opening scene of *Native Son*, Bigger Thomas kills a black rat "over a foot long" in his family's South Side kitchenette apartment (Wright 10). So, too, Hansberry uses the bloody demise of a "rat . . . Big as a cat, honest!" to establish a pervasive reality of ghetto life early in the play (*Raisin* 1.2). Where there is little or no municipal sanitation service or landlord upkeep, rats and roaches thrive. Such implications run counter to dominant myths propping up prosegregation institutions and individuals. When a black South Side infant died of a rat bite, for instance, the landlord denied culpability, saying, "Well, they don't pick up their garbage. Anyway it was a nigger baby and they have a new one every year, so what does it matter?" (Carawan and Carawan 283). Like Gil Scott Heron's song "Whitey on the Moon" and Chicago Freedom Movement songwriter Jimmy Collier's "Rent Strike Blues," the rat in *Raisin* addresses this callous neglect and economic exploitation of ghettoized communities. Such substandard living conditions and negligence, the artists suggest, are criminal, particularly in their endangerment of ghettoized children, who remain the most likely victims of such environmental hazards, including rat bites (Hirschhorn and Hodge e35).

With Beneatha *"on her knees spraying* [pesticide] *under sofa with behind upraised,"* Ruth's tortured response to Travis's encounter with the rodent signals the moral crises faced by parents who raise their children in American ghettos (1.2). Later, when Mama announces she has bought a house in Clybourne Park, despite Ruth's distress at the prospect of living amid Chicago's hostile whites, she "laughs joyously" and puts her hands over her stomach, *"aware for the first time perhaps that the life therein pulses with happiness and not despair"* (2.1). Weighing the dangers of the ghetto against those posed by anti-black terrorism, Ruth determines that she will "scrub all the floors in America . . . if I have to—but we got to MOVE! We got to get OUT OF HERE!" (3.1) The imperative to move refers to both the Younger family's physical departure from Chicago's ghetto and to what Hansberry saw as necessary mass movement to reconstruct the social order. When Beneatha suggests that the "only" way to rid themselves of the roaches and rats they battle in their apartment is to "Set fire to this building," Hansberry rejects not only superficial remedies to inadequate housing conditions, but any form of exceptionalism that allows only a small percentage of black families to escape America's ghettos (1.2).

For Hansberry, the economic exploitation, anti-integration bombs, and organizing activities of the Clybourne Park Improvement Association are absolutely central to *Raisin's* project. Throughout the play, the Youngers exhibit more than what one critic describes as "sensitivity" to the "economic pressures" of ghetto life, or a deficient understanding "that they are engaged in a sociological race war" (Lewis 35). In buying the house in Clybourne Park, Mama asserts her family's right to refute the economic exploitation of Chicago segregation. When the family learns where their new home is, no one is eager to court the wrath of Chicago's white homeowners:

> RUTH: Where is it?
> MAMA: (*Frightened at this telling*) Well—well—it's out there in Clybourne Park . . .
> RUTH: Clybourne Park? Mama, there ain't no colored people living in Clybourne Park.
> MAMA: (*Almost idiotically*) Well, I guess there's going to be some now. . . . (*Raising her eyes to meet [Walter's] finally*) Son—I just tried to find the nicest place for the least amount of money for my family.
> RUTH: (*Trying to recover from the shock*) Well—well—'course I ain't one never been 'fraid of no crackers, mind you—but—well, wasn't there no other houses nowhere?
> MAMA: Them houses they put up for colored in them areas way out all seem to cost twice as much as other houses. I did the best I could. (2.1)

Acknowledging the central role violence plays in maintaining Chicago's racial geography, Hansberry's aesthetics of segregation explicitly connect these Northern experiences to the Jim Crow South. In a scene cut from the stage and first published version of the play, Hansberry brings the Youngers' neighbor, Mrs. Johnson, to report the latest anti-integration bombing in Clybourne Park.

> JOHNSON: You mean you ain't read 'bout them colored people that was bombed out their place out there? . . . Ain't it something how bad these here white folks is getting here in

Chicago! Lord, getting so you think you right down in
Mississippi! [*With a tremendous and rather insincere sense
of melodrama*] 'Course I think it's wonderful how our
folks keeps on pushing out. . . . Lord—I bet this time
next month y'all's names will have been in the papers
plenty—[*Holding up her hands to mark off each word
of the headline she can see in front of her*] "NEGROES
INVADE CLYBOURNE PARK—BOMBED!"

MAMA: We ain't exactly moving out there to get bombed.

JOHNSON: But you have to think of life like it is—and these here
Chicago peckerwoods is some baaaad peckerwoods.

MAMA: [*Wearily*] We done thought about all that Mis' Johnson.
(2.2)

Here, Hansberry employs segregation aesthetics to foment social change:
she exposes the oppressors, as well as the effects of their oppression, systems,
and tools. Emphasizing place—"*here* in Chicago"—four years after the brutal
murder of young Emmett Till in Mississippi, Hansberry's treatment of anti-black
violence in Chicago operates as an instructive rhetorical maneuver. By offering
such stark parallels to the violence of Southern Jim Crow, these comparisons
work to demystify Chicago's complex racist power structures. Collapsing the
distinctions between racial oppression in the North and South—while attending
to the specifics of the local—Hansberry poses the potential for a more unified,
national black struggle. Black Chicago activists themselves employed similar
rhetorical tactics in their 1960s grassroots campaigns against the city's segregated
schools and neighborhoods. Black Southerners, too, recognized important connections between African Americans' struggles in Chicago and emerging movements throughout the South: "Black Chicago," Southern Christian Leadership
Conference leader James Bevel declared, "is Mississippi moved a few hundred
miles north" (Werner 64).

Raisin also directly engages the array of racist discourses in the urban
North, which functioned in tandem to publicly defend and lobby for residential
segregation by threatening violence, miscegenation, venereal disease, and financial
ruin. While whites used blatantly racist language at the grass roots—children sang
in Mayor Daley's neighborhood, for instance, to the Oscar Meyer wiener tune,
"Oh, I wish I was an Alabama trooper . . . then I could kill niggers legally"—they
publicly relied on a coded discourse of civic politics from which race becomes
conspicuously marginalized or absent (Bontemps and Conroy 335–36; Werner
65). So, Chicago politicians and school board officials used seemingly race-less
language to safeguard the city's systems of segregation. Hansberry recognized
that piercing this rhetoric—confirming, in effect, that racism was deliberate and
systemic in Chicago—would prove to be half the civil rights battle.

Hansberry employs Mr. Linder, the chairman of the Clybourne Park Improvement Association "Neighborhood Orientation Committee," to demonstrate the seemingly benign ways in which Northern whites deny racial discrimination, romanticize their own paternalism and repudiate black self-determination. To dissuade the Youngers from moving into Clybourne Park, Mr. Linder draws on a paternalistic language of rights to protect the "hard-working, honest people who don't really have much but those little homes and a dream of the kind of community they want to raise their children in":

> [Y]ou've got to admit that a man . . . has the right to want to have the neighborhood he lives in a certain kind of way. . . . I want you to believe me when I tell you that race prejudice simply doesn't enter into it. It is a matter of the people of Clybourne Park believing . . . that for the happiness of all concerned that our Negro families are happier when they live in their *own* communities. (2.3)

Mr. Linder's speech represents only one rhetorical maneuver by which improvement associations defended segregation in the urban North. Their paternalism was accompanied by two other rhetorical strategies: a battle language of victimization and terrorism, on the one hand, and a language of miscegenation and degeneration on the other. With its talk of "Negro invasions" and "them bombs and things [whites] keep setting off," Raisin engages both the language and the violence of Chicago's housing battle (2.2). Improvement associations in urban centers organized around ideas of "invasions," "battlegrounds," "resistance," and "hold[ing] the line." Furthermore, their militancy functioned beyond the metaphoric: as one former race relations official explained of the postwar years, cities like Chicago and Detroit "did a lot of firefighting in those days" (Sugrue 560; Meyer 89).

Improvement associations combined their battle language of patriotic rights with an emotive rhetoric of "forced mongrelization" (Hirsch "Massive Resistance" 544). Hansberry understood that, in the North, despite its language of property rights and patriotic militarism, "Neighborhood defense became more than a struggle for turf. It was a battle for the preservation of white womanhood" (Sugrue 562). While Walter, Ruth, and Beneatha discuss Mr. Linder's visit, Hansberry cuts to the heart of white Americans' fear of integration:

> BENEATHA: What they think we going to do—eat 'em?
> RUTH: No, honey, marry 'em. (2.3)

Hansberry and Ruth understand that the specter of miscegenation activates a matrix of violence and anxiety. Much like their Southern counterparts,

Northern white supremacists wielded a language of black barbarism and absolute separation to impose the terror of miscegenation: "it won't be long now," workers claimed in Chicago taverns in the wake of the 1954 *Brown v. Board of Education* Supreme Court decision, "and negroes and whites inter marrying will be a common thing and the white race will go downhill" (Hirsch "Massive Resistance" 533).

"Write About the World As It Is and As You Think It *Ought* to Be and Must Be"[9]

Intended to denaturalize segregation and provide imagined alternatives to the existing social order, Hansberry's genuine realism profoundly shaped her revision of *Raisin*'s final scenes. In its original conclusion, the Younger family sat silently in their new living room in Clybourne Park, in the dark, armed, and waiting for the white mob to come (Carter 41; Wilkerson 130). Although Hansberry made several revisions to her manuscript to "sanitize" the play for producers and reduce its length, this is perhaps the most significant revision never restored to the script.[10] Rather than altering the ending to promote assimilation or provide a reassuring sense of inevitable racial "progress," this change in fact proves crucial to maintaining the revolutionary potential of the drama: ending the action prior to the Youngers' arrival in Clybourne Park supplies Hansberry with the only prospect of keeping it real, so to speak, while breaking the cycles of desegregation and ritualized white violence.

Although this revision ultimately invited the widespread celebration of *Raisin*'s "transcendent" conclusion, Hansberry's literary executor Robert Nemiroff points out that even this revised ending "leaves the Youngers on the brink of what will surely be . . . at *best* a nightmare of uncertainty" (*Raisin* 10–11). Frustrated with yet another critic's praise of the play's "accepted and ever popular upbeat ending," Hansberry once huffed in an interview, "If he thinks that's a happy ending, I invite him to come live in one of the communities where the Youngers are going!" (Wilkerson 130; *Raisin* 11). Misreadings of the play's conclusion, especially those that interpret the Youngers' decision to move beyond Chicago's ghetto as "apolitical," distort Hansberry's fundamental point of protest (Wilkerson 122). Directly engaged in an organized movement for black liberation or not, the Youngers remain fully aware that their breech of Chicago's color line will trigger hostility and likely terrorism: as Mama herself explains to the Booker T. Washington-quoting Mrs. Johnson—"we done thought about all that" (2.2).

In the final scene of *Raisin*, Walter Lee rejects the Clybourne Park Improvement Association's offer to buy back the Youngers' house, and the family strikes out for Chicago's embattled racial frontier. But before these events unfold, Asagai insists that this is not the end of the drama. His impassioned speech to Beneatha serves as an answer to the allegedly moderate Mr. Linder's menacing last words: "I hope you people know what you are getting into" (3.1). Representative of the enlightened revolutionary intellectual, and creating a crucial link between Chicago's ghettoized blacks and social movements throughout the so-called Third World, Asagai exhibits no illusions about the processes or costs of social change. "End?" he asks Beneatha, "Who ever spoke of an end?" His use of the future tense enlarges the capacity of Hansberry's genuine realism, and emphasizes the profoundly prophetic quality of her social vision:

> At times it will seem that nothing changes at all ... and then again the sudden dramatic events which make history leap into the future. And then quiet again. Retrogression even. Guns, murder, revolution. And I even will have moments when I wonder if the quiet was not better than all that death and hatred. But I will look about my village at the illiteracy and disease and ignorance and I will not wonder long. (3.1)

Asagai's pragmatic prediction reflects much of the turmoil that would plague African and New World battles for self-determination and social justice in the decades to come. Much as Hansberry had attempted in *Raisin*, the Chicago Freedom Movement of the 1960s endeavored to "stage a crisis" around Chicago's segregated housing and schools, thereby forcing public dialogue, negotiation, and change. But in the face of Daley's Democratic Machine and its loyal black politicians, police brutality, FBI counter-intelligence operations, the real estate industry, white mobs, and the powerful improvement associations, the move-ments—Freedom School boycotts, Unions to End Slums, and open-housing campaigns—collapsed amid repression, assassinations, and fiery ghetto uprisings. The protracted struggle over segregated housing in Chicago was, one movement veteran recalled, "somewhat like war" (Fayer and Hampton 314).[11]

Ultimately, American residential segregation and white flight exposed, in the words of Arnold Hirsch, "the shoals upon which the postwar movement for racial equality would founder" ("Massive Resistance" 523). The 1960s rebellions in Chicago and other black ghettos dangerously expressed African American rage against segregation and white indifference, much as Hansberry had forecast. As the decade passed, Chicago's residential color lines became increasingly stabilized, with the construction of new schools within pre-1950 Black Belt borders (an alternative to allowing black children into less-crowded white schools), contin-ued expansion of the black West Side ghetto, and high-rise public housing like Daley's Robert Taylor Homes extending the ghetto vertically. Between 1960 and 1990, Chicago's white population decreased by 800,000, its white suburbs grew by nearly two million, and more than twenty-five percent of the city's factories closed. By the 1990s, black unemployment approached twenty-three percent and the South Side contained the greatest concentration of public housing in the nation because upward of ninety-two percent of black families lived on government assistance.[12] "Perhaps it is just as well," Baldwin mused, "that [Hansberry] did not live to see with the outward eye what she saw so clearly with the inward one. . . . [T]he horses and tanks are indeed upon us, and the end is not in sight. . . . And it is not at all farfetched to suspect that what she saw contributed to the strain which killed her, for the effort to which Lorraine was dedicated is more than enough to kill a [wo]man" (xx).

Notes

1. *Young* 117.

2. Kamp; Drake and Cayton 182–90; Carter 40–41; Meyer 56–57; Graettinger; Plotkin; Keppel 24.

3. In his chapter on housing segregation in the urban North—entitled "A Raisin in the Sun"—Stephen Meyer identifies this period, from World War II to roughly 1960, as America's most intensely violent period of upheaval over race and housing. Chicago, Meyer and other scholars note, was the most violent city of all. Meyer 115–32. See also Hirsch "Massive"; Mohl 16–23.

4. *Young* 114.

5. In one of her last public appearances, Hansberry spoke of segregation's debilitating effects in personal and broad sociopolitical terms: "I was given, during the grade school years, one-half the amount of education prescribed by the Board of Education of my city. . . . I am a product of [Chicago's segregated school] system and one result is that—to this day—I cannot count properly . . . [or] make even simple change in a grocery store. . . . This is what is meant when we speak of the scars, the marks that the ghettoized child carries through life. To be imprisoned in the ghetto is to be forgotten—or deliberately cheated of one's birthright—at best." ("Scars" 54).

6. On the "moving day" desegregation experience, see Brown 24–59 and Meyer 119. Published the same year as *Raisin's* Broadway debut, Frank London Brown's only novel, *Trumbull Park*, picks up Chicago's desegregation story where *Raisin* ends, and details complex intersections of race, class, gender, and violence in Chicago's most violently integrated housing project.

7. Nemiroff 286–87; Bernstein 22–23; Keppel 177–83.

8. Heron "Whitey."

9. *Young* 257.

10. On the restoration of scenes, see Wilkerson 123–30.

11. Hansberry more deeply explored the relationships between African and black American freedom struggles in *Les Blancs* (1970). See Abell. On Chicago movements of the 1960s see Rice; Ward and Churchill 64–77; Anderson and Pickering 208–340; Hampton and Fayer 297–319, 521–38; Meyer 183–88; Werner 122–24; and Ralph.

12. Hunt 96–97; Rury 121–23; Cohen and Taylor; Hirsch Making; and Werner 145–46.

Works Cited

"45 ADC Mothers 'CAMP IN'—Children Join Protest." *Chicago Defender* 23–31 Oct. 1969: 1.

Abell, Joy. "African/American: Lorraine Hansberry's *Les Blancs* and the American Civil Rights Movement." *African American Review* 35.3 (2001): 459–70.

Baldwin, James. "Sweet Lorraine." *To Be Young, Gifted, and Black*. 1969. Ed. Robert Nemiroff. New York: Vintage Books, 1995.

Baraka, Amiri. "A Wiser Play Than Some of Us Knew." *Los Angeles Times* 22 Mar. 1987, home ed. sec.:41.

———. "Sweet Lorraine." *The LeRoi Jones/Amiri Baraka Reader*, ed. William J. Harris, 2nd ed. New York: Thunder's Mouth Press, 2000. 525–27.

Bennett, Lerone Jr. and Margaret Taylor Goss Burroughs. "A Lorraine Hansberry Rap." *Lorraine Hansberry: Art of Thunder, Vision of Light*. Special issue of *Freedomways* 19.4 (1979): 226–33.

Bernstein, Robin. "Inventing a Fishbowl: White Supremacy and the Critical Reception of Lorraine Hansberry's *A Raisin in the Sun*." *Modern Drama* 42.1 (1999): 16–27.

Blair, Chester. "*A Raisin in the Sun*: The Chicago Connection Linked through Economics, Law, and Literature." *Chicago Bar Association Record* 17 (2003): 33.

Bontemps, Arna and Jack Conroy. *Anyplace But Here*. New York: Hill & Wang, 1966.

Brown, Frank London. *Trumbull Park*. Chicago: Regenery, 1959.

Carawan, Guy and Candie Carawan. *Sing for Freedom: The Story of the Civil Rights Movement Through Its Songs*. Bethlehem, PA: A Sing Out Publication, 1977.

Carter, Steven. "Commitment Amid Complexity: Lorraine Hansberry's Life in Action." *MELUS* 7.3 (1980): 39–53.

Churchill, Ward and Jim Vander Wall. *Agents of Repression: The FBI's Secret Wars against the Black Panther Party and the American Indian Movement*. Boston: South End Press, 1988.

Cohen, Adam and Elizabeth Taylor. *American Pharaoh: Mayor Richard J. Daley: His Battle for Chicago and the Nation*. Boston: Little, Brown, 2000.

Cruse, Harold. *The Crisis of the Negro Intellectual*. New York: William Morrow & Co., 1967.

Daniel, Philip T. K. "A History of Discrimination Against Black Students in Chicago Secondary Schools." *History of Education Quarterly* 20.2 (1980): 147–62.

Drake, St. Clair, and Horace R. Cayton. *Black Metropolis: A Study of Negro Life in a Northern City*. New York: Harcourt, Brace, 1945.

Graettinger, Robert. "*A Raisin in the Sun* as Commentary on *Hansberry v. Lee*." *Chicago Bar Association Record* 17 (2003): 30–33.

Hampton, Henry and Steve Fayer, ed. *Voices of Freedom: An Oral History of the Civil Rights Movement from the 1950s through the 1980s*. New York: Bantam Books, 1990.

Hansberry, Lorraine. *A Raisin in the Sun*. New York: Random House, 1959.

———. *A Raisin in the Sun: The Unfilmed Original Screenplay*. Ed. Robert Nemiroff. New York: Plume, 1992.

———. "The Scars of the Ghetto." *Monthly Review* 41.3 (1989): 52–55.

———. *To Be Young, Gifted and Black: Lorraine Hansberry in Her Own Words*. 1969. Ed. and adapted by Robert Nemiroff. New York: Vintage Books, 1995.

———. "Tribute." *Black Titan: W. E. B. Dubois, an Anthology by the Editors of Freedom-ways*. Ed. Esther Jackson John Henrik Clarke, Ernest Kaiser, and J. H. O'Dell. Boston: Beacon Press, 1970. 17–18.

Hansberry v. Lee. No. 311. Supreme Ct. of the US. 1940.

Heron, Gil Scott. "Whitey on the Moon." *The Revolution Will Not Be Televised*. New York: RCA Records, 1972.

Hirsch, Arnold. *Making the Second Ghetto: Race and Housing in Chicago, 1940–1960*. Cambridge, UK: Cambridge UP, 1983.

———. "Massive Resistance in the Urban North: Trumbull Park, Chicago, 1953–1966." *Journal of American History* 82.2 (1995): 522–50.

Hirschhorn, Randall and Robert Hodge. "Identification of Risk Factors in Rat Bite Incidents Involving Humans." *Pediatrics: The Official Journal of the American Academy of Pediatrics* 104.3 (1999): e35.

Hunt, D. Bradford. "What Went Wrong with Public Housing in Chicago? A History of the Robert Taylor Homes." *Journal of the Illinois State Historical Society* 94.1 (2001): 96–123.

Jacobus, Lee. *Bedford Introduction to Drama*. 3rd ed. Boston: Bedford Books, 1997.

Kaiser, Ernest and Robert Nemiroff. "A Lorraine Hansberry Bibliography." *Lorraine Hansberry: Art of Thunder, Vision of Light*. Special issue of *Freedomways* 19.4 (1979): 285–304.

Kamp, Allen. "The History Behind *Hansberry v. Lee*." *University of California–Davis Law Review* 20 (1986–1987): 481–99.

Keppel, Ben. *The Work of Democracy: Ralph Bunche, Kenneth B. Clark, Lorraine Hansberry, and the Cultural Politics of Race*. Cambridge, MA: Harvard UP, 1995.

Lee v. Hansberry. No. 25116. Illinois Supreme Ct. April 1939.

Lewis, Theophilus. "Social Protest in 'A Raisin in the Sun'." *Catholic World* 190 (1959): 31–35.

Lorraine Hansberry Speaks Out: Art and the Black Revolution. New York: Cademon Records, 1972.

Meyer, Stephen Grant. *As Long as They Don't Move Next Door: Segregation and Racial Conflict in American Neighborhoods*. Lanham, MD: Rowman & Littlefield, 2000.

Mohl, Raymond. "Race and Housing in the Postwar City: An Explosive History." *Journal of the Illinois State Historical Society* 94.1 (2001): 8–30.

Plotkin, Wendy. " 'Hemmed In': The Struggle against Racial Restrictive Covenants and Deed Restrictions in Post-World War II Chicago." *Journal of the Illinois State Historical Society* 94.1 (2001): 39–69.

Ralph, James R. Jr. *Northern Protest: Martin Luther King, Jr., Chicago, and the Civil Rights Movement*. Cambridge, MA: Harvard UP, 1993.

Rice, Jon. "The World of the Illinois Panthers." *Freedom North: Black Freedom Struggles Outside the South, 1940–1980*, ed. Jeanne Theoharis and Komozi Woodard, 41–64. New York: Palgrave Macmillan, 2003.

Rury, John. "Race, Space, and the Politics of Chicago's Public Schools: Benjamin Willis and the Tragedy of Urban Education." *History of Education Quarterly* 39.2 (1999): 117–42.

Sugrue, Thomas J. "Crabgrass-Roots Politics: Race, Rights, and the Reaction against Liberalism in the Urban North, 1940–1964." *Journal of American History* 82.2 (1995): 551–78.

Washington, J. Charles. "*A Raisin in the Sun* Revisited." *Black American Literature Forum* 22.1 (1988): 109–24.

Werner, Craig. *Higher Ground: Stevie Wonder, Aretha Franklin, Curtis Mayfield and the Rise and Fall of American Soul.* New York: Crown Publishers, 2004.

Wilkerson, Margaret. "*A Raisin in the Sun*: Anniversary of an American Classic." *Performing Feminisms: Feminist Critical Theory and Theater.* Ed. Sue-Ellen Case. Baltimore: Johns Hopkins UP, 1990. 119–30.

Wright, Richard. *Native Son.* New York: Harper, 1940.

Housing the Black Body

Value, Domestic Space, and Segregation Narratives

GERSHUN AVILEZ

> We are things of dry hours and the involuntary plan,
> Grayed in, and gray. "Dream" makes a giddy sound, not strong
> Like "rent," "feeding a wife," satisfying a man."
>
> But could a dream send up through onion fumes
> Its white and violet, fight with fried potatoes
> And yesterday's garbage ripening in the hall,
> Flutter, or sing an aria down these rooms
>
> —Gwendolyn Brooks, "kitchenette building"

Valuing Home

"Iron Ring in Housing," a 1940 article from *The Crisis* on the significance of the Supreme Court case *Hansberry v. Lee*, begins by insisting: "There is no right more elemental nor any liberty more fundamental in a democracy than freedom to move where and when you please" (205). Linking together mobility and housing, the article connects these two issues to the rights and privileges of citizenship in a democracy. *Hansberry* takes on residential segregation by confronting that practice not merely as a restriction on domestic space but mainly as a constriction of civic identity. The case intimates that, given the centrality of segregation to restrictive practices affecting citizenship, the relationship of African Americans to places of residence and to domestic space in general is indicative of their relationship to legal structures. The social and legal developments that directly and indirectly encouraged segregated housing during the mid-twentieth century created the conditions for African Americans to feel estranged from their domestic spaces.[1] The feelings of frustration and

131

dissatisfaction with the "kitchenette" apparent in the poem by Gwendolyn Brooks embody the housing problems to come for many African American communities, and such sentiments factor into the representations of domestic space in mid-twentieth-century African American narratives.

Trumbull Park (1959) by Frank London Brown and *Maud Martha* (1953) by Gwendolyn Brooks focus on Black life in Chicago during the 1940s and 1950s, and—like "kitchenette building"—both examine the realities of segregated residential spaces. Accordingly, these novels can be read as segregation narratives. Each text demonstrates how housing policies not only structure where Black people live, but also undermine their relationship to domestic space. Specifically, the texts represent characters as alienated from their domestic spaces due to legal formulations and social perceptions of black domestic space as "valueless." The construction of black-occupied spaces as "valueless" functions within both segregated and integrated spaces and results in "placelessness" for black subjects or the displacement of the black subject from the value more generally attributable to belonging and security within the home.

I recognize two elements of the concept that I call domestic space: the family and the physical structures of homes (houses, apartments, tenement buildings, etc.). Black domestic space in both senses has often been understood as a refuge from the racism and oppression of the social world. bell hooks's theory of "homeplace" as a "safe place where black people could affirm one another and by doing so heal many of the wounds inflicted by racist domination" grows out of this way of thinking (42). Her understanding—situated in a world of racially segregated–integrated neighborhoods—posits black domestic space as a site resistant to effects of oppression. This resistance is rooted in the idea that families are able to create and sustain boundaries that maintain a distinction between interior and exterior space. This ability to distinguish inside from outside is elemental to understandings of domestic space, particularly domestic architecture, that link it to conceptions of interiority.[2] *Trumbull Park* and *Maud Martha* illustrate how representations of domestic architecture and the life it houses reveal not simply black interiority, but also social and legal perceptions of blackness. In these texts, the spatial realities of segregation construct black domestic spaces and continuously encroach upon families and housing structures.

The refusal to integrate public housing projects and the enactment of race-restrictive zoning ordinances demonstrate how on federal, state, and local levels racist practices were encoded into law (Meyer 7). Private groups and practices, however, especially occupy the attention of Brown and Brooks and are central to my discussion. These practices that derive from individual white citizens and their communities were not federal or state legislation; but nonetheless, they assume legal status and uncover the relationship between white privilege and law. Ultimately, they have the force of law in restricting black existence. In particular, I consider neighborhood associations and their tools, racially restrictive covenants, and how their presences directly and indirectly police black domestic spaces in both *Trumbull Park* and *Maud Martha*.[3]

Both the associations and the covenants themselves are based on an understanding of whiteness as property. Property is not simply objects of ownership (like houses), as Cheryl Harris explains, but rather "expectations in tangible or intangible things that are valued and protected by law" (1729). Harris specifies that within "the worlds of *de jure* and *de facto* segregation, whiteness has value, whiteness is valued, and whiteness is expected to be valued in law" (1777). Therefore, narratives that deal with issues of segregation—even if they concentrate on integration—will also be explorations of the value placed on whiteness and the social protection(s) that it is afforded. A legal protection of segregation occurs because there is a value socially invested in whiteness that is not similarly invested in blackness. Such "hypervaluation of whiteness" is apparent in important Supreme Court cases that contend with restrictive covenants such as *Hansberry v. Lee*, *Shelley v. Kraemer*, and *Corrigan v. Buckley*. Regardless of whether the covenant under consideration was upheld or not, none of these cases question the validity of covenants as *legal documents*; all implicitly recognize the white right to exclude black people. There is a fundamental understanding that "a change in color leads to a change in value" and vice versa (Delaney 170). Such cases legalize and protect the right to generate a value-laden boundary between black and white spaces. In the legal discourse, black domestic space not only comes to be seen as a threat to white spaces and to white assessments of "value," but such space also becomes aligned with "valuelessness."

The Limits of Integration: Brown's *Trumbull Park*

The legal protection of segregation finds concomitant social safeguarding of segregation in the work of neighborhood associations, which were organized groups of property owners and their supporters who used legal strategies such as racial restrictive covenants and less formal (and more violent) forms of intimidation to exclude black families from neighborhoods. Chicago felt the presence of these associations particularly, as shown in the reference made to them through the white character Karl Lindner, the representative from the Clybourne Park Improvement Association, in Lorraine Hansberry's play *A Raisin in the Sun* (1959). Lindner visits the Younger family on behalf of his community's association to try to convince this black family not to move into the house they have bought in Clybourne Park: "we are prepared to make your family a very generous offer. . . . Our association is prepared, through the collective effort of our people, to buy the house from you at a financial gain to your family" (118). He comes armed with money to enact social pressure from the whites to ensure a segregated housing community. In justifying the offer, Lindner explains to the Younger family, "a man, right or wrong, has the right to want to have the neighborhood he lives in a certain kind of way" (117). The "certain kind of way" of living that Lindner obliquely references is "white"; the Clybourne Park residents want their neighborhood to maintain this exclusive property.

A similar argument can be made about the efforts to preserve a white community by the South Deering Association, a neighborhood association in *Trumbull Park*. These property owners are much more violent and aggressive in protecting the "whiteness" of their neighborhood depicted by terrorized black families. Brown's novel centers on the Martin family, who move from a black neighborhood in Chicago to a white housing project. When the Martins arrive in Trumbull Park, they are met by a mob; this mob acts as a physical boundary that literally stops black families from moving in, and if the families eventually do so, the hundreds of protestors entrap them in their homes. Often, the maintenance of boundaries can take precedence over what lies inside them because without the boundaries, there no longer can be a way to differentiate. Moreover, boundaries and limits, as Lindon Barrett argues, are the " 'essential' matter of value" because they indicate the same sense of arbitration that the concept of value demands (16). In fact, the mob itself materializes the boundary demarcating the site where value (whiteness) lies—the very boundary or racial "force field" that the covenants attempted to produce and the legal cases to perpetuate. Therefore, the mob's desire to form a physical boundary represents its collective need to instantiate and protect a system of valuation and differentiation.

The formal reiteration and reconstitution of difference at the heart of this valuation is apparent in the mob's irate chant "*Get out, Africans—get out! Get out, Africans—get out! Get out, Africans—get out!*" (27). The insistence on using the term *Africans* to refer to the Martin family is a conscious denial of this (and any) black family's U.S. nationality and citizenship. The chant marks that the Martins, as "Africans," are civic outsiders or foreigners to the space of the neighborhood and consequently are excluded from the rights afforded citizens like the members of the South Deering Association who have a "right" to be housed there.

The chant iterates how both American citizenship and membership in the community are racialized in the minds of the neighborhood association. Later, when a (white) policeman strikes a white member of the mob to calm him down, the captain reproaches this officer by saying, " 'Dooon't [*sic*] rough up these people! They got rights!' " (47). The captain intimates that as citizens of South Deering (and the United States), these protestors have specific guaranteed rights; however, he is not talking about a right to assemble or to protest, but rather a right to a white community, which carries with it a right to protect that community from a black intrusion. If limits and boundaries are about the definition of value, then that which lies outside of the value boundary is arguably without value; in other words, non-whiteness is understood as value-deficient. Accordingly, the South Deering mob attempts to keep out a non-white "valuelessness" that poses a threat to its property and themselves. This sense of raced "valuelessness" becomes an integral element in the delineation of black domestic structures. It is not simply that these structures lack (monetary) value, but rather, that sense of lack gets translated into representations of spaces that are threatening and without value as domestic or familial spaces.

In *Trumbull Park*, Brown comments on the physical structure of black-designated housing. The most typical characteristic of a black family's house in Trumbull Park is broken windows. Bricks, rocks, and cans of sulphur coming from the white mob repeatedly destroy the windows. Black resident Arthur Davis tells the protagonist Buggy Martin: "behind that board there are some windows—at least window frames. The windows have been broken so many times that the Housing Authority put this board up instead of glass. They can't keep replacing the windows, and they *won't* make the cops keep the people from breaking them" (149). The window breaking is a daily, seemingly unstoppable occurrence. This destruction violates the sense of security the homes should offer their residents and does away with any sense of privacy.

A connection of value and violence sheds light on the effects of the white mob's actions in the narrative. The mob literally destroys the economic value of the black families' homes, while simultaneously creating a vector of value. In the calculated acts of destruction, the mob attempts to formulate and sustain its own sense of value against the "irreparable injury" that the black presence seems to guarantee.[4] The symbolic act of valuation is intended to deny value to both blacks and the spaces they occupy and at the same time to resist any perceived change to the larger neighborhood affected by a black presence. One resident's comment, " 'Every place that they've [black people] taken over, they've turned into a slum,' " articulates a belief that black neighborhoods are marked by inferior living conditions and that they likely harbor criminality (Meyer 120). Herman Long and Charles S. Johnson insist: "The ill-kept and unsightly outward aspect of [segregated spaces], with their teeming population, becomes associated in the minds of other city residents with the current occupants themselves, who merely inherited the area in the last stages of usefulness as a dwelling place" (3). Both African Americans and their domestic spaces are seen as undesirable because of the connection to dilapidation and delinquency.

The space of black housing is not merely dangerous, but also confining. Throughout the text, the homes of black residents in Trumbull Park are described as prisons. Buggy Martin insists that Trumbull Park in its regularity and sameness "looked like a great big prison" (84). Moreover, the "book signing" that black families must do to enter and leave their homes because of the mob violence and racist demonstrations by the white rioters produces an atmosphere of incarceration. The signing in and out creates an invasive surveil-lance that is "panoptic-like" in that the black characters' movements are always being monitored and are under constant scrutiny. The result criminalizes the black families, who are the *victims* of the violence. The police presence that should be protecting these families instead inspects and constricts them. The police are less protective forces than prison guards. Arthur alludes to this irony when he asks: "Who are they . . . protecting? Us . . . from the rioters? Or the rioters . . . from us?" (248). Living in Trumbull Park, then, means living in a domestic prison and being transported in police wagons or "cages." In fact, Buggy says, "We were living in a jail, and we went out of Trumbull Park in a cage and came back to Trumbull Park in a cage" (360). Reduced to prisons for criminals, the houses are no longer residential sites for families, and their value has been demoted to that of jail cells.

In light of this construction of carceral space, the moment when one of the members of the crowd calls Buggy a "*jailbird nigger*" becomes central (97). The comment mocks Buggy (and all black residents) who must ride around in a patrol wagon because of the menacing presence of the violent mob. This epithet also reinforces the connection of blackness with criminality. The assumption of whites throughout the novel that black men such as Red or Kevin always have knives—whether they actually do or not—exposes an ingrained reduction of black individuals to *natural* criminal types (35, 206). This connection is basic to the members of the neighborhood association and their desire to keep black residents out of their areas. In the white cultural imaginary functioning in *Trumbull Park*, black physical space is understood as being congruent with the bodies that inhabit it. Therefore, the criminality expected of the black families who move to Trumbull Park is derived from the conflation of criminality with black segregated areas. This criminality is perceived as inhering to the black body itself, meaning that it can be transported along with a black family (along with their furniture) into any neighborhood. Thus, black bodies themselves threaten white spaces. Following this racialized logic, every black body is necessarily concealing a destructive weapon creating a need for race-sensitive boundaries and policies that ensure them.

A consideration of how the narrative portrays familial relations also is vital in understanding how policies influenced the relationship between black subjects and domestic space. In terms of the representations of family structures, *Trumbull Park* is conflicted because families move toward the act of coming together under the difficult circumstances, but the narrative also illustrates how personal relationships were strained. A primary goal of *Trumbull Park* is to emphasize the growing sense of community among the resident black families. Mary Helen Washington contends that Brown's work actually has a "collective protagonist, a community of couples acting" (Foreword xvi). She argues, "with each one of the characters encouraging the others, men and women together, almost in counterpoint, they collectively perform their first acts of defiance" (xiii). The formation of the "vigilante" meeting group—a black "counter" neighborhood association—reflects this idea. Through his experience with the "vigilantes," Buggy manifests an increasing faith in the ability of black people to come together. Earlier in the text he expresses suspicion about "that stuff about Negroes sticking together" (132), but later after the "vigilantes" begin to take action, he insists that what he "had told to Helen about Negroes not sticking together was beginning to soften at the edges and melt away" (260). Brown provides a narrative that is optimistic in terms of group solidarity and cooperation.

Ironically, this growing sense of interfamilial connection is coupled with growing distances within individual couples—a weakening of intrafamilial connections. In thinking about how their lives had changed since they moved into Trumbull Park, Buggy explains that he and his wife Helen had "become so wrapped up in [their] own growing anger that [they] hadn't had time to get the feeling of closeness with the world around [them]" (216). This "anger" is not simply keeping them from the "world," but also distancing them from each other as well. At one of the "vigilante" meetings, Buggy expresses his frustrations that the debate on what the group should do was dividing up households: "I didn't dig all this—I mean, how the wife voted one way and the husband voted the other. Were these wives voting different from the way their husbands were voting just to be contrary? Was there something coming between them that made one do the opposite from the other just for spite?" (271). The narrative signals not only the split between husband and wife, but more importantly it shows Buggy's inability to recognize that these women might have an opinion outside of their husbands'.

This inability, although a reflection of the influence of patriarchal culture, also symbolizes a disconnect between husbands and wives occasioned by life in Trumbull Park.[5] An emotional distancing marks Buggy and Helen's first day in their integrated neighborhood. Buggy criticizes their friend Red and refuses to support him when Red attempts to defend himself against the white mob, whereas Helen indicates her approval of Red's actions and her disappointment with her husband (30). Similarly, the brief reference to William Thomas's relationship with his wife displays this disconnect and the distancing "anger" that Buggy described:

From that minute on, until Mr. and Mrs. Thomas moved out of the project a year later—broken, nervous, talking about divorce, not speaking to each other, not speaking to any of us—William Thomas was never—not even in the closest room, not even in a moving car driving away from Trumbull Park—able to say that the white people were breaking the windows, or setting off the bombs,

or gathering in the mobs that once surrounded his wife and threw
a bomb straight at her. (253)

In the text, there is a close connection between events in Trumbull Park and
the Thomas' marriage. The broken windows and bombs have alienated the Mr.
and Mrs. Thomas from each other, rather than bringing them closer. Although
he does want to proffer a sense of solidarity in his narrative, Brown cannot help
but recognize—even if momentarily or parenthetically—that the actions of the
South Deering Association also can strain and even destroy marital relationships
just as its members continuously destroy house windows.

The idea that white neighborhood associations would have a strong
impact on an integrating black family's relationship to domestic space is not
difficult to imagine. However, the power of *Trumbull Park* lies in the manner
in which it demonstrates the effect that these private associations can also have
on segregated spaces. Neighborhood associations and restrictive covenants did
not only impinge on the lives of African Americans who lived in integrated
spaces; they also structured the lives of those living in segregated spaces. In fact,
these associations and their influence(s) work to collapse the sense of distinction between integrated and segregated space for black families. In Chicago,
white neighborhood associations held blacks from crossing out of segregated
areas. The situations in *Corrigan, Hansberry,* and *Shelley* all reflect a desire
on the part of black families to move outside of the "iron ring" of restrictive
covenants that produced overcrowded and inadequate neighborhoods. Black
families in Chicago and all over the country were trapped for decades in areas
that were increasingly unable to house effectively those who lived there and
whose conditions deteriorated, so much so that the black body itself became
connected with the spatial degradation housing and defining black domestic
space in social and legal discourses.

Brown's novel portrays how the impediment of the boundary line that
neighborhood associations imposed alienated black families from their domestic
structures in nonintegrated areas. Although the novel focuses on integration,
Buggy and his wife initially live in the Gardener building in the segregated part
of Chicago. Buggy points out that he had always lived in the building—like
most of the occupants (15). In fact, the old writings on the building's walls
suggest that the residents' lives are inscribed on the walls (11); their existences
are intimately connected to the building itself. Unfortunately, the narrative
continually aligns the building with death and destruction. The reader soon
discovers that the Gardener is rotting; the novel opens with a description of a
young child, Babydoll, falling from a "rotten porch" on the fourth floor and
dying. This sense of rotting denotes the "valuelessness" of the building.

The implication throughout the narrative is that spaces like the Gardener
building are not "decent" housing (320); in effect, they are not places to raise

a family (safely). Long and Johnson provide a context for the porch that "kills" Babydoll: [Segregated neighborhoods] "tend to exhibit the greatest municipal neglect, not only because the dwellings and surrounding facilities are hardest to keep in repair but because the residents themselves have the least to say about the services provided by the city" (2–3). Helen's discussion with Buggy after Babydoll's death signals that the building suffers from the willful "neglect" of black inhabited space: "Poor Babydoll. I told Mr. Gardner about that porch. It's two or three places there that need fixing. I don't know why the health department don't do something to him, to make him fix this place up" (12). This neglect represents the Martins' lack of control over the conditions in their domestic space, and it is linked to their lack of influence in the social sphere.

Moreover, Brown's narrative figures the Gardener building as a creature that is continually consuming or killing the tenants in the building; it has a destructive agency: " 'Look, look, at that big, ramshackle, firetrap [the Gardener]. Look at it, look at what killed Babydoll' " (9). Later in the narrative, Buggy also accuses the building of killing both his mother and his father (81, 404). If the tenants' lives are intrinsically connected to the building, and the building is rotting (dying), then death becomes part-and-parcel to residency. To live there is to die. Therefore, the building engenders sickness and death, and segregated black domestic space comes to embody these notions.

The Gardener assumes important parallels to the home in Trumbull Park relationally linking black residential conditions in segregated and integrated spaces. Buggy describes his moving out of the Gardener building as "getting out of jail through the front door" (16). In his mind the building is also a kind of jail, like the homes in Trumbull Park; he and his family have exchanged one kind domestic space for another, but the imprisoning nature of the space has remained the same. Even the trope of broken windows forges a parallel between the Gardener and Trumbull Park homes. After Babydoll's death, Buggy is looking up at the building as he says, "Windows, windows, most of them with only one pane. A lot of the windows were broken completely, and in their place were weather-stained, yellowing pasteboards" (9). Broken windows characterize this housing space as well. In some ways, their living conditions do not appear to have changed at all in the move from the Gardener to Trumbull Park.

This troubling similarity is precisely what Buggy observes:

> We were out of the Gardener Building, but now the world around us was icy and mean with the evil stares of the people we had to live with. And the noise of those bombs made the diesel train behind the Gardener Building and the broken banisters seem like maybe I had exaggerated how bad it had been in the first place. I had thought that diesel meant to me the death, dirt, and gloom of the Gardener Building, but it seemed to have caught up with me

in a different way in Trumbull Park. It looked like there was no
place for a broke colored man to go. No hiding place. No place
to run. I felt choked, trapped, and boxed in. (131)

That which the diesel represents, the intangible that brings the "gloom" and
claustrophobia, is as present in the integrated Trumbull Park as it was in the
segregated Gardener; the homes are equally confining. This kind of claustrophobia is exactly what black families had to have felt as covenants restricted their
movement and forced people to live literally on top of one another because of
the limited living space available to them. Ironically, moving to an integrated
space did not mean liberation from this *feeling* of restriction. The different
domestic spaces, then, are haunted by an "unchanging" sameness mandated by
White communities to protect their self-perceived intrinsic value.

Domestic Confinement and Disappointed Domesticity: Brooks's *Maud Martha*

Maud Martha is a strikingly different narrative from *Trumbull Park*. Whereas
Brown's narrative is continuous and linear, Brooks creates a fragmentary poetic
narrative that is made up of "short vignetted chapters" that range in length
with seemingly "no continuity between one chapter and the next" (Washington
454).[6] More important than this structural difference, Brooks never mentions
a restrictive covenant or neighborhood associations. In fact, she places the narrative action entirely in a segregated world. Nonetheless, the novel is driven
by issues of integration (Christian 246), making it as much a text about the
dynamics of segregation and integration as is Brown's later work. What we find
in Brooks's representation of segregated space is an exploration of the world
that neighborhood associations like South Deering had indirectly formed and
directly attempted to stifle through their actions. Unlike Buggy and Helen who
are able to "liberate" themselves from the Gardener, Maud Martha is "narratively"
trapped (or imprisoned) by her domestic space—she does not make it out of
the Gappington Arms kitchenette building by the novel's close.

Maud Martha is not simply trapped in the space of her two-room kitchenette apartment, but rather she also is continuously unsatisfied with it and disgusted
by it. Her initial excitement about her apartment is quickly undermined by the
realities of the space. No matter how much she cleaned with "water containing
melted American Family soap and Lysol every other day" she could not stop
the first roach from arriving (62–63). It is as if a kind of filth inheres in the
building and spreads uncontrollably. This unstoppable roach evidences Maud's
inability to control the sanitary conditions of her home. Such a contaminating
element is what Brooks describes when Maud talks about "the color and sound

and smell of the kitchenette" that spreads to everyone and everything in the building draining the life from it (63). The occupants' bodies become linked to the structural realities of the building.

Whether tenements or houses, segregated domestic spaces to which blacks are relegated exude the substandard. Maud comments on how much she loved the *house* where she grew up, yet the first impression that the reader receives of her childhood home is that it is marked by a sense of inadequacy and unpleasantness: "There was a small hole in the sad-colored rug, near the sofa. Not an outrageous hole. But she shuddered. She dashed to the sofa, maneuvered it till the hole could not be seen. She sniffed a couple of times. Often it was said that colored people's houses necessarily had a certain heavy, unpleasant smell. Nonsense, that was. Vicious—and nonsense. But she raised every window" (17). The impending visit of a young white boy, Charles, causes Maud to have these feeling of anxiety. Although Charles never actually appears in the text, this moment is significant because the presence of a white person—or even the threat of such a presence—introduces questions of value. What the narrative reflects is a consciousness of how white people view black people and their homes, and it shows how such views can structure how blacks see their homes and, accordingly, themselves. Maud's hiding in the bathroom at the end of the chapter is her attempt to prevent Charles from "viciously" seeing her in the way that she believes he sees her home: as valueless. Ultimately, the same kind of rotting that the reader is made aware of in the Gappington and the Gardner is made present in Maud's segregated family home (the "heavy, unpleasant smell" and "outrageous hole") by the mere mention of a white person.

Maud Martha's relationship to these domestic spaces shapes her familial relationship similar to the way domestic space affected marital interactions in Brown's novel. The relationship between the protagonist and her husband Paul is the most significant familial relationship depicted in the text. This marriage unfolds as if there is a nearly insurmountable distance between Maud and her husband; the two are unable to communicate, and they are essentially estranged for most of the narrative. When Maud feels jealous of Maella because Paul is dancing with her at the Foxy Cats Club, she checks her rising anger at this supposed usurper because she decides, "if the root was sour what business did she have up there hacking at a leaf?" (88). Her marriage itself is the root that has *soured*. The "sourness" of the marriage parallels her disappointment with her "rotted" apartment. In fact, Harry Shaw argues that the physical realities of her apartment make Maud Martha feel a disappointment with her marriage (129). Moreover, the chapter that describes her dissatisfaction with her home most specifically, "the kitchenette," is directly followed by a chapter expressing her increasing disinterest in Paul and his desires: he embarrasses her with his crudeness in public and private, and she rejects his sexual advances by suggesting that she instead make sandwiches (65–68). The structure of the narrative connects her feelings about Paul with her frustrations with their living space. This linkage reveals an intimate connection between both of her frustrations (home and husband) and emphasizes the emotional distance she feels from both.

Maud Martha suffers from domestic disillusionment, but this disillusionment does not limit itself to her experiences within her home; it extends to her encounters outside of her domestic space. This "movement" of her disillusionment becomes clear when she takes her daughter Paulette to see Santa Claus. During the visit, Santa Claus shows no interest in Paulette and often ignores the little girl as she speaks:

> "Mister," said Maud Martha, "my little girl is talking to you."
>
> Santa Claus's neck turned with hard slowness, carrying his unwilling face with it.
>
> "Mister," said Maud Martha.
>
> "And what—do you want for Christmas." No question mark at the end.
>
> "I want a wagon, a doll, a bear, a big ball, and a tricycle with a horn."
>
> Silence. Then, "Oh." Then, "Um-hm." (173–74)

This lack of concern causes Paulette to ask her mother, "Why didn't Santa Claus like me?' " Maud Martha tries to make her disappointed daughter believe that Santa had liked her and that he had just been preoccupied; however, she has a lingering fear that her daughter is beginning to recognize the reality of racism and prejudice. Maud Martha hopes that Paulette is not at a point where she would begin to put the pieces together. The chapter ends with a prayer-like moment where Maud Martha wishes: "Keep her that land of blue! Keep her those fairies . . . and Santa's every winter's lord, kind, sheer being who never perspires, who never does or says a foolish or ineffective thing, who never has occasion to pull the chain and flush the toilet" (176). This wish intimates that she does not want her daughter to become disillusioned by racism (just yet).

It is important to note how Maud Martha characterizes this disillusionment. The odd and very particular negative characteristics that are mentioned are essentially those that she connects to her husband Paul. The "toilet" reference stands out especially. After going out to a "musicale" one night, Maud Martha observes that Paul "went immediately into the bathroom." She is frustrated and a bit appalled by the fact that he "did not try to mask his need" at all (66). Paul's behavior is not the behavior Maud Martha expects of her husband; his actions do not represent the domestic life that she had imagined. Moreover, by ending with the image of the "toilet," the text locates the reader squarely within the domestic space with which Maud Martha is unsatisfied, while also evoking issues of sanitation. Maud Martha couches this social disillusionment that she fears for her daughter in the images of disappointed domesticity.

Maud Martha's role as a mother is vital to understanding her feelings about her domestic life. Her relationship to her daughter Paulette reveals much about her marriage in particular (102–7). However, I believe that the way the narrative introduces Maud Martha's second pregnancy in the last chapter points out her rising dissatisfaction with her domestic space. The announcement of this pregnancy is located in the celebratory chapter "back home from the wars!" which describes the moment after World War II when life seemed promising for many African Americans: "There was Peace, and her brother Harry was back from the wars . . . outside it was bright, because the sunshine had broken through the dark green shade and was glorifying every bit of her room" (177). In the chapter, Brooks connects the new pregnancy with this moment so that both appear to be equally promising. Washington appreciates this chapter because she feels that in it Maud is able to free herself, even if momentarily, from the domestic enclosures that have defined her character throughout the narrative (465).

However, just as in Brown's text, there is a parenthetical disturbance of the optimistic narrative; a foreboding elliptical insert interrupts the celebratory tone of the chapter:

> She did not need information, or solace, or a guidebook or a sermon—not in this sun!—not in this blue air!
> . . . They "marched," they battled behind her brain—the men who had drunk beer with the best of them, the men with two arms off and two legs off, the men with the parts of faces. Then her guts divided, then her eyes swam under frank mist. And the Negro press (on whose front pages beamed the usual representations of womanly Beauty, pale and pompadoured) carried the stories of the latest of the Georgia and Mississippi lynching . . .
> But the sun was shining, and some of the people in the world had been left alive. (178–79)

Brooks juxtaposes the images of excited returning soldiers with dismembered men and lynched figures. The reality is that the postwar experience posed difficulties for the struggle for African American freedom, and there was a continuation of racial violence particularly in the South.[7] The insert "places the optimism in the sobering context of the maimed bodies of the soldiers and the news of lynchings" (Andrews 69–70). This elliptical moment in the text, buttressed by references to the "blue sky" and the sun "shining" on both sides, inserts a level of self-conscious irony into the chapter's celebratory tone.

If there is a symbolic parallel between the returning soldiers and the pregnancy being drawn, one must also consider other levels of meaning for the pregnancy because socio-racial realities complicated its counterpart—the soldiers' excitement is undermined by the image of lynching in the text. What another child actually means is *even less room in the two-bedroom kitchenette*. Because of this new child, Maud Martha and Paul will likely need to move, and because one of the last things that we hear about Paul is that he has lost his job (159), such a move is not likely possible. The promise (or threat) of further domestic confinement is what lurks behind the text of the chapter and threatens to emerge, as did the elliptical statement. This understanding provides a productive way to parse a significant statement in the chapter: "What, *what*, am I to do with all of this life?" You-me Park and Gayle Wald explain that "World War II marked the moment when African American men began to organize politically around the war effort to demand their rights as citizens. . . . But where were black women's desires for citizenship and mobility within and between separate spheres being presented?" (278). Park and Wald feel as if Maud Martha's question in the text is actually asking this question about new opportunities for Black women's citizenship and mobility in this period.

This level of meaning may be read in the text, but other, very particular reasons also fuel her question. Maud Martha is actively looking at and thinking about the physical realities of her apartment when she asks this pivotal question. When Maud Martha asks what is she to do with all of this "life," she is asking where is she to put or house all of the "life" that she is carrying: her children. In part, she is asking a question about housing. The novel, then, ends with an unarticulated fear about the realities of the physical domestic space for the black family (the figurative domestic space). Therefore, the question she asks parallels the statement that Buggy makes in Brown's text: "It looked like there was no place for a broke colored man to go. No hiding place. No place to run." Both insist on a lack of a place to house black bodies; a "no-placedness" characterizes their respective experiences.

This "no-placedness" that we can recognize in these texts is actually a social and legal creation that becomes prominent in the African American lived experience. In his discussion of place in *Workings of the Spirit*, Houston Baker argues,

> [for] place to be recognized by one as actually PLACE, as a person-
> ally valued locale, one must set and maintain the boundaries. If one,
> however, is constituted and maintained by and within boundaries
> set by a dominating authority, then one is not a setter of place
> but a prisoner of another's desire. Under the displacing impress of
> authority even what one calls and, perhaps, feels is one's *own place*
> is, from the perspective of human agency, *placeless*. (104)

In Baker's understanding, having one's place defined or controlled by an outside "authority" complicates one's relationship to that place.[8] This idea of constituting and maintaining describes succinctly the social work done by neighborhood associations, racial covenants, and even court cases. Moreover, the establishing of boundaries connected to "place" is the very domain of values (or valuation). Thus, Baker's idea of "placelessness" is intrinsically connected to the idea of "valuelessness" that I have been exploring. We can recognize the "displacing impress of authority" in preventing families from establishing homes past Cottage Grove Avenue in *Maud Martha* and in forcing families to sign in if they want to leave or enter their homes in *Trumbull Park*. Additionally, as Brown's novel illustrates, the structural and psychological realities of segregation that the legal documents and social practices engineered and encouraged did not limit themselves to the actual geographical coordinates of segregated areas. The attempt to confine a subject to a particular place, which characterizes the practice of segregation, can paradoxically engender a feeling of having no place for that subject inside and outside of the segregated area. The sense of having no place travels, as it were, and has the motility of a policing force.

The actual inability to move and the feeling of immobility constitute the sentiment that travels between segregated and integrated spaces. Given this idea, I contend that we can push Baker's conceptualization somewhat further to include this effect by also talking about "spacelessness." Along with the lack of a definite place of value, black bodies do not have the freedom to move that space indicates.[9] The societal investment in whiteness impedes this movement through space, and acts of segregation are structured around this investment. Arguably, it is bell hooks's perception of such "spacelessness" that encourages her theorizing of "homeplace" for African American subjects. My discussion has focused on the relationship that the characters in these narratives have with domestic space, but this relationship is one that is fully intelligible by understanding the place of African Americans in the social realm. It is for this reason that Buggy Martin sees his home in Trumbull Park as a prison and Maud Martha connects the disillusionment of social racism with the disillusionment with her home life. In effect, how the black body is housed in these mid-twentieth-century segregation narratives becomes a representation of how they are "housed" in the body politic: estrangement in one parallels disenfranchisement in the other.

Notes

1. Arnold Hirsch explains how federal policies and organizations meant to dismantle housing discrimination and segregation actually reinforced and extended them in the post-World War II period. There were also social methods of intimidation that discouraged African American from integrating as well as distressed those who did. Such

official and unofficial mechanisms forced African Americans to remain in congested, uncomfortable, and overpriced living spaces (Drake and Clayton 174–80).

2. See Bachelard, *Poetics of Space* and Wallace, *Constructing the Black Masculine.*

3. A race-restrictive covenant is "a mutual agreement entered into by a group of property owners not to sell, rent, lease or otherwise convey a property to Negroes or other particular minorities" (Long and Johnson 10–11).

4. In his discussion, Barrett also calls attention to the significant relationship between violence and value. Additionally, "irreparable injury" is the language used in Corrigan to describe the situation that would be created by African American owning property in the covenant-protected neighborhood.

5. Contributing to this disconnect between husband and wife are the different experiences that black men and women have in Trumbull Park. At one point in the narrative, Buggy realizes that although the men escape the terrors of the mob violence most of the day while they are at work, the women face this harassment all day, every-day (Brown 245).

6. The novel is derived from a sequence of poems that Brooks had written (Melhem 13).

7. See Donald Spivey's and Nikhil Pal Singh's respective discussions of the post-World War II period.

8. Yi-Fu Tuan, whom Baker cites in his own work, differentiates "space" from "place." He explains, "space as that which allows movement"; it denotes having the freedom to move (6). "Place" is "pause": "each pause in movement makes it possible for location to be transformed into place." This pause allows a subject to attach significance to this particular point in space" (12). Thinkers such as Doreen Massey have reconfigured "place" by insisting that it also results from the interaction of social relations so that a network of social forces, such as those embodied in the geographical matrix of segregation, can inform the attachment that an individual has to "place."

9. See note 8.

Works Cited

Andrews, Larry. "The Aliveness of Things: Nature in *Maud Martha*." *Gwendolyn Brooks' Maud Martha: A Critical Collection.* Ed. Jacqueline Bryant. Chicago: Third World, 2002. 69–89.

Bachelard, Gaston. *The Poetics of Space.* Trans. Maria Jolas. Boston: Beacon, 1964.

Baker, Houston. *Workings of the Spirit: The Poetics of Afro-American Women's Writing.* Chicago: U of Chicago P, 1991.

Barrett, Lindon. *Blackness and Value.* Cambridge, UK: Cambridge UP, 1999.

Brooks, Gwendolyn. "kitchenette building." *A Street in Bronzeville.* 1945. Ann Arbor: U of Michigan P, 1975.

———. *Maud Martha.* New York: Harper, 1953.

Brown, Frank London. *Trumbull Park.* Boston: Northeastern UP, 2005.

Christian, Barbara. "Nuance and the Novella." *Life Distilled.* Ed. Maria K. Mootry and Gary Smith. Urbana: U of Illinois P, 1987. 239–53.

Delaney, David. *Race, Place, and the Law.* Austin: U of Texas P, 1998.

Drake, St. Clair and Horace Clayton. *Black Metropolis*, Vol. 1. New York: Harper, 1962.

Hansberry, Lorraine. *A Raisin in the Sun*. 1959. New York: Vintage, 1994.

Harris, Cheryl. "Whiteness as Property." *Harvard Law Review* 106 (8): 1993.

Hirsch, Arnold R. " 'Containment' on the Home Front: Race and Federal Housing Policy from the New Deal to the Cold War." *Journal of Urban History* 26.2 (2000) 158–189.

hooks, bell. *Yearning: Race, Gender, and Cultural Politics*. Boston: South End, 1990.

"Iron Ring in Housing." *The Crisis* 47.7(1940): 205, 210.

Long, Herman and Charles S. Johnson. *People v. Property: Race Restrictive Covenants in Housing*. Nashville: Fisk UP, 1947.

Massey, Doreen. *Space, Place, and Gender*. Cambridge, UK: Polity, 1994.

Melhem, D.H. "Maud Martha, Bronzeville Boys and Girls." *Gwendolyn Brooks' Maud Martha: A Critical Collection*. Chicago: Third World, 2002. 13–32.

Meyer, Steven Grant. *As long as they Don't Move Next door: Segregation and Racial Conflict in American Neighborhoods*. Lanham, MD: Rowman & Littlefield, 2000.

Park, You-Me and Gayle Wald. "Native Daughters in the Promised Land: Gender, Race, and the Question of Separate Spheres." *No More Separate Spheres! A Next Wave American Studies Reader*. Eds. Cathy N. Davidson and Jessamyn Hatcher. Durham, NC: Duke UP; 2002. 263–87.

Shaw, Harry B. "Maud Martha." *On Gwendolyn Brooks*. Ed. Stephen Caldwell Wright. Ann Arbor: U of Michigan P, 1996. 124–37.

Singh, Nikhil Pal. *Black is a Country*. Cambridge, MA: Harvard UP, 2004.

Spivey, Donald. *Fire from the Soul*. Durham, NC: Carolina Academic, 2003.

Tuan, Yi-Fu. *Space and Place: The Perspective of Experience*. Minneapolis: U of Minnesota P, 1997.

Wallace, Maurice. *Constructing the Black Masculine: Identity and Ideality in African American Men's Culture: 1775–1995*. Durham, NC: Duke UP, 2002.

Washington, Mary Helen. Foreword. *Trumbull Park*. By Frank London Brown. Boston: Northeastern UP, 2005

———. " 'Taming all that anger down': Rage and Silence in Gwendolyn Brooks' *Maud Martha*." *The Massachusetts Review* 24 (2): 453–466.

Diseased Properties and Broken Homes in Ann Petry's *The Street*[1]

ELIZABETH BOYLE MACHLAN

> Rent Man waitin' for his forty dollars
> Ain't got me but a dime and some bad news.
> Bartender, give me a bracer, double beer chaser,
> 'Cause I got the low-down, mean, rent-man blues.
>
> —Blues standard

> The shades of the prison-house closed round us all: walls, straight and stubborn to the whitest, but relentlessly narrow, tall, and unscalable to sons of night who must plod darkly on in resignation.
>
> —W.E.B. Du Bois, *The Souls of Black Folk* (1903)

From the "big house" of the plantation to the "big house" of the prison, African Americans have colloquially associated the domestic architecture of the United States with oppression and abjection. Ann Petry's 1946 novel *The Street* brings to life for its audience the deceptive, malignant structures in which Jim Crow housing policies forced many African Americans to dwell, revealing the profound unhomeliness of these marginalized spaces. Due to Petry's "relentless presentation of the dreary despair of the inner cities," critical commentary on *The Street* has tended to engage first and foremost the question of whether her work is simply a "poor imitation" of the depiction of urban racism in Richard Wright's *Native Son* (Christian 11, Henderson 850).[2] I propose instead that *The Street* in fact owes far more to the structural and social preoccupations of the American Gothic than it does to the naturalist tradition, and that Petry positions the apartment house, not the ghetto itself, as the novel's central source of anxiety. To read her Harlem houses merely as metaphors for a troubled urban environment, I suggest, is to minimize the significance of the distinctly domestic horrors they contain.[3] Building on the work of Meg Wesling, who observes that "Petry's interest is not so much in determinist forces as in the

subtleties of social control and the threatening opacity of everyday social relations that racially segregated environments produce"(Wesling 118), my goal is
to locate and explore the ways in which Petry's Gothicized tenement imagines
the specter of segregation and white domination, and to illuminate how the
"peculiar institution" of Harlem's real estate market forced black New Yorkers
perpetually to re-enact Gothic scenarios of familial dismemberment, real and
imagined imprisonment, and sexual intimidation and transgression.

For Petry, the Gothic functions as a border genre, one which monitors the
many moral, cultural, and literal architectures at work in the (Re)construction
of American society. Justin Edwards has described how Gothic conventions
allowed both racist and reformist writers to engage a "racial gothic" discourse
that "employed striking and metaphoric images to filter and give meaning to
the social hierarchies of racial domination and subordination institutionalized
through slavery and maintained in the disenfranchising effects and segregation
laws of the postbellum period" (Edwards xi). The Supreme Court's upholding of
"separate but equal" premise of racial segregation in *Plessy v. Ferguson* (1896) had
demonstrated white America's stake in maintaining a sundered nation-subject,
as well as the psychology, on a national scale, that resisted integration. Wesling
notes that Petry portrays in a very real way "the intricate structural arrangements
that facilitate the economic exploitation of black women and men and the sexual
exploitation of black women by both white and black men" (Wesling 117); any
attempt to defy these hierarchies and cross the thresholds of these segregated
structures, Petry suggests, only defines them more deeply. In *The Street*, Gothic
images are often direct articulations, as opposed to representations, of actual
urban circumstances, since Harlem's houses were—and sometimes still are—sites
of overt racial and economic conflict.

Harlem's Haunted History

In his 1919 essay, Freud describes the uncanny as "what is concealed and
kept out of sight," or, alternately, in spatial terms as "something one does not
know one's way about in" (Freud). Both definitions evoke the constant need
for subjects to re-evaluate their boundaries and demarcate their space, even
within the home. Yet the slippage between home and not-home at work in
the uncanny is not always purely conceptual, or psychological. The history of
Harlem's complex confrontations and negotiations between blacks and whites
demonstrate not only architecture's utility as a tool of social control, but also
how segregation turned a lively neighborhood into the "dark double" of a
predominantly white New York. At the turn of the last century, attempts by
middle-class African Americans to wrest ownership of Harlem's housing stock
from white landlords ultimately resulted in a backlash, articulated by the *New
York Herald* in December 1905:

An untoward circumstance has been injected into the private-dwelling market in the vicinity of 133rd and 134th Streets. During the last three years the flats in 134th Street between Lenox and Seventh Avenues, that were occupied entirely by white folks, have been captured for occupancy by a Negro population.[4]

This "untoward circumstance" prompted Harlem's white landlords and residents to create overtly segregationist organizations such as the Harlem Property Owners' Improvement Corporation. In an attempt to rid Harlem's buildings of their black owners and tenants, corporation members signed "covenants" that "outlaw(ed) future sale and rental of property to colored people" (Osofsky 107). As seen in the passage just presented, white owners used bellicose language to convince others to support their cause: the black "enemy" was "invading" Harlem, and covenants were the first line of defense. The realization that they could not drive the black population out of Harlem completely led to the convening of a sort of mock "summit" with the black community:

Like an enemy negotiating a line of truce, whites called a meeting of Negro real estate men to attempt to draw a voluntary boundary line that would permanently separate the white and Negro communities—a "dead line," it was called. (Osofsky 108)

Defined as the line around a military prison beyond which an escaping prisoner may be shot down, the "dead line" aptly describes the dual dangers of the segregated ghetto: those trapped inside endured squalid, almost penal conditions, whereas those who ventured out risked death at the whim of their captor—white New York—for whom Harlem provoked the "repulsion and distress" characteristic of the uncanny. If New York was a house, Harlem was a dark, cobwebbed basement filled with things better forgotten. Read in this way, Petry's ghetto can be seen as a sort of urban unconscious, a site of repression in its most real and insidious form.

Conventional models of domestic architecture fall apart when applied to living arrangements in the ghetto, a phenomenon illustrated by Petry in the contrast between Lutie's Harlem apartment and the Connecticut home of the Chandlers, for whom she becomes a live-in servant after her husband loses his job. Traditionally, the American home was a private space defined in part by its distance from the workplace.[5] This formulation, however, obviously fails to account for the experience of servants, who may live where they work, or work where others live; it was especially inadequate for black slaves, whose domestic geographies were determined by "the big house," and many of whom aspired to the comparatively cushy life of "house servants." Lutie's position with the Chandlers simultaneously revisits and revises the ambiguous architecture of this economy. As You-Me Park and Gayle Wald illustrate, the very term *domestic worker*, through its conflation of the space of labor and the space of dwelling, is a paradox:

a strict separate spheres analytical framework, with its fetishistic and reductionist separation of *the* public and *the* private, obscures crucial questions about mobility and agency across socially constructed lines of difference. (Park and Wald 612)

Park and Wald argue that the collapse of the distinction between public and private spaces for black women employed by white families points toward the invalidity of conventional definitions of domesticity in the cases of women of color (609). Yet although Park and Wald use Lutie's experience as persuasive evidence of the collapse of the public–private split, their discussion fails to account for how *The Street* upholds other social and spatial segregations: black and white, poor and rich, urban and suburban. Petry emphasizes these dichotomies by locating the wealthy, white Chandler family two hours outside the city, in a semi-rural enclave of Connecticut.[6] Their house is nestled, fairytale-like, in the woods, and Lutie describes it as a "miracle": "Taken altogether it was like something in the movies, what with the size of the rooms and the big windows that brought the river and the surrounding woods almost into the house" (Petry 29).

The design of the house manifests a controlled, aestheticized relationship with the outside world. For the Chandlers, nature is simply an exterior element of interior design, carefully packaged for visual effect by the man-made structure. This manipulation of the environment sharply contrasts with Lutie's lack of control over Bub's view from their window in Harlem: "the rubbish had crept through the broken places in the fences until all of it mingled in a disorderly pattern that looked from their top-floor window like a huge junk-pile instead of a series of small backyards" (50). The Chandlers' house represents how architecture is supposed to work: as a stable system of social organization that allows the family to literally "design" how they appear from the outside. After Mrs. Chandler's brother shoots himself on Christmas morning, the family uses its influence to ensure that the event will be deemed an accident instead of a suicide. One might argue that this event challenges the pastoral perfection of the Chandlers' world; however, the power and prestige of the white family quickly repairs the rift in their social fabric in a way that Lutie cannot emulate. Her closets are barely big enough to contain her clothes, much less her ghosts.

The Architecture of the Veil

In 1935, a decade before *The Street* was published, *The New York Post* observed that "an increasingly impenetrable wall has sprung up around Harlem."[7] Although *The Street* may blur the theoretical boundary between the public and private spheres in terms of women's work, it upholds and reinforces the symbolic "dead line" drawn by the real estate covenants between New York's black and white communities by situating the only two white families Lutie encounters, the Chandlers and the Pizzinis, in residential enclaves to which she has no access. Within Harlem itself, however, architecture fails to demarcate what Henry James referred to in *The American Scene* as "place(s) of passage and place(s) of privacy" (James 125). First among the neighborhood's evils in the eyes of white outsiders was its alleged lack of moral or geographical distinction between "good" and "bad" elements, prompting *Harper's Weekly* to observe as early as 1900 that "the virtuous and the vicious elbow each other in the closest kind of quarters. This is a great source of moral contagion, and vice spreads with great rapidity among the women of such quarters."[8] Although the metaphor of disease was commonly used as a code by white Americans who feared contact with groups regarded as "unhealthy" and/or "foreign," the term *contagion* remained in use in regard to Harlem long after dying out as a rationale for cordoning off other immigrant populations, such as Italians or Jews.[9] Petry appropriates the association of immorality and illness with "close quarters" in the very first pages of *The Street*, when Lutie imagines the typical Harlem tenement: "Because the walls would be flimsy, why, the good people, the bad people, the children, the dogs, and the god-awful smells would all be wrapped up together in one big package"; her reference to "smell(s) that seep" evokes Gothic rot and decay (Petry 8, 16). Her building is an undifferentiated, insubstantial series of spaces that offer little protection or privacy, "like living in a tent with everything that goes on inside it open to the world because the flap won't close," where "the tenants who had apartments would sit on the stairs as though the hall were a theater and the performance about to start" (47, 11).

If, on one hand, flimsy architecture fails to isolate Lutie from her noisy, immoral neighbors, on the other, the "imaginary" walls that divide her and other African Americans from the advantages and security available to the white community are very much intact, and impenetrable. While in Connecticut with the Chandlers, Lutie imagines the white world as a garden she can see, but to which she cannot gain access:

> She was looking through a hole in a wall at some enchanted garden. She could see, she could hear, she spoke the language of the people in the garden, but she couldn't get past the wall. The figures on the other side of it loomed up life-size and they could see her, but there was this wall in between which prevented them from mingling on equal footing. The people on the other side of the wall knew less about her than she did about them. (31)

The image of the wall recasts the Du Boisian veil as a physical structure preventing the union of—or understanding between—the black and white worlds.[10] Lutie, with her knowledge, is excluded from the Edenic atmosphere of the "other side";

the association of whiteness with nature seems to imply that the "dark side" is both urban and fallen. This passage, which posits the wall as an almost organic entity, occurs early in the text, and mutates, as the story progresses, into overt images of obstruction and containment. Unlike Du Bois, who claims early in *The Souls of Black Folk* that he "had no desire to tear down that veil, to creep through" (Du Bois 4), Lutie is determined to get to the other side:

> She had come this far poor and black and shut out as though a door had been slammed in her face. Well, she would shove it open; she would beat and bang on it and push against it and use a chisel in order to get it open. (118)

It is difficult to map the architecture of Petry's analogy and determine whether Lutie is trying to get in, or to get out. By the end of the novel, however, Petry makes it clear that Lutie is trapped inside a symbolically stifling place, an oppressive architecture she attributes explicitly to white oppression: "from the time (Lutie) was born, she had been hemmed into an ever-narrowing space, until now she was very nearly walled in and the wall had been built up brick by brick by eager white hands" (201). These hands are ultimately attached to Junto, the white landlord who conspires to make Lutie his concubine:

> And all the time she was thinking, Junto has a brick in his hand. Just one brick. The final one needed to complete the wall that had been building up around her for years, and when that one last brick was shoved in place, she would be completely walled in. (262)

The image of live burial not only links Lutie's metaphorical imprisonment to Poe's eponymous American Gothic tales, but also, by making Lutie's "real" white landlord the agent of her "imagined" imprisonment, connects the actual architecture of Harlem to the invisible architecture of New York City's *de facto* segregation. For many New Yorkers, both black and white, the refusal of the Metropolitan Life Company in 1943 to lease its Stuyvesant Town Apartments to non-whites signified the city's tacit support for Jim Crow housing policies. For African Americans in Harlem, if not for Henry James, the "one you (were) in" and "the one you (were) not in" was all too apparent, if not in their actual homes, then in terms of where in the city they could safely work, dine, and dwell (James, *AS* 125).

The Urban Gothic

As stated earlier, although Petry's novel calls on the conventions of a range of literary genres ranging from the sentimental to the naturalist, the hybrid that results corresponds most compellingly with the preoccupations of Gothic fiction. Like most Gothic heroics, Lutie is a vulnerable woman in a frightening place haunted by evil agents; on a more complex formal level, the layering of architectural analogies, "actual" architecture, and the social structure of New York City in *The Street* creates a structural *mise-en-abîme* akin to the uncanny atmospheres of Henry James's and Edith Wharton's New York Gothic tales, such as "The Jolly Corner" and "The Bolted Door." If James and Wharton position the Gothic as an "interior" alternative to the increasingly public life of the city, *The Street* drains Gothicism of all romantic resonance, and employs it instead to represent a sort of uncanny realism, a dark urban world in which villains abound and terror is the norm.

Leslie Fiedler famously asserted that "the proper subject of the American Gothic is the black man"; however, female authors familiar with Gothic novels immediately recognized the specific utility of a genre obsessed with "domination and subordination" for describing the experiences of African American women (Fiedler 397, Edwards xi). *Uncle Tom's Cabin* and *Incidents in the Life of a Slave Girl*, as well as Toni Morrison's *Beloved* (1987), are slave narratives packaged as Gothic novels, in which light-skinned black women attempt to escape not only the South, but also their "dark" histories and bodies. Yet Petry makes it immediately clear that Lutie, unlike many black heroines (Stowe's Eliza, Harriet Jacobs's Janie, and Charles Chesnutt's Rena) is not the typical tragic mulatto, but instead the victim of a physical "darkness" that drives her, like Mary Shelley's monster, to diabolical acts—the murder of a man and the abandonment of her son—by a society that refuses to see anything other than her color. Jennifer Greeson has persuasively linked abolitionist texts to urban Gothic fiction from the antebellum era through the two genres' "joint positing of the sexual exploitation of women as evidence of the ills of U.S. society"; by portraying Lutie as the victim of exploitation both as an African American and as a woman, Petry's novel reads as a direct descendant of these complicit genres, minus the optimism of nineteenth-century reformist ardor (Greeson 279). Lutie achieves agency only through monstrosity; the Gothic obsession with personal persecution thus intersects with the urban determinism of naturalist fiction through the figure of the black heroine who, literally trapped within her trauma by the color of her skin, becomes an over determined vortex of psychological, physical, and political repression. The racist "structures" that shape *The Street* are, from Petry's point of view, beyond all hope of reform.

To portray Lutie as a compelling Gothic heroine in depressingly prosaic circumstances, Petry must channel the *thanatos* of the naturalist novel into a single, ominous structure. The building in which Lutie lives both represents and creates a completely new set of domestic disturbances, through which the urban uncanny can be rediagnosed as a symptom of segregation and social control. Mark Edmundson defines the Gothic in part as "the art of possession" (Edmundson 9); although he seems to refer to demonic possession, Harlem's history as a racist playground for unscrupulous landlords like Junto places the white absentee owners—or "possessors"—of black-occupied buildings in a decidedly supernatural position. Like ghosts, white landlords subjected their black tenants to the whims of invisible but potent forces within the supposedly private space of the home; like the victims of hauntings, black occupants of white-owned buildings had no legal or rational means through which to address their persecutors. This lingering white "presence" extended beyond ownership, however, to the actual design of many Harlem houses. Three-fourths of the area's residential buildings were never intended for apartments, but were constructed before 1900 as single-family dwellings for large, well-off white families, making them difficult to divide into affordable flats for black families with fewer children (Osofsky 138). Black residents of Harlem thus occupied "white houses" in more than one sense; they paid rent to white landlords while occupying spaces designed for a far more stable, privileged way of life. Often, the elegance of Harlem's older houses, several of which were designed by the era's preeminent architect, Stanford White, actually contributed to what was regarded as their "degradation," for black families who could not pay the rent were frequently forced to take in "roomers," some of whom would even share a single bed in shifts. Therefore, what Edmundson calls the "house-behind-the-house motif of the Gothic genre" was a very real phenomenon for residents of Harlem forced to make homes out of the same spaces originally built to exclude them (Edmundson 86).

Lutie's apartment offers no such exclusion, but is instead subject to surveillance and intrusion by the superintendent, who, as Junto's agent, can come in and "mak(e) himself at home" as he pleases (Petry 121).[11] Literary buildings often have been interpreted as architectural embodiments of the qualities of their inhabitants; Petry reverses this equation by insinuating that the superintendent "stands for" the building in human form.[12] Lutie's first traumatic experience takes the form of an imaginary but ultimately prescient rape that intertwines her fear of the superintendent with her fear of the space:

> Suppose I'd been left standing here in the dark of this little room, and he'd turned out his light. Suppose he'd started walking toward me, nearer and nearer in the dark. And I could only hear his footsteps, couldn't see him, but could hear him coming closer until I started reaching out in the dark trying to keep him away from me, trying to keep him from touching me—and then—then my hands found him right in front of me. (16)

Petry plays with actual, formal, and chronological architecture to convey an atmosphere of menace made stronger by the sense, shared by reader and protagonist, of having seen—or read—it all before, evoking Freud's definition of the uncanny as "something repressed which *recurs*" (241, emphasis in orig.).

Park and Wald aver that, in *The Street,* "domesticity offers no protection from the social; rather, domestic spaces are those that interiorize the violence of the outside world" (Park and Wald 617); yet Petry's metaphors alert us to the disturbing fact that there is as much, if not more, to be afraid of inside the house as there is outside. Lutie's son Bub endures extreme apprehension when his mother leaves him alone in the apartment at night, and his fear very clearly responds to the uncanny aspects of the apartment itself:

> When she wasn't there, he was filled with a sense of loss. It wasn't just the darkness, because the same thing happened in the daylight when he came home from school. The instant he opened the door, he was filled with a sense of desolation, for the house was empty and quiet and strange . . . frightening and cold. But when she was in it, it was warm and familiar. (134)

The words Bub uses to describe his mother identify her, not the apartment, as "home." Lutie is "warm and familiar"; without her, the space is desolate, "strange," and "frightening"—quintessentially uncanny. Although urban reformers lamented the forlorn images of black children with house keys tied around their necks, left to fend for themselves while their mothers worked, Bub, like Lutie, is safer on the street than in the house.[13]

"Unloose Me!": Tied to the Tenement

The most persuasive evidence of the horror of the Harlem interior lies in the staging of the text's two most violent scenes inside apartment buildings, as opposed to in the street. Lutie's imagined rape in the first chapter foreshadows the superintendent's attack on her midway through the book; the building itself is implicated in their confrontation:

> She screamed until she could hear her own voice insanely shrieking up the stairs, pausing on the landings, turning the corners, going down the halls, gaining in volume as it started again to climb the stairs. And then her screams rushed back down the stairwell until the whole building echoed and re-echoed with the frantic, desperate sound. (148)

In this passage, Lutie's voice moves futilely through the building seeking refuge and finding none. The superintendent attempts to pull Lutie through "the partly open cellar door" (148); she tries frantically to escape into the street. The real danger for Lutie involves her absorption into the body of the house, as well as the hierarchy of repression and exploitation it enforces. Oddly, Lutie is rescued by a sort of ghost: Mrs. Hedges, the madam who lives on the ground floor of the building, and who greets Lutie from her window when she first comes to look at the apartment. Mrs. Hedges, horribly burned in a house fire years before when her excess weight prevented her from squeezing out a window, spends most of the book in that liminal position between the house and the street, and seems to be omniscient about the world on both sides of the door—*and* the veil. She also is a procuress, who interrupts the rape not in order to save Lutie, but to save her *for* the white landlord Junto; early on, she informs the superintendent to stay away from the young woman because " 'There's others who are interested' " (60). Clad in a "big white nightgown" that "moved gently from the draft in the hall," Mrs. Hedges has, in Lutie's mind, "the appearance of some creature who had strayed from another planet" (148). Although Lutie sees her as extraterrestrial, we can also easily read the white-clad Mrs. Hedges as a spectral representative of Junto's power over his black tenants and employees. Hearkening back to Lutie's ghostly status in her own home, as well as the dark double she plays at the Chandlers', Petry's supernatural, in its emphasis on the contrast between black and white, becomes a symbol of society's failure to integrate the most separate of its spheres. Only specters—representatives of "real" agents, as opposed to the agents themselves—can pass through the literal and symbolic walls to escape Du Bois's "prison-house" of segregation.

If Mrs. Hedges stands for the whites' ghostly potency, the superintendent represents the decay that results from entombment in white-owned architecture. Mrs. Hedges tells him: "You done lived in basements so long you ain't human no more. You got mould growin' on you" (148), once again casting the building, as opposed to the street, as the primary source of degeneracy and danger. Although the superintendent's desire is manifested as a direct physical threat, his overt longing for Lutie actually indicates his impotence in comparison to the insidious transactions invisibly conducted by Junto. To make Lutie pay for her refusal to give in to his advances, the superintendent tricks her unsupervised son into stealing mail for him, a crime that lands the eight-year-old boy in a white-run reform school, where Lutie eventually abandons him, literalizing an imprisonment that was previously only symbolic.

More than any other moment in *The Street*, Lutie's hyperbolically Gothic nightmare entwines Lutie's architecture with her anxiety:

> The building was chained to [the superintendent's] shoulders like an enormous doll's house made of brick. She could see people moving inside the building, drearily climbing the tiny stairs, sidling through the narrow halls. Mrs. Hedges sat on the first floor smiling at a cage of young girls . . . [Lutie] screamed and screamed and windows opened and the people poured out of the buildings—thousands of them, millions of them. She saw that they had turned to rats.

> The street was so full of them that she could hardly walk. They
> swarmed around her, jumping up and down. Each one had a
> building chained to its back, and they were all crying, "Unloose
> me! Unloose me!" (122)

Lutie's dream imagines a literal link between the monstrosity of the superintendent and the structure of the apartment house. One could argue that he
and the others turn into rats only after they reach the street; however, their
continued inability to leave the buildings behind strongly suggests that their
inhumanity is a direct effect of the architecture they inhabit. It is significant, I
think, that Petry uses the unusual word "unloose" as opposed to "free"—even
semantically, freedom is not an option. Through these images, Petry suggests
that, for the superintendent, for Lutie, and perhaps for all poor black residents
of Harlem, domestic architecture has become the antithesis of the safety, security, and comfort it represents for whites—in effect, the antithesis of society
itself. Although the houses of rich white families like the Chandlers protect and
reinforce their privileged status despite their "interior" conflicts, Petry's "doll's
house" both imprisons its inhabitants and devolves them into vermin, as if the
malignancy of the ghetto has actually reversed human progress. The end result
of segregation, Petry suggests, is not "separate but equal" communities, but an
ideal white world that exists at the expense of a black dystopia.

   The Street reaches its real climax in Boots's luxurious apartment, where
Lutie, desperate to free Bub, goes to ask for money. Although Boots also owes
his livelihood to Junto, he resolves to rape Lutie himself before handing her over
to his boss. He locks her into the apartment from the inside and begins to beat
her; Lutie, who may be the first literary heroine to put this eponymous Gothic
object to good use, bludgeons him to death with a "heavy iron candlestick" (266).
Driving each blow is a scene from her past; although she begins with the street,
Lutie's litany of disappointment becomes immediately and entirely interior:

> First she was venting her rage against the dirty, crowded street.
> She saw the rows of dilapidated old houses; the small dark rooms;
> the long steep flights of stairs; the narrow dingy hallways; the little
> lost girls in Mrs. Hedges's apartment; the smashed homes where
> the women did drudgery because their men had deserted them.
> She saw all of these things and struck at them. . . . Finally, and the
> blows were heavier, faster, now, she was striking at the white world
> which thrust black people into a walled enclosure from which there
> was no escape . . . (266)

Once again, Petry's prose depicts architecture as much more than a metaphor;
the buildings themselves are agents for an oppressive, racist society. That Lutie
kills Boots, who is black, instead of Junto indicates Petry's belief that all efforts

to struggle against white domination are ultimately futile, making racism a weapon that its victims ultimately wield against each other. Segregation may be an "exterior" phenomenon inflicted on African Americans by a reactionary white society, but its most chilling effects, for Petry at least, are manifested on the dark side of the wall, within the architecture of African American experiences, relationships, and families. Lutie, unable to face the even-more-real imprisonment that will result if she is caught and convicted of murder, takes money from Boots's wallet and catches a late-night train to Chicago, leaving Bub behind.

It is tempting to read the novel as evidence of the futility of domesticity for black city dwellers in the face of streets Petry characterizes as "the North's lynch mobs . . . the method big cities used to keep Negroes in their place" (200). Although this analogy attributes considerable—and legitimate—agency to Harlem's streets as enforcers of New York City's *de facto* and *de jure* segregation, it cannot account for the relentless pull of the interior on Petry's characters, particularly Lutie, the superintendent, and Mrs. Hedges. Lutie and Mrs. Hedges blame the building for the Super's psychosis, thinking, "He had been chained to buildings until he was like an animal" (121). In this simile, architecture, which traditionally separates the "interior" of civilization from the "exterior" wilderness, is aligned with savagery, as opposed to society or culture, drawing attention to the fact that what Kim Ian Michasiw calls "the primary defensive function of place" imagines a world where we know which side of the wall is safe (Michasiw 238). Even critics who interpret Lutie's street—and Harlem itself—as microcosms of a racist public sphere fall into the trap of exteriorizing its interior spaces without asking what, exactly, makes Petry's architecture so inexorable, even as she insists to her reader, in the last lines of the novel, that "it was that street. It was that God-damned street" (Petry 270). Larry Andrews writes that Lutie "sees her street, and by extension the city, as her monstrous antagonist;" paradoxically, however, he also characterizes "the dominant images of the novel" as "claustral and suffocating" (Andrews 196). In a similar vein, Carol Henderson surmises that the following:

> as an institution, the street functions outside mainstream society, creating its own microcosm within the infrastructures of larger social systems; it is often depicted as a university of higher learning, lawless and brutal in the punishment it yields to those who fail to learn from its "hands-on" training. (Henderson 851)

In yet another of New York City's many unmappable spatial metaphors, Henderson situates the street "outside mainstream society" and "within the infrastructure of larger social systems" simultaneously. These analogies, considered in light of Harlem's original status as a white oasis, forge an uncanny link between the ghetto and the suburb, both clearly demarcated, primarily residential locales parasitically dependent on the city proper for economic sustenance—but on vastly different scales. Harlem's buildings, Petry suggests, have become warped monuments to the institutionalized inhumanity of a fundamentally racist society.

The Street stands at the crossroads of literary convention, political activism, and domestic discourse, "a place where," Claudia Tate asserts, "domestic plots of social optimism (became) outmoded, and explicit depictions of social alienation and racial protest commence to satisfy the expectations of twentieth-century black readers" (Tate 210). Lutie's flight to Chicago results in not only her abandonment of her son, but also the abandonment of the home as a site of safety and potential redemption for African American families. Petry posits domestic architecture as a material manifestation of racism, as well as the broken, lost promises of Reconstruction and (re)integration. Black New Yorkers, she suggests, as the exploited tenants of the white-owned city, are forced to dwell within a segregated system over which they have no control. Perhaps, like Stowe and Jacobs, Petry hoped that readers who had never seen a ghetto might be pulled in by the age-old draw of the Gothic haunted house, which, as Michasiw points out, "defines a scene, terrain, geography, for something terrible" (Michasiw 237). Literary conventions may seem odd vehicles for political and social reform; however, the Gothic iconography so evident in The Street vividly conveys the dire need for government intervention against all-too-real urban horrors that might otherwise go unnoticed, and unchallenged. Freud writes, "an uncanny effect is often and easily produced when the distinction between imagination and reality is effaced, as when something we have hitherto regarded as imaginary appears before us in reality, or when a symbol takes on the full function of the thing it symbolizes" (Freud 243). By portraying entombments and hauntings not as white bourgeois thrills but as facts of black urban life, Petry creates a world far more frightening than any imagined by Ann Radcliffe, or E.T.A. Hoffmann, one in which the monsters are far more real than the reforms intended to destroy them.

Notes

1. "Diseased properties" comes from the 1935 "Preliminary Report on the Subject of Housing," from the papers of Fiorello LaGuardia (qtd. in Osofsky, 141).

2. Although Henderson herself does not hold this view, her words accurately express the opinions of other critics such as Bernard Bell, who describes The Street as "a conventional novel of economic determinism in which the environment is the dominant force against which the characters must struggle to survive" (178).

3. See Harris-Lopez's chapter on "Architecture as Destiny? Women and Survival Strategies in Ann Petry's The Street" in which she writes: "the options available to characters

(in *The Street*) center around the larger enclosures of the city of New York, of which the smaller, domestic enclosures are but a microcosmic representation" (68).

4. Reprinted in Schoener 1979.

5. In a chapter devoted to Emily Dickinson, Diana Fuss writes: "The rise of interiority in nineteenth-century America was made possible by the growing distinction between public and private space. During Dickinson's lifetime, houses became increasingly privatized as commercial labor moved out of the home and into the town or factory" (Fuss 25).

6. Petry grew up in Old Saybrook, Connecticut, where her father was a pharmacist. In a 1988 interview with Mark Wilson for *MELUS*, when asked about the inspiration for *The Narrows*, she described her own upbringing in terms of the separation between the family business and the home: " 'The drugstore was the public part of our lives. My parents never let it intrude on their private lives. They created a whole separate world' " (Wilson 72). Although it may seem unlikely that a small-town pharmacist, whose business relied on knowledge of the private ailments of his neighbors, could successfully keep apart his professional and private spheres, Petry's idealized recollection of her childhood home as "a whole separate world" makes Lutie's futile search for a safe place to raise her son all the more poignant.

7. From the *New York Post*, March 3, 1935.

8. From "The Negro in New York." *Harper's Weekly*, Dec 22 1900.

9. Tuberculosis was in fact rampant in Harlem, primarily because of the lack of public health programs in the neighborhood, and the inability of the understaffed, underfunded Harlem Hospital to provide services for the entire area. In 1942, soldiers in New York during World War II were actually forbidden to visit Harlem for fear that they would pick up venereal diseases from black prostitutes.

10. Du Bois writes: "Then it dawned on me with a certain suddenness that I was different from the others; or like, mayhap, in heart and life and longing, but shut out from their world by a vast veil. I had thereafter no desire to tear down that veil, to creep through: I held all beyond it in common contempt, and lived above it in a region of blue sky and great wandering shadows. . . . Alas, with the years all this fine contempt began to fade; for the worlds I longed for, and all their dazzling opportunities, were theirs, not mine" (Du Bois 4).

11. Lutie's body, as well as her space, is watched by Mrs. Hedges and the superintendent and subject to invasion by the superintendent, who attempts to rape her. For a more detailed discussion of this aspect of the text, see Hicks.

12. See, for example, Marilyn Chandler's *Dwelling in the Text: Houses in American Fiction*, Berkeley: U of California P, 1991.

13. Although the term *latchkey kid* only entered the parlance of the white middle and upper class in the past twenty years or so, records dating back to 1900 show that the children of working black mothers were often left home alone unsupervised (Osofsky 147).

Works Cited

Bell, Bernard. "Ann Petry's Demythologizing of American Culture and Afro-American Character." *Conjuring: Black Women, Fiction, and Literary Tradition*. Eds. Marjorie Pryse and Hortense J. Spillers. Bloomington: Indiana UP, 1985, 105–15.

Bremer, Sidney. *Urban Intersections: Meetings of Life and Literature in American Cities.* Urbana: U of Illinois P, 1992.

Briefel, Aviva, and Sienne Ngai. " 'How Much Did You Pay For This Place?': Fear, Entitlement, and Urban Space in Bernard Rose's *Candyman.*" *Camera Obscura* 37 (1996): 71–91.

Du Bois, W.E.B. *The Souls of Black Folk.* 1903. New York: Penguin Books, 1996.

Edmundson, Mark. *Nightmare on Main Street: Angels, Sadomasochism, and the Culture of Gothic.* Cambridge, MA: Harvard UP, 1997.

Edwards, Justin D. *Gothic Passages: Racial Ambiguity and the American Gothic.* Iowa City: U of Iowa P, 2003.

Fiedler, Leslie. *Love and Death in the American Novel.* New York: Doubleday, 1960.

Freud, Sigmund. "The Uncanny." *The Standard Edition of the Complete Psychological Works of Sigmund Freud.* Ed. James Strachey. London: The Hogarth Press, 1953.

Fuss, Diana. *The Sense of an Interior: Four Writers and the Rooms That Shaped Them.* New York: Routledge, 2004.

Greeson, Jennifer Rae. " 'The Mysteries and Miseries' of North Carolina: New York City, Urban Gothic Fiction, and Harriet Jacobs's *Incidents in the Life of a Slave Girl.*" *American Literature* 73.2 (2001): 277–309.

Hakutani, Yoshinobu and Robert Butler, eds. *The City in African American Literature.* Madison, NJ: Fairleigh Dickinson UP, 1995.

Harris-Lopez, Trudier. *South of Tradition: Essays on African-American Literature.* Athens, GA: U of Georgia P, 2002.

Hicks, Heather. " 'This Strange Communion': Surveillance and Spectatorship in Ann Petry's *The Street.*" *African American Review* 37.1 (2003) 21–38.

James, Henry. *The American Scene.* 1907. New York: Penguin Books, 1994.

———. "The Jolly Corner." *The Complete Stories of Henry James 1898–1910.* New York: The Library of America, 1996.

Michasiw, Kim Ian. "Some Stations of Suburban Gothic" In *American Gothic: New Inventions in a National Narrative.* Eds. Robert K. Martin and Eric Savoy. Iowa City: U of Iowa P, 1998, 237–57.

Osofsky, Gilbert. *Harlem: The Making of a Ghetto 1890–1930.* New York: Harper & Row, 1966.

Park, You-me and Gayle Wald. "Native Daughters in the Promised Land: Gender, Race, and the Question of Separate Spheres." *American Literature* 70.3 (1998): 607–33.

Petry, Ann. *The Street.* New York: Pyramid Publications, 1961.

Schoener, Allan, ed. *Harlem on My Mind.* New York: Dell, 1979.

Wesling, Meg. "The Opacity of Everyday Life: Segregation and the Iconicity of Uplift in *The Street.*" *American Literature* 78.1 (2006) 117–140.

Wharton, Edith. "The Bolted Door." *The Collected Short Stories of Edith Wharton, Vol. 2.* New York: Scribner: 1968.

———. *The Decoration of Houses.* Eds. John Barrington Bayley and William A. Coles. New York: W.W. Norton, 1978.

In the Crowd series, Untitled #4 (Oklahoma, 1911). Archival ink print, 14 × 11 inches. Image courtesy of the artist, Shawn Michelle Smith.

Section IV

Exporting Jim Crow

This section moves deliberately outside the familiar contexts of the Jim Crow South and the *de facto* segregation of the urban North. With transnational, Pan-African, and cross-ethnic approaches, the studies in this section help us to understand what happens when something like Jim Crow pops up in other places, or when writers place Jim Crow in global frames. Gary Totten discusses the famous political work of Ida B. Wells-Barnett, as well as others such as Frederick Douglass, in the context of her transnational anti-lynching tour, to show how she consciously presents her own U.S. black body as a platform of protest. Like Totten, Eve Dunbar, too, is interested in tropes of violence in the South and its implications in a Pan-African context, arguing that Richard Wright treated the South and its peculiar practices as fodder for consciously regional fiction during Wright's later expatriate years. Together, Totten and Dunbar provide fresh ways of thinking about how segregation and its related practices informed the role of the South in the national and global literary imaginations. In another transnational approach to Jim Crow, Ruth Blandón looks carefully at the revealing but undernoticed role of Latin America in James Weldon Johnson's well-known *The Autobiography of an Ex-Coloured Man*. Although Johnson could never escape the effects and attitudes of his own experience with U.S. race relations, Latin America served as a trope for him to protest the injustice and unnaturalness of Jim Crow-style segregation.

Embodying Segregation

Ida B. Wells and the Cultural Work of Travel

GARY TOTTEN

Writing about the return voyage from her first trip to the United Kingdom in 1893, Ida Wells notes two "delightful" circumstances of the journey: "[f]irst, there were few if any white Americans on board. Second, there were fifteen young Englishmen in one party. . . . [who] were as courteous and attentive to me as if my skin had been of the fairest" (*Crusade* 113). She identifies this voyage as the first time that white people had extended to her "the courtesy they would have offered to any lady of their own race" (113), emphasizing the racially segregated nature of her environment and experience up to this point. Yet her shipboard experience does not utterly surmount segregation's logic because she also reports that the Englishmen "seemed to take great pleasure in shocking onlookers by their courteous and respectful attention to me" (113). Wells reveals that such courtesy depends on a racialized and hostile context for its effect, which emphasizes her position as exotic "Other," the highly visible and racially marked object of the young men's spectacle of civility. Wells's travel experience encourages us, in the words of Farah J. Griffin and Cheryl J. Fish, to rethink the specific "significance of mobility and its relationship to subjectivity" for black travelers (xiv). During her anti-lynching tours in the United Kingdom in 1893 and 1894, Wells draws on the general tropes of travel and the specific relationship between mobility and subjectivity in black experience to critique U.S. segregation and its resulting violence. This critique appears in the autobiographical account of her 1893 tour and in her column, "Ida B. Wells Abroad," published in the Chicago *Inter-Ocean* detailing her 1894 tour. Although the title of her column emphasizes her position as traveler, Wells resists tourist spectacle in both the column and autobiography to promote the cultural work of her travel and to establish herself as a credible and embodied eyewitness of segregation and lynching. Ultimately, the act of traveling as a form of cultural work (rather than tourist pleasure) functions as a trope for the ways that African Americans might resist historical narratives of segregation and inequality and move toward greater cultural power. In her transatlantic writing, speaking, and traveling, Wells's mobile black body becomes corporeal proof of the potentially empowering aspects of physical and cultural mobility.

The Cultural Work of Travel

In the preface to her autobiography, Wells notes that she writes her life story for young black readers who know "little of our race's history" beyond the Civil War, so that they will understand "how the agitation against the lynching evil began" (4). The important work of Wells's anti-lynching campaign is well illustrated by her published pamphlets before and after her trips to the United Kingdom (respectively, *Southern Horrors: Lynch Law in All Its Phases* [1892]; *A Red Record: Tabulated Statistics and Alleged Causes of Lynchings in the United States, 1892–1893–1894* [1895]). Her autobiography and column from abroad also focus on the difficult work of achieving equality and exposing the horrors of lynching. Although the tropes of travel and tourism are evident in her column, most likely appealing to readers eager for dispatches from a special correspondent abroad, Wells's column functions chiefly as a polemic against lynching. By positioning her writing and traveling persona against familiar tropes of leisure travel, she rejects not only the role of tourist, but also the various images of the black traveler constructed in other key African American texts, such as those by Olaudah Equiano, Mary Seacole, Frederick Douglass, A.B.C. Merriman-Labor, or Matthew Henson. Equiano's (1789) and Seacole's (1857) picaresque narratives frequently emphasize the adventure and fantastic sights of travel, while Douglass's characterizes the author as a tourist at a Robert Burns monument in Scotland in 1846 and at Egyptian historical sites and museums in his unpublished travel diary of 1886–1887. In *Britons Through Negro Spectacles* (1909), Merriman-Labor adopts the persona of a witty tour guide and cultural critic of London's spectacles, whereas Henson registers the romance of exploration in *A Negro Explorer at the North Pole* (1912).

Wells distances her travels from the tourist spectacle and romantic adventure emphasized in many of these works. Indeed, when the Memphis *Daily Commercial* suggested she was simply a "Negro Adventuress" and vilified her work, she responded in her May 28, 1894 *Inter-Ocean* dispatch that if the same effort to "conceal the facts were exercised to put a stop to lynching," she would not need to rehearse such atrocities (*Crusade* 169).[1] By dissociating her travels from romance and spectacle and insisting on the truth of the barbaric lynching incidents she describes, Wells also defines her work and travel against the fantastic, which, as Hélène Christol argues, often becomes "a crucial literary mode" in the context of the black Atlantic (164). Wells's rejection of both the touristic and the fantastic produces what Paul Gilroy terms the black Atlantic's "redemptive critique" (71). Retracing the historical transatlantic routes of the Middle Passage, Wells's travel alludes, in the words of Peter Linebaugh and Marcus Rediker, to the "transformed . . . experience of work" that resulted as trading routes were established and peoples throughout the transatlantic world were forced into slavery and servitude (327). However, unlike Africans traveling the original Middle Passages "literally suspended in the 'oceanic' " dimensions or "*nowhere*" of the Atlantic's "undifferentiated identity," to borrow Hortense Spillers's terms (72), Wells challenges notions of enforced travel, slave labor, and diminished subjectivity through the liberated mobility, definitive agenda, and cultural work of her trips abroad. In doing so, she reimagines slavery's transatlantic passages as routes that mobilize black bodies to resist segregation and violence and move toward empowerment.

In her first *Inter-Ocean* dispatch, published April 2, 1894, Wells draws connections between her travels abroad and the United States' oppressive racial atmosphere. Following the "suppression" of her Memphis newspaper, the *Free Speech*, in May 1892, she was unable to generate U.S. concern for her anti-lynching work (128), but discovered sympathetic audiences in the United Kingdom in 1893; these paved the way for her second tour in 1894. She admits the strangeness of going abroad when, logically, more good might come of such a campaign in the United States, save that "we, as a race, cannot get a hearing in the United States" where both "[t]he press and pulpit" are silent about, and thus complicit in, lynch law (131). She hopes that the example of the English press and clergy in denouncing lynching will produce a similar response in the United States (131). Wells's need to cross national borders to accomplish her aims illustrates Gilroy's argument that the "modern political and cultural formation" of the black Atlantic derives its specificity "through [a] desire to transcend both the structures of the nation state and the constraints of ethnicity and national particularity" (19). Wells exhibits the desire to escape such limitations when she characterizes her experience in Europe as a rebirth (*Crusade* 135), language that indicates, as Gilroy suggests, the transformative nature of transnational experience (19). Unlike many African Americans abroad, who, as Carolyn Karcher reminds us, either settled permanently in Europe or embraced Pan-Africanism, Wells, although eventually returning to the United States, underwent "an alteration of consciousness akin to both a religious conversion and a change of nationality" (Karcher 135) and emphasized the right of individual African Americans to emigrate to Africa or remain in America, a position typifying, according to Karcher, "the transnationalism of the Black Atlantic" (135).

Wells's April 9, 1894 article from Liverpool, reveals her developing transnational consciousness and its role in her anti-lynching campaign. She reminds readers that Liverpool was the English center of "slave interests" from the Elizabethan period to the British abolition of slavery in 1807 and that the majority of the slave ships traversing the black Atlantic "were built in the

Liverpool docks and owned by Liverpool merchants" (*Crusade* 133). As Wells describes Liverpool's investment in the slave trade, however, she notes that the city "has learned . . . [it] can prosper without the slave trade or slave labor" (135). Liverpool's complex slave history provides a dramatic backdrop for the distinctions that Wells draws between the segregated United States and a progressive Liverpool, where a "colored person" can ride in public transportation without insult, stay in hotels and eat in restaurants without incident, and freely move about in art galleries and churches (135). "[I]t is like being born into another world," she writes, "to be welcomed among persons of the highest order of intellectual and social culture as if . . . one of themselves" (135). As further proof of her increased physical and cultural mobility, she notes that in two weeks' time she has, by invitation, delivered ten speeches refuting the idea "that Negro men are despoilers . . . of white women" (136). She juxtaposes the cultural message of her travels with the slander of white transatlantic American travelers who "draw a picture of the isolated district in the South where great hordes of ignorant and dangerous Negroes swarm; of the inadequacy and delay of the law; and then ask, 'What would you do if your wife or daughter were so assaulted?' " (136). Wells counters the assumptions about African Americans supported by such rhetoric through her frequent reference to the mobility and respect that she enjoys in the United Kingdom.

Wells again emphasizes her increased mobility and the urgency of her cultural work abroad in her May 19, 1894 article, in which she declares that she has "been so constantly traveling and speaking" that she has been unable to write (*Crusade* 153). Her unrelenting schedule also prevents her from sightseeing. She contrasts her travel agenda with that of the tourist, acknowledging the attractions awaiting the tourist in the United Kingdom but representing herself as a committed advocate for justice who rejects the temptation to sightsee rather than to work. In an earlier article of April 23, 1894, Wells describes potential tourist attractions, including Manchester's shipping interests (143–44), the opening of its great Canal by Queen Victoria, the "public buildings . . . black with the centuries of smoke and dust," and the convenient layout of its art galleries (145), but then devotes the majority of the article to the anti-lynching theme. Similarly, in her June 25, 1894 article, Wells opens with travel guide-like observations, mimicking tourists' complaints about the weather or cramped railway compartments (171), but these details of tourist culture become the vehicle through which she critiques U.S. segregation, noting that "primitive as are these railway carriages, I as a Negro can ride in them free from insult or discrimination on account of color, and that's what I cannot do in many States of my own free (?) America" (172). Further invoking tourist tropes, she notes that the "charm of antiquity and historic association" is evident throughout London, including the home of her host, P.W. Clayden (editor of the *London Daily News*), across the street from Dickens's London residence and only a few minutes' walk from the British Museum (173–74). But she writes that she is "too engrossed in the work which brought me here" to act the tourist at the British Museum, the Royal Academy, or Westminster Abbey (174).

Wells's depiction of travel as cultural work anticipates Booker T. Washington's transatlantic travels two decades later recorded in *The Man Farthest Down* (1912), which he similarly characterizes as work rather than pleasure. He travels to Europe to gauge the conditions of Southern blacks in relation to the European laborer, a comparison that allows him to promote industrial education. To better experience working conditions in Europe, he asserts that he must "leave the ordinary beaten track of European travel and . . . plunge into regions which have not been charted and mapped, and where ordinary guides and guide-books are of little or no avail" (9–10). Working against the "conspiracy" of the tourist culture that tempts him to waste time on the "dead" and unchangeable past found in cathedrals, museums, cemeteries, or ruins, he hopes to experience "the grime and dirt of everyday life" among Europe's laboring poor (13). Unlike Wells, however, Washington seems willing to ignore historical slavery and contemporary segregation to promote industrial education, and is even somewhat acquiescent on the subject of lynching. Furthermore, in *The Man Farthest Down*, Washington sometimes characterizes slave history as a series of romanticized adventure stories, thus distancing himself from the historical specificity and material reality of slavery and its legacy of segregation and violence.[2]

In contrast, Wells's notion of cultural work does not ignore slavery's historical legacy and the lasting conditions of segregation and violence in the United States; rather, her articles and lectures are steeped in them. Not only does she share specific examples of lynchings with her British audiences (and at one breakfast meeting passes around an image of the lynching of C.J. Miller [*Crusade* 178]), but also connects her work and trip to the historical work of other black leaders and to the narrative of black struggle against segregation. In her autobiography, Wells registers the important differences between her own approach and Washington's, differences that are informed by their fundamentally different attitudes about segregation in the United States.

Her acquaintance with Washington began when she wrote to him on November 30, 1890, praising his "manly criticism of our corrupt and ignorant ministry" (*Booker T. Washington Papers* 3:108). Her admiring letter masks her nuanced opinion of Washington, however, for she was displeased that he would choose Boston as the city from which to voice complaints against the moral and intellectual inferiority of the southern black clergy, and she wrote an editorial in the *Free Speech* criticizing him (*Crusade* 41). Her 1890 letter to Washington implies her displeasure: "I have long since seen that some one of the name & standing of yourself, *among ourselves*, must call a halt and be the Martin Luther of our times in condemning the practices of our ministers" (*Booker T. Washington Papers* 3:108). Her emphasis of the phrase "among ourselves" suggests that a black person must perform this critique, but it also implies that such critique should be *kept* within the black community. Indeed, she notes in the autobiography that although there might be truth in Washington's statement, "it was a wrong thing for him to have made that criticism in a white paper so far away from home [in the North]. When the people needed such criticism, I felt he ought to have done as we did—tell them about it at home rather than tell our enemies abroad" (*Crusade* 41).

Later, Wells would become an outspoken critic of Washington, particularly of his unwillingness to oppose lynching more firmly, and she was consistently critical of his accommodationist stand on segregation, which she saw as ultimately fostering attitudes and stereotypes leading to violence against African Americans. According to Wells, Washington refused to ally himself with her and the Afro-American Council because of their radical politics (265) and he seemed more interested in promoting his theory that blacks "had better give attention to trying to be first-class people in a jim crow car than insisting that the jim crow car should be abolished" (265). As Patricia Schechter explains, Wells also was critical of Washington's characterization of blacks in his speeches and jokes and "blamed [him] personally for circulating negative stereotypes of black people to whites—especially those of the chicken thief and the lay-about, uneducated 'darky' preacher," stereotypes that supported "assumptions about black criminality and moral deviance and traveled all too quickly to a supposed inclination to rape" (*Ida B. Wells-Barnett* 130). Years after Wells's trips abroad, when Julius Rosenwald (president of Sears Roebuck and a Tuskegee supporter) regaled Wells and the NAACP with an account of Washington's "chicken-stealing stories" delivered at a Standard Club meeting, Wells rejoined, "a great many of us cannot approve Mr. Washington's plan of telling chicken-stealing stories on his own people in order to amuse his audiences and get money for Tuskegee" (*Crusade* 331). In perhaps her most succinct criticism of Washington's position, Wells exposes the direct relationship between Jim Crow and lynch law: " 'Mr. Washington knows . . . that lynching is not invoked to punish crime but color, and not even industrial education will change that' " (qtd. in Schechter, *Ida B. Wells-Barnett* 131). Unlike Washington, whom Wells sees as willing to voice criticisms of black people "abroad" in the U.S. North, Wells journeys overseas to spread her anti-lynching message among international allies rather than among enemies within her "own free (?) America," as she states in her *Inter-Ocean* June 6, 1894 article, where she cannot even ride a railway car "free from insult or discrimination on account of color" (172).

"Truth Compelled Me": Wells as Embodied Eyewitness

Such references to the physical realities of her segregation experiences are replete throughout her columns and autobiography, and Wells uses such experiences to lend authority to her anti-lynching work abroad. The corporeal ramifications of her work and travel—its physicality in contrast to the disembodiment of the traveler's gaze—are apparent in the autobiographical account of her first trip to England in 1893, in which Wells reprints an article from *Ladies Pictorial*, the British women's magazine. The article describes how she was "dragged out of a railway car in Tennessee and on refusing to go in to the 'Jim Crow car,' was left behind in the station, to the great delight of the passengers who stood up on their seats and applauded the action of the conductor, baggage master, and stationmaster in expelling her" (*Crusade* 108). The article suggests the legitimizing function and emotional appeal that Wells's firsthand experiences with segregation could have on audiences: "[a]ny one who has traveled through America knows the horrors of the 'colored car,' and will sympathise with Miss Wells" (108). Furthermore, in contrast to Washington's contention that racial uplift is a natural result of African Americans' hard work and conciliation, Wells's experience reveals that "as the Negro advances in education and in the qualities of good citizenship, the disinclination to allow him civil rights becomes deeper" (109). This validation of Wells's experience and message lends authority to her lynching accounts, her "appeals for a fair trial and legal punishment" (109), and her insistence that black education and progress alone will not counter deeply entrenched segregation and the violence it generates.

Wells's exile from Memphis in 1892 also grants her authority as a witness to the violence generated by segregation. While traveling in the North, she received word that "a committee of leading citizens" had destroyed the offices and type of the Memphis *Free Speech* newspaper (which she partly owned), threatening death to anyone who revived the paper (*Crusade* 61–62). The destruction of the newspaper occurred in retaliation against a May 1892 editorial in which Wells had dared to challenge the "thread-bare lie that Negro men assault white women" (*Crusade* 65). "If Southern white men are not careful," Wells wrote, "they will over-reach themselves and a conclusion will be reached which will be very damaging to the moral reputation of their women" (65–66). She expressed similar ideas in *Southern Horrors*, her anti-lynching pamphlet of the same year, in which she characterized black men as "Afro-American Sampsons who suffer themselves to be betrayed by white Delilahs" (*Southern Horrors* 31). The retaliation against the editorial was swift, and on learning that her home was under surveillance by the lynchers "who promised to kill [her] on sight" (62), she took a position at the *New York Age* and continued her anti-lynching work in the North. "They had made me an exile and threatened my life for hinting at the truth," she wrote, and she felt that she "owed it" to herself and the race "to tell the whole truth" (62–63) once in New York where she "could do so freely" (69). Wells argued that lynching was not motivated by black men raping white women, but by black economic success (64): her controversial editorial had been inspired by the lynching of three black businessmen who were threatening white business interests. Lynching was a way to " 'keep the nigger down' " (64), she argued, the vehicle to sustain inequality and "stifle Negro manhood" when segregation and other forms of social and political injustice became less efficient (71).

Wells alludes to these incidents from her own experience throughout her *Inter-Ocean* dispatches, linking her work in England to her earlier antiracism work in the United States and extending to her transatlantic trip the image that she had constructed of herself as an exile within her own country with nothing to lose for telling the whole truth about lynching. In Liverpool, she notes that although "grieved" to do so, "truth compelled me to say that lynching is spreading in the states" (135). In Manchester, writing about her criticism of Frances Willard and others, Wells notes that she seeks only "to tell here what truth has compelled me to say as to the words and actions of some of our American Christians and temperance workers, when asked by British friends to do so" (152). In Bristol, when explaining how Southern churches refused to admit African Americans, Wells was "asked if Northern churches knew of this discrimination and continued fellowship with the churches which practiced it." "Truth compelled me to reply in the affirmative," she says, and to describe the prejudice northern churches practiced in an attempt to court "the good will of the South" (155). Wells's statements emphasize the kind of work and the amount of truth-telling necessary to challenge segregation and lynch law.

However, if, as Bederman notes, lynching was for northerners in the United States, largely "an imaginary scenario, constructed and fed by depictions in newspapers and literature" (46), then this scenario was certainly the case for the British, as well. Wells works against the assumptions of these imaginings on both sides of the Atlantic to argue for her own authenticity as an eyewitness of such events, adopting a trope that is readily apparent in most travel narratives: that of the seeing eye. Early in her autobiography, she notes that journalism gave her "an outlet through which to express the real 'me' " (31), and in the *Inter-Ocean* column she works to convey the sense that readers are not only getting her real self but also the real story. She inserts into her column excerpts from other journalists' newspaper and magazine articles that note her unimpassioned voice (147) as well as the absence of rhetoric in her speeches (150); thus, she further establishes her objectivity as a traveling eyewitness.

Yet Wells's authority as eyewitness to segregation's horrors chiefly depends on the embodiment of her seeing eye within a black female body that has been marked and despised through segregation and threatened with death by a Memphis lynch mob. Her public visibility as an anti-lynching proponent counters the many ways that, as Schechter notes, "black women were totally invisible in the dominant lynching story" ("Unsettled Business" 292). Schechter observes that Wells began this unmasking of black women in *Southern Horrors*, where she "made black women visible in the dynamics of southern lynching and sexualized racism" as victims of lynching and rape ("Unsettled Business" 296), "assert[ing] black women's claim to outraged womanhood traditionally reserved only for white women" (297–98).[3] According to Schechter, *Southern Horrors* explicitly "connect[s] the 'private' crime of rape to the 'public' crime of lynching" (301), making visible the violence against black women. Even while exposing the abuse of black bodies, however, Wells retains a desire to "shield the bodies of African Americans, especially women," from "complete exposure" that might perpetuate racist stereotypes (*Ida B. Wells-Barnett* 114). Another risk was the kind of humiliation that could result from some of Washington's discourse, for example. Not only does Wells draw attention to black women's complex relationship to the lynching issue but also, as Nicole King has observed, she expands "the definition of lynching 'victims' to include not only those hanging in the trees but the entire black community—the collective public body that lynching was meant to terrorize through the example of the particular, dead, victim" (95).

Wells's own mobile and public body also acts as a material sign to her British audiences of the collective body targeted by lynchers. Indeed, as I have implied, Wells's tour, speeches, and even her demeanor can be viewed as performative.[4] In her biography of Wells, Linda McMurry notes Wells's interest in public performance and the stage, having "toyed with the idea of becoming an actress" (169), implying the ease and pleasure with which she might have taken up the lecture circuit. The disturbingly public and "masculine" aspects of her lecturing performances were problematic, however, for the way they blurred distinctions between notions of men's and women's work (Schechter, "Unsettled Business" 307–9). As Bederman points out, to lecture on issues related to sexuality (such as rape) was hardly proper feminine behavior for a young unmarried woman, and she often quoted graphic descriptions of lynchings from Southern U.S. newspapers (63), avoiding direct discussion of the unseemly details herself.

Wells also presented herself as a model of virtue and womanly attributes to counter rumors about her unsavory past. Schechter notes that white racists and newspapers labeled her "a 'black harlot' in search of a 'white husband,' . . . 'a prostitute bent on miscegenation,' . . . [and] a 'slanderous and nasty-minded mulatress' " ("Unsettled Business" 305). In her autobiography and elsewhere, Wells insisted on her virtue, requesting that a minister who had suspected her of unseemly behavior use the pulpit to detract his aspersions. Wells writes, "I wanted him to know at least one southern girl, born and bred, who had tried to keep herself spotless and morally clean as my slave mother had taught me" (*Crusade* 44). In a June 12, 1886 diary entry, Wells described two exemplary models of womanhood (*Memphis Diary* 77–79), which she further developed in her portrait of proper black womanhood titled "The Model Woman: A Pen Picture of the Typical Southern Girl," published in the *New York Freeman* 18

February 1888 and offered as a "pattern" for young black women (*Memphis Diary* 189). Yet Wells also worried about appearing too feminine, concerned over the effects of her tears during a New York speech in which she described her exile from Memphis and her resulting loneliness and homesickness. (She used similar language to detail these experiences in the chapter of her autobiography titled "The Homesick Exile.") Although Wells excised demonstrations of sentimental weakness from subsequent public appearances, King suggests that Wells was caught in "the paradoxes of being a Victorian feminist activist": "in order to convey the 'truth' Wells was required to perform according to a conventional 'role,'" and her performance of womanly sentiment often worked in her favor (92). Indeed, Wells sometimes underscores her conventionality even while exposing segregation's absurdity, emphasizing, for example, in her description of the young white Englishmen's courtesies on her return voyage in 1893, how their attentions confirm that they recognize her as a "lady" (*Crusade* 113).

Wells links her performances of respectability and womanliness to her segregated experience to expose the irrational logic of lynch law. She lifts up the lynched black body as evidence against lynching but also offers her own body as the embodiment of segregated experience in the United States.[5] One form of this embodiment appears in her anti-lynching pamphlets, which often displayed her name and an image of her face on the covers, raising important "questions about power and identity," as Schechter suggests, and, in the case of *Southern Horrors*, "qualif[ying] the effect" of Douglass's "authenticating" letter of introduction ("Unsettled Business" 302). Theorizing the importance of embodiment in travel texts, Marguerite Helmers and Tilar Mazzeo note that "[h]istorically, the implied presence of the body has been one of the ways in which travel writers guarantee the authenticity of their accounts. As a matter of convention, travel writers have assured their readers that their representations have a source in 'first-hand' or 'eye-witness' experience"; thus, through such "narrative posturing, the travel account insists that someone actually went somewhere" (267). Wells's narrative posturing as an eyewitness to segregation and lynching, then, not only involves having been somewhere in terms of travel, but also emphasizes that she has "been there" as a black women experiencing racial discrimination and threats of violence. Helmers and Mazzeo further contend that "[w]hile the textual and imaginary body is never contiguous with the 'real' body of a writer, the conventions of the genre promise that its representations have their origins in the materiality of both the subject and the object" (268). In Wells's case, there appears an even more direct link between the textual and actual body of the writer, as well as between the lynched bodies she describes in her column (often vicariously through newspaper accounts) and the images of actual bodies (such as C.J. Miller's) that she presents to her audiences.

Wells's use of real, textual, and photographed bodies invokes the tensions between the body and the gaze. Theorists of the gaze have suggested that scopic desire leads to the erasure of the seeing body to focus on the gaze itself, which becomes an ideological apparatus of empire, according to Mary Louise Pratt, and is assumed to originate in a colonizing white male body. As indicated by the scene described at the beginning of this essay, with Wells as a black female spectacle on board the ship, her black body is the object of the white male gaze but that body *also* embodies a counter gaze that registers the reactions of others to its disruptive presence. Radhika Mohanram suggests that the erasure of the corporeal in colonial texts acts as a sign of imperial power and access to knowledge of the object (16), a process well illustrated by Edward Said's theory of Orientalism. But scholars such as Lila Harper and Sara Mills remind us that the erasure of the body is more complicated for female writers or writers of color whose actual bodies can be read as signs of difference. Female travelers and female travelers of color are both seeing and seen, positions that, as Helmers and Mazzeo contend, "the speaking subject constantly negotiates" (270). Thus, although Wells, as a black female traveler, gazes back, she also finds herself inter-pellated, to borrow Louis Althusser's term, simultaneously "hailed" as subject by dominant American and European culture, functioning as both eyewitness and embodied racial spectacle. That is, she is a racial body, a segregated body, and even, as her experiences in Memphis show, a potentially lynched body.

We might ask how, in this play of presence and absence, Wells negotiates the erasure of the body that characterizes travel writing as a genre. On occasion, she seems to resist her position as spectacle (as her positive representation of her shipboard experience with the young Englishmen reveals). Additionally, she distances her writing and experience from the sometimes spectacular and fantastic elements of other black travel writing through the emphasis on her cultural work and firsthand eyewitness critique of segregation and lynching. In these instances, she appears to deflect attention away from her body to concentrate on the fruits of her transatlantic travel and labor or the objects of her critical gaze. But her function as an embodied racial spectacle (toward which the placement of her image on the cover of her pamphlets seems to gesture) sometimes erupts through the carefully orchestrated rhetoric of her texts. Her experience as a shipboard spectacle for the young Englishman is one example. Another occurs at the end of her May 19, 1894 *Inter-Ocean* article that describes meeting Lady Jeune, wife of an eminent British jurist, who assures Wells of a London audience with her friends, "for she thinks they ought to know that the Negro race is not the degraded one she had been led to believe" (*Crusade* 159). Lady Jeune wanted Wells to persuade her friends that African Americans are not a "race of rap-ists" (71), but the event also can be read as a chance for Wells to demonstrate, through her own body, bearing, and intelligence, that African Americans are not degraded; she is corporeal proof, in this case, against degradation.

Wells's position as a spectacle, and the ways that she turns such moments to her advantage, is further emphasized by her discussion of Douglass's appearance at the Chicago World's Fair. African Americans had been denied representation at the fair, and Wells had written a pamphlet distributed at the fair denouncing this exclusion. However, Douglass was allowed to participate as a representative of Haiti.[6] In her *Inter-Ocean* article of May 28, 1894, Wells notes that the British assume "that such a man [as Douglass], a product of American civilization, was a more wonderful tribute to America's greatness than all the material exhibits stored in the white city" (*Crusade* 163–64). Although such a statement turns Douglass into a visible product of U.S. civilization, Wells also signifies on the objectification of Douglass as the most important "exhibit" in the "white city" of America when she notes that "[t]he Negro hopes that some day the United States will become as great intellectually and morally as she is *materially*" (164). Because Douglass is the material manifestation of American greatness, this phrase could also be read as a hope that the United States "will become as great intellectually and morally" as are already Douglass and African American culture. Douglass (and by extension all African Americans) becomes the truly fine American *material* in this case.

Such ideas coincide with Griffin and Fish's suggestion that the complexities of black subjectivity are often revealed in black travel writing, in this case through Wells's material exhibitions of both respectability and racial injustice. Through these exhibitions, Wells typifies the black Atlantic's "insider–outsider duality" of consciousness (Gilroy 186), what W.E.B. Du Bois would refer to as "double-consciousness" (215). Karcher emphasizes that this duality is most apparent in Wells's position between two worlds, Britain and America, and in her negotiation of these respective audiences (141), sometimes representing herself "as an outsider forced into exile by her native land and pleading with strangers for acceptance, sometimes as an insider welcomed as a guest of honor in circles from which her white compatriots would have banned her" (142), and sometimes identifying herself as an American (145), "conjur[ing] up for her American audience the picture of a world without Jim Crow" (144). Wells's negotiation of these various positions is apparent in her autobiography where, as Schechter notes, Wells reveals how her British audiences "keyed skin color to [her] credibility" (*Ida B. Wells-Barnett* 24). Her hostess, Mrs. Clayden, noted that Wells might have achieved greater success abroad if she "had been a few shades blacker" (*Crusade* 214), when only a few pages earlier, Wells had expressed the relief of being among people who judge a person on more than "the color of the skin" (212). Schechter reminds us that Southern racists "questioned Wells's authority *through* her body" (*Ida B. Wells-Barnett* 105; emphasis added), drawing attention to her multiracial status as white, African American, and American Indian and suggesting that her perspective might thus be "tainted," a charge that she also encountered in London, and to which she replied, "if I have any taint to be ashamed of in myself, it is the taint of *white* blood!" (qtd. in Schechter, *Ida B. Wells-Barnett* 25). From this perspective, Wells seems involved in a complex performance of transatlantic identity as a woman, a traveler, and an African American of multiracial ancestry.

However, Wells's embodied performances of identity are not simply demonstrations of transatlantic double-consciousness. Her corporeal fabrications of identity operate as a chain of signifiers masking or destabilizing the supposed grounds (or transcendent signifieds) of various organizing identities that her detractors want to assign her or between which she wants to fluctuate. This play of identity is conversely related to a process within the lynching issue in which "the rape charge" served a "masking function" for the racist grounds on which segregation and lynching rested (Schechter, "Unsettled Business" 295). As Robyn Wiegman helpfully explains, "a feminist politics of antiracist struggle . . . is not simply invested in bringing the black woman into critical view but [in] trac[ing] the historical and theoretical contexts that shape her absence and that speak more broadly to the intertwining relationship between patriarchy and white supremacy" (84–85). The relationship between patriarchy, white supremacy, and black female identity is apparent in Wells's performances as an anti-lynching agitator abroad, through which she challenges essentialist notions about her identity (and thus emphasizes its fluid nature) and exposes the masked patriarchal and racist grounds for segregationist thinking in the United States.

Traveling Through History

As Wells's body takes on the cultural weight of various identities, it becomes clear that they not only weigh her down but also mobilize her because they are the means through which she places her body into circulation. Transatlantic travel propels the body of the writer and the text, supplying Wells with opportunities to function as an unrooted body in transit between continents and identities. The relationship between Wells, the writer, who is actually in motion, and the way that motion is inscribed in the text aesthetically and culturally, emphasizes the passages of black transatlantic history on which her travels and texts rest. History is always already lurking in the background of Wells's travel texts, both exposed and elided. Even in the process of denying tourist culture (which would include history as spectacle) she evokes history, but in ways, as shown here, more strategic and transformative than a traveler such as Washington.

Traveling through space and history across transatlantic routes both past and present, Wells invokes and complicates the narratives and histories of slavery, segregation, and lynching. In her June 25, 1894 article, Wells notes that women are not allowed on the floor of the British House of Commons, but must stand in the ladies' gallery behind a "cage" of wire netting barring their access (*Crusade* 174). This image of women caged and segregated recurs in a more horrific form in her description of an African American woman "boxed up in [a] barrel into which nails had been driven and rolled down hill in Texas" (154). This link between the British Parliament's segregationist policies and the particularly cruel murder of the Texas woman in a sort of lynching cage allows Wells to critique the various cultural cages of segregation. Furthermore, in the image of the cage we find echoes of slavery's devices of torture and containment, replete in the literature of slavery and conquest from J. Hector St. Jean de Crèvecoeur's "man in a cage" in *Letters from an American Farmer* (1782) to the iron muzzles and shackles of Equiano's *Interesting Narrative*, and the "garretted" existence of Harriet Jacobs/Linda Brent in *Incidents in the Life of a Slave Girl* (1861).

By manipulating the tropes of history and travel, Wells embraces the shifting surfaces and essences of black female identity. Describing the contours of this complicated subjectivity, Spillers writes, "I am a marked woman. . . . a locus of confounded identities. . . . so loaded with mythical prepossession that there is no easy way for the agents buried beneath them to come clean." She continues, "In order for me to speak a truer word concerning myself, I must strip down through layers of attenuated meanings, made an excess . . . over time, assigned by a particular historical order, and there await whatever marvels of my own inventiveness" (65). Wells enacts this unearthing (and, on occasion, masking) by way of her travel experiences, demonstrating that subjectivity is as mobile as the ships of the Middle Passage, the image of which, as Gilroy notes, focuses our attention on the "circulation of ideas" and people in the transatlantic world (4). Schechter calls attention to the shifting terrain of Wells's project and body when she notes that "Wells's efforts against lynching shed light on the ways in which black bodies became the site of a shifting contest over civil rights and physical integrity, over human dignity and social power. The body in question, whether that of the lynching victim or the African American woman critic, was impossible to represent as a state of biological fixity demanded by Americans to bring order to an uncertain world" (*Ida B. Wells-Barnett* 84). Wells embodies this refusal to be fixed not only in her own subjectivity but also in her mobility as a traveler and travel writer as she moves through time and physical space. She extends these principles of instability to her project of shifting the very ground out from under preconceived notions about segregation. Wells's linking of her own embodied subjectivity to the segregation issue reveals how, to borrow Stuart Hall's words, "[i]dentity is formed at the unstable point where the 'unspeakable' stories of subjectivity meet the narratives of history, of a culture" (115). Significantly, Wells manages to speak from the unstable point at which she combines the unspeakable stories of lynching with the histories of segregation. She achieves this voice in the act of traveling and rewriting a colonizing history in which the black woman, heretofore mobilized as slave and captive, now travels as the embodied eyewitness of historical trauma in resistance to contemporary injustice. In doing so, Wells reveals, in Spiller's words, the potential for an African American woman to acquire "the *insurgent* ground as female social subject" and "rewrite after all a radically different text for a female empowerment" (80).

When such "redemptive critique" is read within the context of black travel experience from Douglass to Washington, we can better appreciate how Wells's complex transatlantic perspective contributed, literally and metaphorically, to the brave rhetoric of her anti-lynching narratives and, more broadly, to antisegregation arguments in the late nineteenth century. This transatlantic distance emphasizes the increased mobility of post-emancipation African Americans and, in Griffin and Fish's terms, allows Wells to reimagine black mobility and subjectivity in a way that would expand options for improving the status and identities of African Americans in the late nineteenth century. If there is finally any stable ground underneath Wells's embodied performances of subjectivity and segregation it rests on the facts around which she organizes her final dispatch of July 7, 1894, in which she writes that "[a]ll the vile epithets in the vocabulary nor reckless statements cannot change the lynching record of 1893" (*Crusade* 186). She concludes with her own quote published in the *Inter-Ocean* two weeks earlier:

> [i]f I am become an adventuress for simply stating facts, by what name must be characterized those who furnish these facts? However revolting these lynchings, I did not perform a single one of them, nor could the wildest effort of my imagination manufacture one to equal the reality. If the same zeal to excuse and conceal the acts were exercised to put a stop to these lynchings, there would be no need for me to relate nor for the English press to give ear to these tales of barbarity. (187)

In this statement, she claims the authority to speak truth to segregation's lies, the power to expose those who perpetuate racial violence, and the right to name them according to their vile actions. The imperative to do so becomes part of her important cultural work in the United Kingdom and is sustained by her own position as an embodied eyewitness and traveler.

Notes

1. All references to Wells's *Inter-Ocean* column are from *Crusade for Justice: The Autobiography of Ida B. Wells*, which reprints the articles.

2. For an extended discussion of Washington's problematic relationship to black history and travel in *The Man Farthest Down*, see my article, "Southernizing Travel in the Black Atlantic."

3. In her essay on the Thomas–Hill hearings, Elsa Barkley Brown explores ways that we continue to elide the lynching of black women (102).

4. Schechter (*Ida B. Wells-Barnett*) and King also discuss Wells's performative identity but not in the context of travel and travel writing.

5. For an analysis of Wells's embodiment in relation to U.S. citizenship, see Piepmeier.

6. Wells resented the fair's belated sponsorship of a "Negro Day" and signaled her displeasure with Douglass's decision to speak at the event by boycotting his speech. However, after reading about the speech in the papers the next day, she "went straight out to the fair and begged his pardon for presuming in my youth and inexperience to criticize him for an effort which had done more to bring our cause to the attention of the American people than anything else which had happened during the fair" (*Crusade* 119).

Works Cited

Althusser, Louis. "Ideology and Ideological State Apparatuses (Notes towards an Investigation)." *Lenin and Philosophy and Other Essays*. Trans. Ben Brewster. New York: Monthly Review Press, 1977. 127–86.

Bederman, Gail. *Manliness and Civilization: A Cultural History of Gender and Race in the United States, 1880–1917*. Chicago: U of Chicago P, 1995.

Brown, Elsa Barkley. "Imaging Lynching: African American Women, Communities of Struggle, and Collective Memory." *African American Woman Speak Out on Anita Hill–Clarence Thomas*. Ed. Geneva Smitherman. Detroit: Wayne State UP, 1995. 100–24.

Christol, Hélène. "The African American Concept of the Fantastic as Middle Passage." *Black Imagination and the Middle Passage*. Ed. Maria Diedrich, Henry Louis Gates, Jr., and Carl Pedersen. New York: Oxford UP, 1999. 164–73.

Crèvecoeur, J. Hector St. John de. *Letters from an American Farmer*. 1782. New York: Fox, Duffield, 1904.

Douglass, Frederick. "Letter from Scotland." 1846. *Always Elsewhere: Travels of the Black Atlantic*. Ed. Alasdair Pettinger. London: Cassell, 1998.95–97.

———. "A Month in Egypt." 1887. *Always Elsewhere: Travels of the Black Atlantic*. Ed. Alasdair Pettinger. London: Cassell, 1998.209–14.

Du Bois, W.E.B. *The Souls of Black Folk*. 1903. *Three Negro Classics*. New York: Avon, 1965. 213–389.

Equiano, Olaudah. *The Interesting Narrative of the Life of Olaudah Equiano, or Gustavas Vassa, the African. Written by Himself*. 1789. New York: W. Durrell, 1791.

Gilroy, Paul. *The Black Atlantic: Modernity and Double Consciousness*. Cambridge, MA: Harvard UP, 1993.

Griffin Farah J. and Cheryl J. Fish, eds. Introduction. *A Stranger in the Village: Two Centuries of African-American Travel Writing*. Boston: Beacon Press, 1998. xiii–xvii.

Hall, Stuart. "Minimal Selves." *Black British Cultural Studies: A Reader*. Eds. Houston A. Baker Jr, Manthia Diawara, and Ruth H. Lindeborg. Chicago: U of Chicago P, 1996. 114–19.

Harper, Lila M. *Solitary Travelers: Nineteenth-Century Women's Travel Narratives and the Scientific Vocation.* Madison, NJ: Fairleigh Dickinson UP, 2001.

Helmers, Marguerite and Tilar J. Mazzeo. "Introduction: Travel and the Body." *Journal of Narrative Theory* 35.3 (2005): 267–76.

Henson, Matthew Alexander. *A Negro Explorer at the North Pole.* New York: F. A. Stokes, 1912.

Jacobs, Harriet A. *Incidents in the Life of a Slave Girl.* 1861. Ed. Jean Fagan Yellin. Cambridge, MA: Harvard UP, 1987.Karcher, Carolyn L. "Ida B. Wells and Her Allies Against Lynching: A Transnational Perspective." *Comparative American Studies* 3.2 (2005): 131–51.

King, Nicole. " 'A Colored Woman in Another Country Pleading for Justice in Her Own.' " *Black Victorians/Black Victoriana.* Ed. Gretchen Holbrook Gerzina. New Brunswick, NJ: Rutgers UP, 2003. 88–109.

Linebaugh, Peter and Marcus Rediker. *The Many-Headed Hydra: Sailors, Slaves, Commoners, and the Hidden History of the Revolutionary Atlantic.* Boston: Beacon Press, 2000.

McMurry, Linda O. *To Keep the Waters Troubled: The Life of Ida B. Wells.* New York: Oxford UP, 1998.

Merriman-Labor, A. B. C. *Britons through Negro Spectacles; or, A Negro on Britons. With a Description of London.* London: Imperial & Foreign Company, 1909.

Mills, Sara. *Discourses of Difference: Analyses of Women's Travel Writing and Colonialism.* New York: Routledge, 1993.

Mohanram, Radhika. *Black Body: Women, Colonialism, and Space.* Minneapolis: U of Minnesota P, 1999.

Pettinger, Alasdair, ed. *Always Elsewhere: Travels of the Black Atlantic.* London: Cassell, 1998.

Piepmeier, Alison. *Out in Public: Configurations of Women's Bodies in Nineteenth-Century America.* Chapel Hill: U of North Carolina P, 2004.

Pratt, Mary Louise. *Imperial Eyes: Travel Writing and Enculturation.* New York: Routledge, 1992.

Said, Edward. *Orientalism.* New York: Pantheon, 1978.

Schechter, Patricia A. *Ida B. Wells-Barnett and American Reform, 1880–1930.* Chapel Hill: U of North Carolina P, 2001.

———. "Unsettled Business: Ida B. Wells Against Lynching, or, How Antilynching Got Its Gender." *Under Sentence of Death: Lynching in the South.* Ed. W. Fitzhugh Brundage. Chapel Hill: U of North Carolina P, 1997. 292–317.

Seacole, Mary. *Wonderful Adventures of Mrs. Seacole in Many Lands.* London: James Blackwood, 1857.

Spillers, Hortense J. "Mama's Baby, Papa's Maybe: An American Grammar Book." *Diacritics* 17.2 (1987): 65–81.

Totten, Gary. "Southernizing Travel in the Black Atlantic: Booker T. Washington's *The Man Farthest Down.*" *MELUS* 32.2 (2007): 107–31.

Washington, Booker T. *The Booker T. Washington Papers.* 14 vols. Ed. Louis R. Harlan. Urbana: U of Illinois P, 1972–89.

———. *The Man Farthest Down: A Record of Observation and Study in Europe.* 1912. Garden City NY: Doubleday, 1913.

Wiegman, Robyn. *American Anatomies: Theorizing Race and Gender*. Durham, NC: Duke UP, 1995.

Wells, Ida B. *Crusade for Justice: The Autobiography of Ida B. Wells*. Ed. Alfreda M. Duster. Chicago: U of Chicago P, 1970.

———. *The Memphis Diary of Ida B. Wells*. Ed. Miriam DeCosta-Willis. Boston: Beacon Press, 1995.

———. "The Model Woman: A Pen Picture of the Typical Southern Girl." 1888. *Memphis Diary* 187–89.

Wells-Barnett, Ida B. *A Red Record*. 1895. *On Lynchings*. Ed. Patricia Hill Collins. Amherst, NY: Humanity Books, 2002; 55–151.

———. *On Lynchings*. Ed. Patricia Hill Collins. Amherst, NY: Humanity Books, 2002.

———. *Southern Horrors: Lynch Law in All Its Phases*. 1892. *On Lynchings*. Ed. Patricia Hill Collins. Amherst, NY: Humanity Books, 2002; 25–54.

Black Is a Region

Segregation and American Literary Regionalism in Richard Wright's *The Color Curtain*

EVE DUNBAR

What has my geographical position on earth have to do with the faults or merits of a book?

—Richard Wright

"I am a rootless man," Richard Wright declares very early in *White Man, Listen!* (1957). The simple utterance captures the tie between his statelessness and his humanity: "I declare unabashedly that I like and even cherish the state of abandonment, of aloneness; it does not bother me; indeed, to me it seems the natural, inevitable condition of man, and I welcome it," says Wright (*White Man* 17). Many will note that Wright's statement is colored by his acquaintance with French existentialism; but if we consider that his personal and literary roots are grounded in Jim Crow America—roots publicly solidified with the publication of his autobiography *Black Boy* (1945)—the statement illuminates the complex relationship among geography, blackness, and humanity in Wright's work. The connectivity between these subjects is what Paul Gilroy challenged us to explore more deeply in his foundational *The Black Atlantic* (1993). For Gilroy, Wright's work while living in Paris symbolized black writing that contradicted the "ethnic absolutism" that has historically characterized black political culture (Gilroy 5). Gilroy understands Wright's movement away from the particularity of African American life and culture in the United States to topics as far ranging as Spanish religion and Asian identity as a move toward anti-essentialism.

Yet, paying close attention to tension among race, roots, and humanity in Wright's travel writing, I encourage a reconsideration of the uneasy literary ties that bound Wright to American racial segregation, even in his most global writing. What follows is an exploration of how "Rootless" Wright remained

185

tethered to the U.S. racial constructs by the conventions of American literary regionalism and, by extension, racial segregation's role on black American writing. Moving past common criticism of Wright's expatriation as either time spent alienated from African American concerns or as maturation beyond a provincial focus on African American culture, I argue that Wright's attachment to African Americans exhibits something much deeper than alienation. When we consider the relationship between books like *Black Boy/American Hunger* and *The Color Curtain* (1956), Wright's struggle with American literary regionalism—which I conceive in this essay as a type of literary segregation—informs his struggle to understand black Americans in a global context. This essay takes seriously Gilroy's call for an increased focus on Wright's travel writing, but concentrates on the role American racial segregation played in one of his most geographically alien texts, *The Color Curtain*. To state my aims more clearly, I argue that Wright is not the complete "anti-essentialist" that Gilroy contends. Rather, Wright remained deeply attached to an essentializing notion of African Americaness into the mid-1950s, while simultaneously positing the necessity of racial–political nonalignment. The conflicting impulses to essentialize black Americans while calling for their political nonalignment produced a fractured narrative around African Americaness that Wright found impossible to remediate, but necessary to represent.

Black Boy solidified Wright's standing as one of the most important African American voices of mid-twentieth century regarding U.S. race relations. As a coming of age story about racial segregation, *Black Boy* places Wright in step with the black literary tradition dating back to slave narratives, which often underscores freedom's dependence on literacy and northern migration. Interestingly, however, as early as *Black Boy*, Wright prophesied not only his inability to escape the American South, but also the possibility that sentiments born in Southern soil might bloom elsewhere. "Yet, deep down, I knew that I could never really leave the South, for my feelings had already been formed by the South, for there had been slowly instilled into my personality and consciousness, black though I was, the culture of the South," Wright writes in the final pages *Black Boy*. "So, in leaving, I was taking part of the South to transplant in alien soil, to see if it could grow differently, if it could drink of new and cool rains, bend in strange winds, respond to the warmth of other suns, and, perhaps, to bloom" (228). His quest to transplant in alien soil, not Northern, points to Wright's early understanding that uprooting would be necessary to achieve a sort of human dignity unheard of in American for blacks.

Wright's decision to characterize his final travel destination as "alien soil" also is interesting in light of *Black Boy*'s notorious publishing history. *Black Boy* is the truncated version of Wright's original but posthumously published novel, *American Hunger*. If it had been published as Wright intended, with its deleted second section titled "The Horror and the Glory," *Black Boy* would have recounted his struggles as a black man in the American South *and* North. Because unlike *Black Boy*, *American Hunger* ends not with Wright being delivered into the optional-laden North, but with literature/writing as his only true redeemer. Wright asks and answers,

> What had I got of out living in the south? What had I got out of living in America? I paced the floor, knowing that all I possessed were words and dim knowledge that my country had shown me no examples of how to live a human life. . . . I wanted to try to build a bridge of words between me and that world outside, that world that was so distant and elusive that it seemed unreal. I would hurl words into this darkness and wait for an echo, and if an echo sounded, no matter how faintly, I would send other words to tell, to march, to fight, to create a sense of the hunger for life that gnaws in us all, to keep alive in our hearts a sense of the inexpressibly human. (452–53)

With these final words he seeks to use writing to catapult himself outside of segregated America, which places his blackness at the center of his identity, not his humanness. Wright articulates a critical humanist agenda that would become the foundation of his future writings. And as the ending of *American Hunger* makes clear, Wright perceives his humanist agenda as incompatible with American reality.

Recently, critic Jeff Karem tracked the revision process that turned *American Hunger* into *Black Boy* to uncovered the story of how a few Book-of-the-Month Club judges coerced the construction of a positive U.S. national image. In the midst of World War II, two judges deemed it best not to offer as damning a critique of the United States' race relations as Wright offered in the last pages of *American Hunger*. Instead they encouraged him to stop the text at the moment before protagonist Wright leaves the South for Chicago in order to "curtail his 'questing adventure' and confine his work to his 'roots,' " (701). Karem contends, "Confining Wright's autobiography to his Southern childhood . . . served to blunt the political impact of his work" (701), and thereby confined Wright's "criticism exclusively to the South," producing a text that could "pay tribute to American ideals as a whole," and be "a national affirmation, not a national indictment" (704). Wright made the revisions the Book-of-the-Month Club suggested, and *Black Boy* garnered the club prize and the inevitable commercial and critical success (the royalties from *Black Boy* would sustain Wright up until the last years of his life). But Kareem also argues that, as a result, Wright emerged "less an artist and more a conduit of factual and folkloric knowledge," and his text, once made regional, "ascribed authority to Wright based on the truths of his Southern past," thereby lessening his "threatening potential for the American present" (708). *Black Boy* is made a regionalist text and, as such, offers the Wright no narrative access to the future. Instead, Wright creates the "literature of memory."

In light of the closing of *American Hunger*—"I would hurl words into this darkness and wait for an echo, I would send other words to tell, to march, to fight, to create a sense of the hunger for life"—to have Wright's words made impotent by generic restrictions undermines his power and potential. Wright wants his words to change the future but some critics deaden them—this is important to note because they do this after praising his gritty, naturalist novel, *Native Son* (1940). But if we consider blackness the ultimate segregated region in the United States, to write from that position is to always be creating regional literature. This is especially true during the 1940s, when the legal, economic, and psychic conditions of segregation shaped life in both the American North and South. Blacks literally and literarily occupied a space outside the confines of mainstream, white America. Unable to escape the critical expectation to produce regionalist writing (with texts like *Uncle Tom's Children*, *Native Son*, and *Black Boy* under his belt), Wright spends the rest of his career attempting to get out of regionalism's shadow. I argue he does this in two ways in *The Color Curtain*. First he leaves the United States and assumes a rootless, exilic stance. And second, he treats African Americans as regional characters within his own texts.

"A Basic Southern Occasion": Establishing Black as a Region

American literary regionalism is the genre of the alienated. It is constituted by narratives about alien places and the people who inhabit them. Growing out of the late nineteenth- and early twentieth-century American realist tradition,[1] regionalism has historically been a literature defined by where and who it is not: urban, white, middle class and male. In the imagined community of the United States, regionalist texts perform the cultural work of bringing the margins to the center, allowing an anxious (urban, white, middle-class male) readership to take stock of its national cultural holdings with the hope of allaying concerns regarding its own fragmentation. Ann Kaplan argues that the differences implied by U.S. regionalism, with its attention to vernacular language and "alien" land-scapes, allowed the nation to imagine a controlled reconstitution in the midst of societal upheavals like war, urbanization, and immigrant influx. Additionally, regionalist texts allowed "mainstream" readers the opportunity to solidify their sense of modernity and progress through fiction produced at the margins, in places and by people who exist outside time and troubles of "cosmopolitan development" (Kaplan 251). To that same end, Eric Sundquist characterizes regionalism as the "literature of memory" (508), which confines it the hegemonic cultural work of centralizing the reader's subject position and solidifying the temporal distance of the region and its inhabitants from the reader.

Many contemporary revisionists have worked to redeem regional writing from its pejorative status,[2] especially by tracking the reception of such writings. Although this is a valid concern, it does not necessarily account for the sense of burden that minority or female writers often experienced when associated with the genre. The burden of the particular has long been associated with African American writers. Regionalism, with its attention to presenting the margins to the center, allowed numerous African American writers access to the publishing world, while at the same time keeping their representations segregated from the national narrative. According to Richard Brodhead, "Regionalism made the experience of the socially marginalized into a literary asset, and so made marginality itself a positive authorial advantage" (117). In the late nineteenth century Charles Chesnutt earned early success for his collection of dialect stories, but his later attempts at selling novels that tackled seriously the problems of the color line proved the American readership uninterested in African American commentary on national issues. The problem of a dual audience,[3] one black and one white, plagued James Weldon Johnson's ability to render racial protest into the novel form while being commercially viable and pleasing to a white audience that expected a "pleasant excursion into black life as local color" (Andrews xvi). So, although many postbellum American writers entered the literary fold through the regionalism, unlike their white, male contemporaries, most African American writers were later unable to orchestrate an easy escape from the genre (Brodhead 116).

In his essay "Regional Particulars and Universal Statement in Southern Writing," writer Albert Murray senses the continued dangers of regionalism for the Southern writer. Murray states that the Southern writer must "[process] into artistic statement, [stylize] into significance" the "regional particulars—the idiomatic details, the down home conventions, the provincial customs and folkways" (3). Murray is pushing black writing out of the regional and into the universal to facilitate an escape from regionalist othering. Because if the writer does not create a work of art with "broad applicability," Murray argues, "time and again . . . it has to be rejected as too exclusive, too narrow, or . . . too provincial. Too Southern. Of some down home significance, perhaps; if you like that sort of thing. But not of very much immediate use elsewhere" (4). Still more direct, Murray says writers must "[treat] a basic Southern occasion as a basic American occasion which is in turn a basic contemporary occasion, and thus a basic human occasion" (4). Murray's statement encourages a move away from the particular to themes that will not alienate readers.

Because he addresses the particular, geographically specific situation of being a Southern writer and writing about the South, Murray's statement resists the easy replacement of "Southern" with "black." However, we might be able

expand his concerns to African American writers because African American literary (cultural) production has historically had the American South at its core. As
Houston Baker notes, "black modernism is not only framed by the American
south, but also is inextricable—as cognitive and somatic process of performing
blackness out of or within tight spaces—from specific institutionalizations of
human life below the Mason-Dixon" (26). So when Murray says "Southern"
he is talking primarily about the black Southern writer. The parallel becomes
more pronounced if we consider the drastic difference in issues raised between
his statement on Southern writing and the issues raised by a white Southern
writer like Flannery O'Connor. O'Connor makes it clear that burden of being
a Southern, regional writer is no burden at all: "To call yourself a Georgia
writer is certainly to declare a limitation, but one which, like all limitations, is
a gateway to reality. It is a great blessing, perhaps the greatest blessing a writer
can have, to find at home what others have to go elsewhere seeking. . . . and
most of you and myself and many others are sustained in our writing by the
local and the particular and the familiar without loss to our principles or our
reason" (54). More important, however, is O'Connor's understanding that the
region, particularly the South, needs no translation by or for Northerners and
is best when appreciated by locals. Although white Southern writers may face
the task of having their stories considered integral to the national narrative,[4]
black writers face the task of creating black humanity. Unlike Murray, who feels
the need to strive for a human story over a Southern (black) story, O'Connor
never questions the humanness of the art she produces. Because the burden of
having once been property is not easily shaken off, Murray's striving for the
status of humanness is part and parcel of the African American literary tradition,
which began with Phyllis Wheatley's poetry, found itself articulated in Du Bois's
The Souls of Black Folk, and continues to serve as motivation for many African
American writers.[5] In this monumental way, Murray's view of regional writing
differs from Southern peers like O'Connor, Faulkner, and Twain, all of whom
found their way to literary production through forms of regional writing, but
for whom the need to transcend the region in order to achieve humanity was
not so pressing. Murray's statement exposes the deep-seated quest for humanness, which also is part and parcel with a quest for perceived universal themes
and characterizations. Such humanity and universality is an achievement that
holds the promise of desegregating the American literary canon. Yet, the quest
for universalism at the expense of African American particularism does very
little to deconstruct the literary racial hierarchy; it merely condemns those
black texts that are perceived as aligning themselves with local articulations of
blackness. That is, universalism frames "blackness" as a pejorative region without
recognizing its complexity as a counterpublic sphere.[6]

 Understanding the fear of literary segregation is central to understanding
many black authors' quest for perceived literary universalism, and is especially

telling in the case of Richard Wright. As early as 1937, Wright understood and articulated the stakes involved in the creation of African American letters in his essay "Blueprint for Negro Writing." He understood that there was an entire counterlife created by American racial segregation that shaped black writing. In "Blueprint" Wright argues that this counterlife, though in many ways disabling, could also create a black social consciousness that exposed and changed black life in the United States. Because he was still living in the United States and was still a member of the Communist Party, Wright saw black writing as part of a nationalist enterprise. In "Blueprint" he notes that "Negro writers must accept the nationalist implications of their lives," because these implications form the foundation of the reality of black life in the United States. Nationalism is double-veiled in Wright's essay; first, he uses it to signify the black counterpublic created by racial segregation, and second, it signifies African American experience that is particular to living as a second-class member of the U.S. nation-state. Like Du Boisian "double-consciousness," Wright dictates that black writing must represent the particular lived experience of *Negroes* in *the United States*. Yet, similar to his desertion of the Communist Party because of the limitations it placed on black-centered progressive politics, Wright found the United States unfruitful soil for his psychological, physical, and artistic development and in 1947 he emigrated to Paris. Because Wright visited the United States infrequently before his death in 1960, it would be easy to argue that he abdicated his sense of responsibility to American race relations. But any such characterization of Wright would fail to understand how his post-1947 artistic vision. Biographer and critic Michel Fabre suggests that Wright believed that in order to save America he had to save the world (320). From 1947 onward, Wright's creative and political blueprints—the two were never separate for him—ceased to be confined to the provincial landscape that he articulated in "Blueprint for Negro Writing." Instead, his time spent in France offered him access to an international human enterprise, but he continued to struggle with how and when to represent African American particularity and whether or not its particularity could ever achieve humanity on U.S. soil.

Wright, Regionalism, and Segregation Transplanted to Alien Soil

In spring 1955, Richard Wright, U.S. émigré in Paris, flew to Bandung, Indonesia to attend the Bandung Asian-African Conference. Bandung participants represented twenty-nine free and independent nations (e.g., China, India, Indonesia, Japan, Burma, Egypt, Turkey, the Philippines, Ethiopia, etc.) for whom the discussion of both of nonalignment and Afro-Asian solidarity was critical. With the cold war in full swing, as well as the fallout from the Korean War, Vietnam's struggle for independence, and the general push for decolonization by various African and Asia countries underway, the world of color was ripe for a conference promising change through solidarity. Wright was drawn to Bandung by his status as a person of color, and he attended the conference in order to witness something momentous: the human race gathering to develop community, as his wife put it. Bandung was part of a larger transnational political trend in Wright's life. From his involvement with Alioune Diop in the 1946 inauguration of *Presence Africaine* to the 1956 First International Congress of Black Writers and Artists, Wright was deeply involved and invested in creating and honing what was to become the archive of negritude. With Leopold Senghor, Aimé Césaire, Alioune Diop, George Padmore, C.L.R. James, George Lamming, a young Frantz Fanon, and various other black artist and thinkers, "the need to disseminate African culture was a priority for Wright" (Fabre 319). The company he kept influenced his work by providing him another portal through which to address modernity's dehumanization. Thus, his time at the Bandung conference marked Wright's continued commitment to international activism that gave voice to not only members of the African diaspora but also to disenfranchised people of color across the globe.

    The Color Curtain is Wright's homage to Bandung's vision of Third World solidarity. It reads like an ethnographic document and centers around Wright's recounting of interviews he conducted with a few self-selected Asians and Euro-Asians, all of whom he describes by their representative types: colonial subject, westernized Asian educator, full-blooded Indonesian, and so on. The text is part of the body of work known as Wright's "travel writings," which includes *Black Power: A Record of Reactions in a Land of Pathos* (1953), *The Color Curtain, Pagan Spain* (1957), and *White Man, Listen!* (1957) (see Smith xi). Consistent with his other travel writing, *The Color Curtain* illustrates Wright's skill as ethnographer and journalist. But I am most fascinated by the lack of inflection Wright chooses to give the interviewees he encounters and recounts in the text. As John Reilly points out, "in none of his reported conversations does Wright make an attempt to preserve a sense of natural verbal exchange or to create verisimilitude. Instead he emphasizes the content of informal talk as though it were delivered without inflection, tone, or the dynamics of dialogue that provide 'color' and reveal animation. . . . They are spokespeople without unique voice" (512). This lack of inflection is an important feature because it might be used to mark and maintain distinctions between Wright's provincially (regional) African American texts, which always feature some element of dialect or highlight the black counterlife created by racial segregation. Moreover, Reilly's critique of Wright's character renderings in *The Color Curtain* for their lack of *color* and uniqueness—qualities privileged within regionalist literature—can be best understood as symptomatic of Wright's departure from American regionalism. Wright's empirical voice situates him as a powerful narrator, unfettered by conventions of regionalism; in fact, Wright's voice takes the tone of ethnographer.[7]

Wright's decision to forgo the voice of regionalist for that of ethnographer is more complicated then substituting one genre for another, even if the genres are kin. However closely linked the two forms of writing, American literary regionalism consistently makes Wright the author-subject; a writer, but a writer whose blackness and Southernerness are central to the perceived success of the subject matter. Conversely, through ethnographic travel writing, Wright creates *othered* subjects and situates his authorial voices as stemming from his astute understanding of ethnographic journalism and global perspective, rather then from his own racial identity. For example, although *The Color Curtain* is told in the first person and recounts Wright's travels and interactions, his status as a participant-observer requires that he is always officially an outsider to the material conditions he is recounting. And playing with the "insider–outsider" role that James Clifford notes is foundational to participant observation,[8] Wright is able to toe the line between concerned activist and disassociated ethnographer. In either case, Wright's blackness grants him the "rapport" (Clifford 34) necessary for this sort of ethnography: "In my questioning of Asians I had had one tangible factor in my favor, a factor no Westerner could claim. I was 'colored' and every Asian I had spoken to had known what being 'colored' meant," contends Wright (*CC* 25). But rapport is merely a trick of the participant-observer, because Wright never fully assimilates his blackness into the narrative of the Bandung conference.

Moreover, this role as "outsider" is crucial to Wright's own self-creation. According to S. Shankar, "the outsider . . . is the privileged possessor of an uncommon knowledge regarding power and society, as well as the agent capable of acting on this knowledge. In Wright's consciously abstract and metaphysical argument in [*The Outsider*], the outsiders are agents of change, through not always for the better" (6). Although Shankar is speaking of Wright's novel *The Outsider*, I believe Shankar's description can also be said of Wright's more ethnographic writings. Thus, in disregarding his status as regionalist writer for that of outsider, Wright is able to exist outside of systems that seek to sever his creative agency through casting him as merely a native informant-narrator. Wright's outsider status is what Gilroy privileges, but the role of African Americans in *The Color Curtain* makes clear that not everyone has access to the position of "outsider."

There are three African American "characters" in *The Color Curtain*, all of whom are unassimilable into the milieu of Bandung in Wright's account. Although they are moved by the conference's goals, they just do not fit within the movement's framework because of their ties to American racial segregation. Additionally, unlike Wright, they have no authorial control over their characterization. For example, Wright tells the story of Mr. Jones, "a light brown,

short, husky man who, according to American nomenclature, was 'colored' "
(*CC* 176). Jones, a mechanic in Los Angeles, is so moved by the potential of
the Bandung conference that he exhausts his life's savings to get to Indonesia.
A man whom Wright in one long paragraph describes as "colored" four times
and as "obscure" once, Jones seems out of place at the conference. Wright notes
that Jones, "felt that he belonged to a 'colored' nation, that he was out of place
in America . . . so this brown man came thousands of miles to feel a fleeting
sense of identity, of solidarity, of religious oneness with others who shared his
outcast state. . . . And brown Mr. Jones, watching the wily moves of tan Nehru
and yellow Chou En-Lai, understood absolutely nothing of what was going
on about" (*CC* 177). Forgetting about the problem of our not hearing about
Jones's experiences in his own voice, Wright's closing statement hems Jones into
the margins of the United States, while also disallowing him the privilege that
Wright himself employs throughout the book: a necessary amount of objective
removal and global perspective. For Wright, Jones is "obscure," meaningless
to the larger discussion of anti-colonialism and nonalignment being discussed
at Bandung. And although it happens to be a problem of language, the same
problem Wright should have, Jones seems out of place precisely because he
comes directly from Los Angeles and lacks the geographical distance that would
separate him from American nationalism. So, geographical distance becomes key
to Wright's conception of humanity and authorship.

Likewise, Wright recounts Adam Clayton Powell's experience at the
conference. Powell, a well-known black pastor and a Congressman from New
York, made his way to Bandung as the U.S. government's only official conference observer. Wright notes that Powell, a light-skinned black man, had to
be introduced to conference participants as black because he was taken to be
white. Whether or not Wright is attempting to slight Powell or merely "report
the facts," Wright attributes some of the half-hearted response to Powell to his
perceived "whiteness." Wright reports that Powell's address "stressed the colored
population of the United States" and that it "is to be recalled that, with the
exception of Congressman Powell, no delegate or observer at Bandung raised
the Negro problem in the United States" (*CC* 178). Although the content of
Powell's speech, which stressed the importance and improvement of African
Americans within the United States, might have prompted Wright and the
other conference goers' dismissal, Wright omits a description of Powell's speech
in *The Color Curtain*. Instead, Wright opts to describe the Negro problem as
"child's play compared to the naked racial tensions gripping Asia and Africa"
(*CC* 178). In short, not only does Wright's narration locate Powell's rhetorical
failure in his visibly miscegenated and nationally segregated body—a particular
marker of U.S. slavery and segregation in this narrative—but Wright also determines that the concerns of African Americans have little global worth. Within
this anti-colonial space, Wright's dismissal of Powell represents the dismissal of

the sort of African American counterpublic articulations that Paul Gilroy finds counterproductive to an anti-essentialist agenda.

The final example of Wright's segregated inclusion of African Americans and their concerns centers around a conversation Wright has with a white American reporter about her roommate, whom she describes as being a "black, *real* black [woman]" (*CC* 184, emphasis added). Soon after she meets Wright, the white journalist reveals that she is seeking his advice because she believes her black roommate might be practicing voodoo. She describes the black woman's nightly ritual as involving a blue light and the scent of something. After a few questions, Wright determines what the black roommate does not want her white roommate to know: that she is straightening her hair with a hot comb and a Bunsen burner once the lights go out. It's a simple misunderstanding that has grave ramifications for Wright's textual representation of black Americanness. Because the exchange continues with Wright informing the white journalist that her black roommate straightens her hair simply because she is self-loathing (*CC* 187), the interaction could be read as Wright's attempt to represent the American racial allegory, which highlights white American benightedness with respect to black Americans. Wright offers this black women's "shame" to the white journalists (and readers) as an object lesson in the international colored population's inferiority complex, a topic with which he feels the conference is reckoning. Yet, when the white woman asks what she can do to change this he responds by saying "Nothing. It's much bigger than you or I. Your father and your father's father started all this evil. Now it lives with us. First of all, just try to understand it. And get all that rot about voodoo out of your mind" (*CC* 188). Wright does to these female journalists, Mr. Jones, and Powell what the Book-of-the-Month judges did to him just a decade earlier: he regionalizes them by confining their concerns to a temporal past, thereby blunting the force of African American (and progressive white) resistance to U.S. racial segregation.

How does one make sense of the faith Wright has in the power of an event like Bandung alongside his seeming lack of active engagement with American racial segregation, which seems so out of place in *The Color Curtain*? Considering Wright's Pan-African work in Paris and his investment in international activism, his decision to narrate the interaction with the journalist is complicated by his apathy regarding the potential of his object lesson. Because Wright and this white woman talk in his hotel room, the conversation is removed from the primary conference space. As with Wright's critique of Powell's speech to the Bandung attendees, American racism is too specific to be explored on the international public stage, and possibly the Bandung participants. Instead, Wright recreates the intimacy of American racial segregation in his hotel room. Possibly due to these other African Americans' continued geographical and intellectual association with the United States, Wright seems to find it difficult to integrate their narratives into the framework of global solidarity and nonalignment.

Even after Bandung, it is difficult for Wright to rhetorically fuse the particular concerns of African Americans in the United States with his growing interests in a more "universal" theme of the human struggle for dignity. His tendency to marginalize African Americans in *The Color Curtain* is indicative of his continued negotiation concerning the textual "value" inherent in African American cultural production located in the United States. Concerned with the "discursive economy of Wright's text," Shankar imagines a metaphorical economic system where the "value-coding" of a text originates from outside the text (5). Shankar contends that in *Black Power,* Wright, unable to make sense of his own blackness while in his ancestral home of Africa, oscillated between relegating colonial Africa to prehistory and embracing the continent's potential for anti-colonial revolution (18). So, Wright is caught in the trap of privileging Western rationalism and textual production, while also wanting to rearticulate such coding. For Shankar the resulting tension between the West and non-West is palpable in Wright's *Black Power.*

It stands to reason that this tension continues beyond *Black Power.* In fact, Wright's relationship to African Americans and regionalism in the international context typifies the vexed position that the black American writer must often occupy in order to make his or her writing matter in the present and, more importantly, in the future. The years Wright spent in Europe were dogged by accusations that ranged from having an outdated sense of U.S. race relations because his post-*Black Boy* writings failed to capture the racial nuance created by the burgeoning civil rights movement in the United States, to a sense that his internationalism had taken him too far from his expertise in African American life. Torn between two creative worlds—African American regionalism and Pan-African, humanist solidarity—Wright would find very little solace in his attempts to bridge them. From his imagined magnum opus "Celebration," which he envisioned would tie his novel *Savage Holiday* (1954) and two unwritten novels that explored the lives of Montezuma and a pathological teenage girl in New York,[9] to his travel writings, Wright met constant critical disinterest in the Unites States. During the last years of his life, Wright's publishers, editors, and his own literary agent tried to get him to go back "home" creatively. Confounded by negative reviews and the general push to move back into the *black region,* Wright asked his agent, "What has my geographical position on earth got to do with the faults or merits of a book?" (Fabre 468). The answer: everything. Looming financial instability gave critics' concerns more weight then they might have, and Wright continued to his death trying to make the regional mesh with his global perspective.

Paul Gilroy commends Wright for his ability to resist ethnocentrism and for his willingness to live between insider and outsider status. But I hope that I have shown that such resistance on Wright's part was not without its own share of racial essentialism, in the form of regionalizing and political segregation of African Americans in *The Color Curtain*. Likewise, Wright was marred by his attempts to desegregate his creative vision, as is evident from a warning he received from his agent Paul Reynolds just two months before the *Color Curtain*'s American publication:

> It seems to me—and of course I'm only guessing now—that as you have found greater peace as a human being, living in France, and not being made incessantly aware that the pigmentation in your skin sets you apart from other men, you have at the same time lost something as a writer. *To put it another way, the human gain has been offset by a creative loss.* (Fabre 432, emphasis added)

Obviously, the exchange rate between the particular and the anti-essential for African Americans is a complex transaction. Wright may have transplanted but was never able to fully cultivate African American concerns in the alien soil, so his example begs us to think further about how best to value African American regional particularism without forgoing the possibility of African American global agency favored by Gilroy. We must know that Mr. Jones's and the unnamed black journalist's African American identity and humanness do not make them segregated outcasts, but actually facilitate their relevance to both global and local counterpublic articulations.

Notes

1. The division between American literary realism and literary regionalism is blurry at best. American literary realism, which American regionalism is traditionally considered a subgenre (with all the connotations of "sub" being played upon), has its roots in the late nineteenth century and coincides with the rise of technology. Realism, according to William Dean Howells, depicted "the simple, natural, and the honest," and resisted romantic representations of humanity.

2. See, for example, Fetterley and Pryse's *Writing Out of Place*. Elsewhere, Fetterley argues that regionalism, which for her is nearly synonymous with nineteenth-century women's writing, is inherently an "un-American" genre (878) that allows "persons made silent or vacant through terror to tell stories which the dominant culture labels trivial," and "change our perspective and thus to destabilize the meaning of margin and center" (887).

3. Andrews argues that Johnson was able to overcome this burden by employing autobiography because whites were more receptive to that genre than the novel. It is important to note that *The Autobiography of an Ex-Coloured Man* is also a travel narrative featuring the narrator's traversal through many remote and marginal locations.

4. Robison examines how the South vacillates in meaning and importance to the United States. Sometimes the site of what America is not, sometimes the nostalgic site of what it wishes it could be again, according to Robison, the American South is often

treated as the symbolic register of the nation's relationship to race. But even Robison's analysis of how race affects the South's national importance, fails to consider how African Americans in the South register their own national longings and belonging.

5. Toni Morrison notes that the tension between the particular and the universal is a constant concern for African American writers. Specifically, many black writers believe they are burdened with the task of making the particular experience of blackness readable to white people. Morrison renounces this sentiment in black writing because she sees little value in universalism and, instead, relishes in the local/regional. See her interview in Taylor-Guthrie.

6. See Dawson's *Black Visions* for more on the black counterpublic.

7. Robison contends that ethnography, like regional writing, serves the cultural function of providing mainstream readers an authoritative introduction to new cultures. Ethnography and regionalism both create an outside observer and "enact through their very form, a hierarchical relationship between observer and observed that assumes the superiority of the voice that 'looks down upon what the other is' " (64).

8. Clifford describes ethnographic participant observation as a method that places the ethnographer between "inside" and "outside" of the events she is recording. The value of this particular type of ethnography is that it allows the impression of dialectical interaction between author and subjects, but still privileges the voice of the ethnographer and her ability to make sense of the culture being described.

9. For more detailed description of this failed writing project, see Michel Fabre's *The Unfinished Quest of Richard Wright.*

Works Cited

Anderson, Benedict. *Imagined Communities: Reflections on the Origin and Spread of Nationalism.* New York: Verso, 1983.

Andrews, William. Introduction. *The Autobiography of an Ex-Coloured Man.* Ed. William Andrews. New York: Penguin Books, 1990.

Baker, Houston, Jr. *Turning South Again: Re-thinking Modernism/Re-reading Booker T.* Durham, NC: Duke UP, 2001.

Brodhead, Richard. *Cultures of Letters: Scenes of Reading and Writing in Nineteenth-Century America.* Chicago: U of Chicago P, 1993.

Clifford, James. *Predicament of Culture: Twentieth-Century Ethnography, Literature, and Art.* Cambridge, MA: Harvard UP, 1988.

Dawson, Michael. *Black Visions: The Roots of Contemporary African-American Political Ideologies.* Chicago: U of Chicago P, 2001.

Fabre, Michel. *The Unfinished Quest of Richard Wright.* New York: William Morrow and Co., 1973.

Fetterley, Judith. " 'Not in the Least American': Nineteenth-century Literary Regionalism." *College English* 56 (1994): 877–95.

——— and Marjorie Pryse. *Writing Out of Place: Regionalism, Women and American Literary Culture.* Chicago: U of Illinois P, 2003.

Gilroy, Paul *The Black Atlantic: Modernity and Double Consciousness.* Cambridge, MA: Harvard UP, 1993.

Judy, Ronald. "Paul Gilroy's *Black Atlantic* and the place(s) of English in the global." *Critical Quarterly* 39 (1997): 22–29.

Kaplan, Ann. "Nation, Region, and Empire." *The Columbia History of the American Novel.* Ed. Emory Elliott. New York: Columbia UP, 1991.

Karem, Jeff. " 'I Could Never Really Leave the South': Regionalism and the Transformation of Richard Wright's American Hunger." *American Literary History* 13 (2001): 694–715.

Murray, Albert. "Regional Particulars and Universal Statement in Southern Writing," *Callaloo* 38 (1989): 3–6.

O'Conner, Flannery. "The Regional Writer." *Mystery and Manners: Occasional Prose.* Eds. Sally Fitzgerald and Robert Fitzgerald. New York: Farrar, Straus, & Giroux, 1961.

Reilly, John. "Richard Wright and the Art of Non-Fiction: Stepping Out on the Stage of the World." *Callaloo* 28 (1986): 512

Robison, Lori. "Region and Race." *A Companion to the Regional Literatures of America.* Ed. Charles Crow. Malden, MA: Blackwell Publishing, 2003.

Shankar, S. "Richard Wright's *Black Power*: Colonial Politics and the Travel Narrative." *Richard Wright's Travel Writings: New Reflections.* Ed. Virginia Smith. Jackson: UP of Mississippi, 2001.

Smith, Virginia Whatley. Introduction. *Richard Wright's Travel Writings: New Reflections.* Jackson: UP of Mississippi, 2001.

Sundquist, Eric. "Realism and Regionalism." *The Columbia Literary History of the United States.* Ed. Emory Elliot. New York: Columbia UP, 1988.

Taylor-Guthrie, Danille, ed. "Language Must Not Sweat: A Conversation with Toni Morrison." *Conversations with Toni Morrison.* Jackson: UP of Mississippi, 1994. 119–28.

Wright, Richard. *American Hunger.* New York: HarperPerennial, 1993.

———. *Black Boy.* New York: The World Publishing Company, 1945.

———. "Blueprint for Negro Writing." *Richard Wright Reader.* Eds. Ellen Wright and Michel Fabre. New York: Harper, 1978.

———. *The Color Curtain: A Report on the Bandung Conference.* 1956. Jackson: UP of Mississippi, 1995.

———. "The American Writer in a Democratic Society." (Carl Miller/1938). *Conversations with Richard Wright.* Eds. Keneth Kinnaon and Michel Fabre. Jackson: UP of Mississippi, 1993.

"¿Qué Dice?"
Latin America and the Transnational in James Weldon Johnson's *Autobiography of an Ex-Coloured Man* and *Along This Way*

RUTH BLANDÓN

Transnational connections—whether real or fantastical—were a matter of psychological and emotional survival for African Americans who endured Jim Crow laws and segregation. Connections to the Latin Americas, specifically, helped debunk the insidious logic of race and racism in the United States, and questioned segregation based on such "race logic." For instance, as early as 1852 Martin Delany, in his *The Condition, Elevation, Emigration, and Destiny of the Colored People of the United States,* proposed Mexico, Nicaragua, and New Grenada (present-day Colombia and Venezuela) as places that presented no obstacles and offered boundless opportunity in regard to racial freedom and economic exploitation. The migration discourse within black communities by the early twentieth century was a reaction against Jim Crow laws that corralled people defined as legally "black" into a space in which they were more subjects of the United States rather than citizens with the legal rights and protections that citizenship suggests. This domestic focus on migration also has a transnational presence: the physical crossing of national borderlines, as Delany once claimed, could offer respite from racism. But as Johnson proves, the strategic use of language can be a means by which to escape the constraints of racism and segregation laws, while also complicating assumptions about race and axiology. Transnational migration and language masquerade facilitate border crossings and ambiguous readings of the body, while also calling into question the fixed relationship of identity to culture and nation.

James Weldon Johnson's first and only novel, *The Autobiography of an Ex-Coloured Man,* (1912) and his autobiography, *Along This Way,* (1933) complicate the idea of travel and migration as solutions to U.S. racism and segregation laws. Although his observations on the more malleable workings of race in Latin American cultures greatly influenced the creation and depiction of the unnamed ex-coloured man in his novel, the unnamed (and arguably unnamable) protagonist is simultaneously the embodiment of segregation and also its negation. Was it possible, as Johnson's novel suggests, that one could befriend, live next to, and even marry someone who appeared white but was indeed black as defined by U.S. law? The paranoia and fear about the specter of "invisible blackness," as sociologist F. James Davis describes, is what prompted laws that defined blackness and thus established legal separation between the races (56). Johnson's novel, however, depicts a racially ambiguous man who jumps a constructed and legal color line at will. He thus poses both an epistemic and axiological dilemma for those who read (and misread) him from the outside and also for himself. As the ex-coloured man negotiates his identity, much of his racial passing is passive, for in strategically using language in his masquerade, he complicates the readability of his body by performing social class and culture, but also by placing the burden of determining racial, cultural, and legal status on those who read and decipher him.

As both Johnson and the ex-coloured man observe, culture, any culture as long as it is not African American culture, trumps race in terms of access to the benefits of citizenship and cultural capital. African Americans are undoubtedly considered part of U.S. history and thus part of the U.S. narrative, but as Johnson's own experience, as well as that of the ex-coloured man's, suggest, African Americans function as a foil within that narrative of peoplehood. Rogers M. Smith, for example, posits that nation-building and the corresponding edification of peoplehood depend on narratives. These stories function, he states, to clarify and justify to a nation's people, "who is to be segregated or killed, and who is instead to be fully included as an equal. There cannot be 'imagined communities' without mental images of what those communities should be and who should be in them" (48). Those imagined communities are made up of people and the non-people who help them define themselves as such. The strategic employment of the Spanish language, in both Johnson's novel and in his autobiography, and his use of dialect in the novel, however, are the means by which Johnson questions the function of African Americans in the United States narrative, the concept of racial taxonomy, contradictory cultural hierarchies, and race/culture-based segregation laws. All the while, Johnson illumines the psychic implications of crossing borderlines—whether those borderlines are national, ethnic, or racial—and the alternative, which is to stay confined within United States parameters and remain the segregated self.

Race laws, whether in the United States or throughout the Latin Americas, are informed by complicated understandings of race. By featuring Latin American ideas about race and culture in his novel and autobiography, however, Johnson sheds light on what he perceives as a more benign racial environment for African Americans, while he describes the pleasure and pain of cultural absorption and identitarian malleability. For example, Davis documents that, "some not-so-light mulattoes passed by taking Latin names and moving to an appropriate locale" (56). Although this type of "passing" was common, Davis notes that many who passed for Latin American "found that passing was easy but that the emotional costs were high, and some therefore returned to the black community" (56). Nonetheless, what is clear here is that people who would typically be categorized as "colored" or "black" had the ability to manipulate perception, and consequently, taxonomy through the acquisition of the Spanish or Portuguese languages, and also through the changing of surnames.

Language may place one within a specific cultural and national context, and when combined with color, may mean the difference between life and death. No image illustrates this better than that of a Moroccan man, described by Booker T. Washington in *Up from Slavery* (1901), finding that his language exempts him from the racism and violence that his color elicits:

> I happened to find myself in a town in which so much excitement and indignation were being expressed that it seemed likely for a time that there would be a lynching. The occasion of the trouble was that a dark-skinned man had stopped at the local hotel. Investigation, however, developed the fact that this individual was a citizen of Morocco, and that while traveling in this country he spoke the English language. As soon as it was learned that he was not an American Negro, all the signs of indignation disappeared. The man who was the innocent cause of the excitement, though, found it prudent after that not to speak English. (60)

In this case, the English language, in tandem with the Moroccan man's coloration, resulted in a misreading of cultural context, taxonomy, and position on the U.S. social ladder. Most urgently, however, it also determined the man's lack of access to civil rights and protection under U.S. law upon being read as "black." It is only when he is contextualized outside of the institution of slavery and outside the institution of blackness that he is made exempt from racist taxonomy and axiology. His status as foreigner and guest are only then returned to him, as well as the rights that go along with this status. The contradictions, hypocrisy, and illogic that could pronounce a man "black," nearly cause his lynching, and then result in a retraction of the indictment mirrors the often contradictory workings of U.S. race law. This also illustrates that the initial perceived offense is not one of race or color; it is based on perceived deviation from prescribed roles in the national narrative. The Moroccan man must immediately assert his own identity through language and through strategic silence in order to resist domestic understandings of race that are foreign to him and that may prove deadly. Domestic understandings of race, although familiar to citizens, are not necessarily comprehensible to its citizens, especially those whose citizenship is greatly compromised because of race and racial taxonomy in the United States. As Johnson finds out in his youth and quite by accident, however, race and taxonomy are not fixed things, especially when bodily readability is obscured by perceptions of foreignness. If race could be read according to what side of the border one stepped and according to the language one spoke, what did this expose about race in the domestic narrative? What was Johnson's role in this story of peoplehood and of citizenship? Johnson's time as a diplomat in the Latin Americas would expose the arbitrary and manipulative underpinnings of the U.S. national narrative. His observations on race would also confuse his own identitarian place in the world.

"Any kind of a Negro will do . . ."

Throughout his autobiography Johnson repeats the phrase, "any kind of a Negro will do; provided he is not one who is an American citizen." These observations and conclusions, brought about through the simple act of speaking a language other than English, comprise the crux of Johnson's novel, *The Autobiography of an Ex-Coloured Man*. Johnson thus debunks a binary understanding of race that can be toppled with the mere utterance of a few foreign words. In the process, he exposes U.S. constructions of identities that seem to be caught between black and white, that are simultaneously African, European, Native American, and sometimes Asian, all the while invisible, and yet given access to citizenship and white cultural capital. The observations, moments of astonishment, and cross-cultural experiences described by Johnson while living in the cigar-factory town of Jacksonville, while cohabitating for years with the Cuban Ricardo Rodriguez Ponce, and then while on diplomatic duty in Venezuela and Nicaragua, irrefutably shaped the lens with which he viewed race. It also influenced how he represented the workings of racial constructions within U.S. borderlines. It was while in Venezuela, Johnson recalls, "I began in earnest work on *The Autobiography of an Ex-Coloured Man*, of which I had already made a first draft of the opening. The story developed in my mind more rapidly than I had expected that it would; at times, outrunning my speed in getting it down" (*ATW* 238). Johnson's autobiography places him in the Latin Americas as he wrote *The Autobiography of an Ex-Coloured Man* and also upon its 1912 publication. He began diplomatic duties in the U.S. Consular Service in Venezuela and Nicaragua in 1906, so some of his observations while in Latin

America, which are documented in *Along This Way*, influenced his depiction of the ex-coloured man and his adventures.

Johnson's observations on the complexities of race, and how they exposed the illogic of segregation laws, started in Jacksonville, Florida, long before he embarked on his diplomatic duty. Johnson tells a story in *Along This Way* that questions how variants such as language and culture disrupt the readability of race. A train conductor orders Johnson and Ricardo Rodriguez Ponce, the Cuban student who was at that time staying with the Johnsons, to move to the car designated for "colored people," despite the fact that they had purchased first-class tickets. "But we have first-class tickets; and this is the first-class car, isn't it?" Johnson protests. Although the conductor warns them about the trouble they will face if they insist on staying in the car, Rodriguez Ponce, not fully understanding the conversation, turns to Johnson and asks "*¿Qué Dice?*" ("What does he say?") Johnson explains to him in Spanish. Johnson then states:

> As soon as the conductor heard us speaking a foreign language, his attitude changed; he punched our tickets and gave them back, and treated us just as he did the other passengers in the car. . . . Fifteen years later, an incident similar to the experience with this conductor drove home to me the conclusion that in such situations any kind of a Negro will do; provided he is not one who is an American citizen. (64–65)

The idea of national constraints on African Americans is especially important, for it simultaneously questions black identity outside U.S. borderlines. In speaking the Spanish language, the train conductor takes Johnson and Rodriguez Ponce outside the institution of blackness, outside the codes and laws of race segregation, and sets them in a third and more ambiguous cultural space. Racial confusion that leads to law and policy confusion on trains is a common trope in African American literature. Johnson, however, highlights foreign language as a weapon and defense against U.S. race laws while he also ruptures the assumption that race (or color) is the primary factor that determines how one is situated legally and socially.

Fifteen years after this experience, Johnson describes a second incident in which he this time consciously manipulates language as he travels from Jacksonville to New York. Whereas the train incident involving Rodriguez Ponce quite by chance disclosed to Johnson the power that the Spanish language had in contextualizing him, this later incident plays out like theater. Upon entering one of the compartments containing five men, Johnson is scrutinized immediately. One of the men is a veteran of the Spanish-American war and is just returning from Cuba. His familiarity with Latin America prompts him to turn to his father and refer to Johnson's hat: "Dad, there's a genuine panama hat" (88). The hat is passed around, and Johnson observes that as soon as the war veteran notes the Havana-stamped lining, he turns to him and asks "Habla Vd. español?" Johnson answers, "Sí, Señor" (88). Johnson adds, "There upon he and I exchanged several commonplace phrases in Spanish; but in a short while his knowledge of that language was exhausted, and general conversation in English was resumed" (88–89). It is only after this exchange, which contextualizes him outside of the United States, that, ironically, he is no longer perceived as an interloper. As a matter of fact, states Johnson, "the whole party spent the time in the smoking compartment, talking, joking, laughing. The railroad official went into his bag and brought out his private flask of whisky, from which each of us, including the preacher, took several samples, all drinking out of the same glass. Before we reached Savannah a bond of mellow friendship had been established" (89). After his "newly made friends" debark in Savannah, Johnson says, "I went to bed repeating to myself: In such situations any kind of a Negro will do; provided he is not one who is an American citizen" (89). Johnson may repeat the same words that he does after describing the first train incident, but this situation plays out differently. Although initially perceived as having a very specific role in the context of the national narrative, as soon as he is situated outside the narrative, his status rises in the eyes of the other men in the compartment. In this scenario, Johnson participates in a ruse while at the same time coolly observing the nuanced differentiation of race that takes place in the context of travel and with the use of the Spanish language. In other words, by participating in and even directing this experimental theater, he puts theory into practice.

Given Johnson's observations on how language could affect the perception of identity and also what rights and social niceties were bestowed (depending on said identity) in the United States, it is no wonder that people defined by law as three-fifths of a human being, therefore "black" and subjugated, sought out the possibility of migration and immigration. In addition to being sympathetic toward "blacks" in the United States, Latin Americans did not subscribe to the same type of racial categorizations and hierarchies. Whereas U.S. laws had established a binary enforcement of race in which one was either black or white, Charles Wagley documents that Latin Americans understand race in terms of "social races" rather than "genetic race." Additionally, Wagley contends that the criteria involved that determines social races varies throughout the Latin Americas, thus making it difficult to identify consistent rules about race (13). The understanding of race in the region in which Johnson found himself at the time was and is blurred. Julian Pitts-Rivers, for instance, notes that "skin color is merely one of the indices among physical traits that contribute to a person's total image. It is not necessarily more significant than hair type or shape of eye" (62). Moreover, he adds, "in Latin America, a person with non-white physical traits may be classed as white socially" (63), concluding:

> The problem of race relations in North America and Latin America are, therefore, fundamentally different. One concerns the assimilation of all ethnic groups into a single society; the other, the status distinction between persons who have been assimilated for hundreds of years but who are still distinguished socially by their appearance. The two are comparable only at the highest level of abstraction. (67–68)

Never quite able to reconcile competing ideologies on race and color, Johnson was constantly startled by "integration" in Central and South America. As Johnson vacationed from his duties as Nicaraguan consul in San José, Costa Rica with his wife Grace a few years later, he recalled strolling the streets and then entering a church upon hearing singing. He was astonished to find that, "the preacher was a jet-black Negro. The congregation was composed of a few Negroes and overwhelmingly of Costa Ricans. That constituted the most curious sight we saw in Catholic San José" (275). Johnson's assessment of this scene as "curious" establishes his inscription in U.S.-specific racial roles and mores. Most tellingly, Johnson himself segregates the congregation, separating the "Negroes" from the "Costa Ricans." As Johnson's language betrays, he relegates "Negroes" to race rather than nation, thus exposing the unconscious subscription to a U.S. notion of peoplehood that excludes him. Despite the racial and cultural freedom that migration promises, the internalization of segregation results in a segregating eye/I.

It also results in a *segregated* eye/I. The link between the segregating and the segregated eye/I is one that is inextricable, for one does not occur without the other. It follows that when one segregates, differentiates, and categorizes, that one also will situate and compartmentalize oneself accordingly. Consider, for example, Johnson's description of the limits of cultural absorption, in which he unconsciously situates himself: "there were some things that appeared to be shortcomings in the Venezuelans and Venezuela that I felt I could discuss only with [Cuban consul] Zangroniz, of all the *foreign* language men in Puerto Cabello. Even so, on my side, I sensed limitations; for I realized that, after all, in language, religion, and traditional background, Zangroniz and the Venezuelans were one" (235, emphasis added). Although Johnson underscores the limits and porosity of cultural boundaries, his own problematic position as an agent of U.S. interests in the Latin Americas influences his subject position. It is curious, for instance, that he would describe the Spanish-speaking and

Cuban Zangroniz as a "foreign language" man in Venezuela—a slip that betrays his interpellation of the U.S. imperialistic machinery, and also of its domestic segregation codes and laws.

"The miracle of my transition . . ."

Despite the fecund field of theoretical and rhetorical complexities that Johnson's novel provides, it is commonly noted that the ex-coloured man is stuck between two worlds—the black and the white. Although it is true that the ex-coloured man's parents are identified as "white" and "colored," the ex-coloured man is actually able to transcend binary constructions that assume that the United States is solely black and/or white, if only temporarily through language and while working in a cigar factory.

From the beginning, the ex-coloured man is a child without cultural training. His father is absent for the most part of his life and his mother is silent about her contribution to his cultural heritage and ancestry. The ex-coloured man "learns" culture through books and consequently has an extrinsic relationship with his culture as well as with the abstract concepts of culture and ethnicity. After losing his money in Atlanta and, along with it, his academic aims, he continues his ethnographic and phenotypic studies in the cigar-factory town of Jacksonville. He betrays a growing fascination with the ambiguity and unreadability of appearance. As he sits at the breakfast table with his fellow boarders, he describes his new environment in which the lines between race, color, and culture are increasingly blurred for him, and in which the ability to read appearance and literally interpret language becomes impaired. "There were eight or ten of them," he describes. "Two, as I afterwards learned, were colored Americans. All of them were cigar makers in which the color-line is not drawn. The conversation was carried on entirely in Spanish, and my ignorance of the language subjected me more to alarm than embarrassment" (31). The ex-coloured man then speaks of their barrage of Spanish—none of which he could understand.

There are two important insights that occur for the ex-coloured man during this experience of "illiteracy" and language confusion: the first is that he himself cannot distinguish and thus, in his mind's eye, segregate the Cubans from the "colored Americans." He consequently makes the quick taxonomic transition in his mind from culture to race upon the disclosure and discovery that, despite the language being spoken, not all at the table are Cuban. The second insight is that despite his immediate taxonomic separations, language unites all of those at the table, thus blurring the "color line" that is ever present in the ex-coloured man's mind and is the source of all his anxiety. Why does this cause him more alarm than embarrassment? What separates him from everyone else is language, not color, nationality, or even culture. Even the "colored Americans," to whom he believes he should feel connected, are more connected to the Cubans through language than they are to him, thus producing in him the fear that he is in essence connected to no one, no culture, and no race. In this case, language undermines the stability of identity for him—an aim and strategy that he will later undertake and implement. The title, which identifies the narrator as "ex-coloured" has been misinterpreted as meaning "ex-African American" or "ex-black." Perhaps the title that Johnson originally had in mind—*The Chameleon*—would have lent itself to a broader interpretation of what it means to pass through or transcend boundaries that otherwise are thought of as fixed. As the ex-coloured man seeks to extricate himself from the confines of fixed identity, he draws on the transnational space to cultivate an ambiguous identity through the conscious and unconscious performance of race and culture that all the while debunk fixed notions of race.

The Autobiography of an Ex-Coloured Man begins in retrospect, as the perpetually unnamed and anonymous ex-coloured man discloses his story—a sad tale of finding himself between cultures, between races, and between worlds. Ultimately, this in-between state leaves the narrator with no cultural identity whatsoever. Despite an ending that leaves the ex-coloured man in a state of identitarian limbo, his attempt to free himself from the confines of legal "blackness" depicts cultural play that (although causing him to slip through the cracks of culture and race) help expose the tenuousness of racial taxonomy in the United States. What has remained unexplored thus far is how the ex-coloured man uses the Spanish language to linger in the third space that is Latin America before he makes the choice to become white.

The need for a third space that offers psychological alleviation from the toll that a binary enforcement of race takes on the psyche is most apparent at the defining moment when the ex-coloured man's grade-school teacher asks him to sit down after having asked all of the white boys to stand up in class for a count. She continues the count by then asking all of the "colored" boys to stand up. This time she insists that the future ex-coloured man stand up. The result is devastating to the young boy and he woefully recalls, "when school was dismissed I went out in a kind of stupor. A few of the white boys jeered me, saying, 'Oh, you're a nigger too.' I heard some black children say, 'We *knew* he was colored' " (7, emphasis added). The idea of "knowing" is not only about epistemology, but is also tied to social power and the power to name. It is the difference between naming and *being* named, and about who controls racial, social, and legal identity. In other words, it is about power relations and how a performative utterance can determine identity, taxonomy, axiology, and consequent quality of life, including access to legal protection under the constitution, and one's place in the national narrative of peoplehood.

The ex-coloured man marks this moment in which his identity is changed forever as, "the miracle of my transition from one world into another," and recalls, "I did indeed pass into another world" (9). He simultaneously describes both a death and a birth, as well as foretells his choice to pass from one world to another at will. That identity, personhood, citizenship, and the rights that are part of full citizenship in the United States can so drastically change in an instant and, most poignantly, at the naming by those with social and legal power, is more the crux of this story than is the theme of racial betrayal.

After being publicly identified by his white teacher, the ex-coloured man recalls thereafter being instructed on his legal standing and social value by a white author. He reads Harriet Beecher Stowe's *Uncle Tom's Cabin or, Life Among The Lowly* (1852), indignantly declaring it a "direct misrepresentation" (18), and sadly remarks, "it opened my eyes as to who and what I was and what my country considered me; in fact, it gave me my bearing. But there was no shock; I took the whole revelation in a kind of stoical way" (19). The ex-coloured man may express disgust at Tom's powerlessness, but he is strangely silent about the characters who cross racial, state, and ultimately, legal lines in Stowe's novel. Neil Brookes points out the action conveyed through the ex-coloured man's silences: "His attempts to narrate a life of concealment and disguise produce a text that can only be understood through what it conceals, through the gaps and the unspoken" (84). It can also be understood through what is subtle or coded. The ex-coloured man's silences are just as interesting (if not more so) than his disclosures, for the lack of mention of characters who pass color and culture lines within Stowe's novel seems to indicate that the act of passing registers so deeply for him as to be unutterable.

After reading Stowe's *Uncle Tom's Cabin*, the ex-coloured man embarks on a trip to the South to attend Atlanta University. There he observes people through the lens of the novel, and lives out a sort of *Uncle Tom's Cabin* fantasy. As he makes his way through the South he bestows distinct dialect to characters within his narrative according to physical characteristics and class—very much *à la* Stowe. When he seeks to rent accommodations from a proprietor whom he describes as "a big, fat, greasy looking brown-skinned man" (24), and he stipulates his intentions to only stay for two or three days, he reports the proprietor's response: "Oh, dat's all right den . . . You kin sleep in dat cot in de corner der. Fifty cents please" (24). The role of language that the ex-coloured man has established is one that he links to region, race, color, and social class. He attempts to shape the reader's perception of not only his travels, but also the people he encounters through the strategic use of dialect. Through the shift between dialect and King's English, he makes himself distinct from others as he sees fit, maintaining a class-based, cultural, and, arguably, a race-based segregation at his will and pleasure. Even when jumping transnational lines through what he perceives as cultural immersion, the ex-coloured man uses language to distinguish himself, in the process either refusing to connect or unwilling to do so. Interestingly, within the mire of dialect, the cost of the room is crystal clear. Anything to do with money is not lost in translation for the ex-coloured man and, as this passage indicates, he clearly understands the language of economic exchange. He does not, however, understand the true worth or true cost of things.

The ex-coloured man has never been taught to internalize "culture" or "race," and he learns about both through surface observation and through the superficial reading and analysis of books. He can observe either only through the surface reading of physical signs such as color, phenotype, and class signifiers, as well as through aural signs such as language, which he immediately recognizes as having the power to shift the perception of others in terms of bodily readability, interpretation, taxonomy, and legal identity. There is, however, some value and accuracy in some of the ex-coloured man's observations. As he becomes more acquainted with his co-workers in the cigar factory and he begins to learn about some Cuban history, he begins to distinguish the difference in how race is read in Cuba as opposed to how it is read in the United States. As he converses with one of his Cuban co-workers, they touch on the subject of Cuban independence. This being the "subject nearest his [companion's] heart," the ex-coloured man describes his co-worker's story:

> He was an exile from the island, and a prominent member of the Jacksonville *Junta*. Every week sums of money were collected from *juntas* all over the country. This money went to buy arms and ammunition for the insurgents. As the man sat there nervously smoking his long, "green" cigar, and telling me of the Gomezes, both the white one and the black one, of Maceo and Bandera, he grew positively eloquent.[1] (33)

The reference to the Cuban Revolution reflects Johnson's own exposure to and knowledge of the Cuban exile community in Jacksonville as well as knowledge of the political organizing that went on in cigar-factory communities and in the cigar factories themselves. It also indicates a consistent character sketch of an ex-coloured man who cannot read beyond the surface and insists on distinguishing and segregating according to race. This is especially pronounced given his highlighting of the "white" and "black" Gómezes (Máximo Gómez and Juan Gualberto Gómez, respectively). The ex-coloured man notes here how names do not distinguish one Gómez from the other, and it is unclear whether it is he or his co-worker who mentions "color" in a Cuban context—a curious insertion, because Juan Gómez is famous not only for the fight for Cuban independence, but also for pushing forth the idea of *el hombre sin adjetivo* [man without adjective]. Nonetheless, the ex-coloured man notes that these men are spoken of in the context of Cuban nationalism with no compromise of citizenship, duty, or honor. He realizes, just as he did at the breakfast table at which language seemed to congeal a group while transcending cultural boundaries, that here lies a take on race and culture far different from that of the dominant U.S. culture, and that there are competing concepts of peoplehood.

As these "border crossings" are linked to and facilitated by language, the ex-coloured man finds it necessary to learn the Spanish language. He documents his method and process for learning, and painstakingly describes how his landlord helps him learn Spanish, how he practices with his colleagues at the cigar factory, and how he begins to read Cuban newspapers and Spanish literature. "I was able in less than a year to speak like a native," he boasts, and concludes his bluster by letting the reader know, "it was my pride that I spoke better Spanish than many of the Cuban workmen at the factory" (34). Although the ex-coloured man's linguistic gifts mirror Johnson's facility with language, it is clear, within the context of the novel, that his being able to speak "better" Spanish than any of his co-workers is an impossibility. This assertion suggests that the ex-coloured man associates the mastery of language with the mastery of grammar and speech. In other words, for the ex-coloured man, to speak "correct" Spanish means to speak a standardized Castilian Spanish, an insensitive bias that privileges Spain at a time when Cuba strives for its independence, and that simultaneously betrays his ignorance about culture(s) and language variance, as well as his superficial understanding of language, idioms, culture, and affiliation. His preoccupation with "purity" of language hint at his internalized notions of racial purity, and his perception of himself as essentially soiled and split.

"I had formulated a theory of what it was to be colored, no I was getting the practice," declares the ex-coloured man (34). His theory about what it is to be "colored," what it means to be "raced," differs from and becomes a resistance to the imposition of race and taxonomy in the United States, much like the resistance to the one-drop rule on the part of Latin Americans as described by F. James Davis: "many Hispanic Americans with black ancestry resist the rule if they can" (133). Davis describes a consequent sort of compromise: "[Latin Americans] may accept and make use of the marginal status position, adopting a marginal identity rather than a black identity, perceiving and dealing objectively with the black and the white communities both while not being fully a part of either, and often being a liaison person between the two" (150). Davis's language suggests a deviation from "the rules," and thus an imperialistic imposition of law and social mores on a people who do not subscribe to the one-drop rule. The cigar-factory town and the factory's cultural space provide an alternative culture that defies the U.S. culture at large. Indeed, the ex-coloured man gets practice in being "colored" or, more precisely, *of color* in the United States, and yet is able to remain outside the margins of what it means to be legally black. Armed with the Spanish language, the ex-coloured man can and will put theory into practice.

After traveling to Europe as a wealthy man's companion, the ex-coloured man finds himself in the South once again, and experiences a horror that will mark the second turning point in his life. He witnesses a man being dragged into town, and just as rope is put around his neck, someone yells, "Burn him!" (88). As people scramble for fuel, oil, and the torch, the ex-coloured man describes that the man was "too stunned and stupefied even to tremble" (88). But then the writhing begins, as do the groans and screams. All the while, the ex-coloured man stands powerless, fixed to the spot where he witnesses not only the murder, but also the yells and cheers from the crowd. The horror of this murder and of witnessing this atrocity do not turn into rage for the ex-coloured man. Curiously, his horror turns to shame: "A great wave of humiliation and shame swept over me. Shame that I belonged to a race that could be so dealt with; and shame for my country, that it, the great example of democracy to the world should be the only state on earth, where a human being would be burned alive" (88). The ex-coloured man may have suspected the existence of a national and formative narrative of peoplehood that excluded him, but this moment confirms his suspicions and his role within said national story. As he projects himself onto the man being lynched, he is stripped of his human worth, and inextricably confined within national boundaries.

If, for the ex-coloured man, identity means nothing beyond surface readings of culture that can be performed through language masquerades, and has nothing to do with community and familial ties, then the ex-coloured man's words in which he describes his (in)action after the lynching take on a sadder and more profound meaning: "When I decided to get up and go back to the house I found that I could hardly stand on my feet. I was as weak as a man who had lost blood" (89). The words are simultaneously metaphoric and prophetic. The ex-coloured man projects himself onto the lynched body because, despite his masquerade, he still feels a part of the African American community, thus illustrating the limits of jumping cultural lines and making theater out of language, culture and identity.

"I was occupied in debating with myself the step which I had decided to take," the ex-coloured man remembers. "I argued that to forsake one's race to better one's condition was no less worthy an action than to forsake one's country for the same purpose" (90). After he deliberates, he finally comes to the conclusion that seals his fate, which is to be neither "black" nor "white," and yet at the same time to reject neither: "I finally made up my mind that

I would neither disclaim the black race nor claim the white race" (90). This passage refutes literary critics who argue that the ex-coloured man decides to pass for "white" upon witnessing the lynching. In fact, he continues to describe his somewhat passive intentions, stating, "I would change my name, raise a mustache, and let the world take me for that it would; that it was not necessary for me to go about with a label of inferiority pasted across my forehead" (90). Indeed, the ex-coloured man decides to participate in what I can only describe as "passive passing," since he decides to let the world read his identity as it wills, imposing taxonomic categorization and value on his body as deemed by changing social mores and fashion.

Neil Brookes claims that the passing is not simply a theatrical performance or an impersonation. Rather, he states, it is the "physical manifestation of a psychological quest to understand oneself in a society where to be black was often not to have one consistent self but to have a double self" (86). To Brookes's call for a psychological understanding of passing as an act in which the subject negotiates his own identity, I add that for Johnson the act is most importantly an act of social defiance and legal resistance. The position claiming that the passing subject is an imposter who violates a racial and social contract, assumes a racial and essential self that must be legally defined and segregated. This is a position that works only domestically, within the parameters of the one-drop rule, and that falls apart in the Latin Americas and in the context of being Latin American.

This act of legal and social defiance is less admirable in light of the ex-coloured man's economic ambitions: "I had made up my mind that since I was not going to be a Negro, I would avail myself of every possible opportunity to make a white man's success; and that, if it can be summed up in any one word, means 'money' " (91). Economic capital is less valuable than the cultural capital gained in being "non-black." The ex-coloured man "betters [his] condition" by acquiring a position in the South American department of a downtown wholesale house in New York, and here he rhapsodizes on his good luck: "My knowledge of Spanish was, of course, the principal cause of my good luck; and it did more for me; it placed me where the other clerks were practically put out of competition with me" (91–92). Beyond winning him a coveted position, the Spanish language also allows him to be not only non-black, but, in fact, "Latin American." He attempts to transcend a bifurcated identity or a sense of internal race segregation through the creation of what he perceives to be a third space, which provides space for legal transgression and repudiation, but nonetheless garners him access to white cultural capital.

For the ex-coloured man, culture trumps race, as he learns in the cigar factory, and culture is malleable and can be performed. Because he conflates culture and identity, identity is also malleable and can be performed as well.

All notions of identity remain at a surface level for the ex-coloured man, something of which he never seems quite conscious until he meets and falls in love with a white woman. It is then that he worries, "up to this time I had assumed and played my rôle as *a white man* with a certain degree of nonchalance, a carelessness as to the outcome. . . . My acting had called for mere external effects. Now I began to doubt my ability to play the part" (94, emphasis added). It is not until he falls in love with and begins to court a white woman that he explicitly describes himself as "a white man." This is the climatic moment that he consciously crosses an invisible line that seals his fate. The ex-coloured man turns his head from Latin America as a locus of adoptable identity and a livable life, eastward toward Europe instead. The ex-coloured man's union with the white woman in conjunction with North American and European perception that deemed Latin Americans racially and culturally inferior could explain his shift in geographical focal point. According to Smith, the perception that Latin Americans were inferior to North Americans or to Europeans was because of the "biological and cultural admixture with indigenous peoples and imported Africans" (107). In shifting his gaze from Latin America to Europe, the ex-coloured man moves from the perception of having probable African and indigenous ancestry at some point in his lineage, toward making that ancestry improbable. In other words, he lightens and probably whitens assumptions about his ancestry, whether to the outside world, to his children, or to his created self.

The possibility of identitarian freedom in a third space is lost for the ex-coloured man upon declaring himself white and in making the conscious decision to confine himself to a white life upon marrying this woman. Before marriage and during courtship, he confesses himself to her, however. He states, "under the strange light in her eyes I felt that I was growing black and thick-featured and crimp-haired" (96). Soon after, he confesses his shameful truth: "This was the only time in my life that I ever felt absolute regret at being colored, that I cursed the drops of African blood in my veins, and wished that I were *really* white" (96–97 emphasis added). The two eventually marry and they have two children—a girl, whose description he quickly glosses over, only noting that she has "hair and eyes dark like mine," and a boy, upon whose description he sensuously lingers: "fair like his mother, a little golden-headed god, a face and head that would have delighted the heart of an old Italian master" (99). It seems at first that the ex-coloured man lingers on the description of his son because he is so much like his white mother, but on closer examination, it is clear that the ex-coloured man has linked the child to himself with the genealogical language of fantastical ancestry. Consider, for example, the description of his son's face and head as something that would have delighted an old "Italian master," and the ex-coloured man's description of himself that just precedes that of his son: "I am certain, too, that, in spite of my Italian-like complexion, I was as red as a beet" (93).

The repetition of the Italianate descriptions serve multiple purposes: His subtle self-description, coupled with that of his son's, further his own passing and assures his son's social, racial, and cultural positions as non-black. This passage also betrays the ex-coloured man's moving away from an ambiguous racial identity, to one that is firmly rooted in Europe, a subtle movement that is also exhibited in the European spelling of the novel's title, and of the words "rôle" and "programme" toward the end of the narrative.[2] The ex-coloured man's wife dies giving birth to this "god"-like son, and the ex-coloured man is left alone, locked in a white world with an identity that is both secret and a public performance. He reflects, "it is difficult for me to analyze my feelings concerning my present position in the world. Sometimes it seems to me that I have never really been a Negro, that I have been only a privileged spectator of their inner life; at other times I feel that I have been a coward, a deserter, and I am possessed by a strange longing for my mother's people" (99). In the end, he observes, "I am an ordinarily successful white man who has made a little money . . . I have sold my birthright for a mess of pottage" (99–100). Most critics tie the selling of his birthright with implied denial of his African American heritage as he consciously enters the "white" world. Jennifer Schulz, for example, argues, "Johnson's work confirms that one cannot refuse participation in the racial contract; to attempt to do so is to mistakenly believe that one can remake oneself entirely—transcend the racial contract—simply by changing geographical location, passing for white, or reclassing oneself" (34). The notion of the racial contract described here must be put into the context of an arbitrary national narrative in which one group forces another into subservience in order to define themselves as a people. Moreover, Johnson situates this racial contract in transnational contexts, in the process calling into question its irrevocability, its validity, and the foundational fictions that make up the national narrative.

"Trespassing with a false passport"

Johnson negotiates blurred borderlines—racial, national, and legal—with his depiction of the polyglot progeny. In the process, Johnson explores the pull of cultural ties and national ties when pitted against intolerable, domestic living conditions and the promise of utopia across national lines. Some critics such as W. Lawrence Hogue, however, have blurred the line between author and character, thus aligning Johnson's race and color politics with that of the fictional ex-coloured man's, going so far as to charge Johnson with performing for a white audience:

in this attempt to reassimilate back into this regime the ex-coloured man and Johnson, wishing to uplift the race by showing how African Americans can practice the values of the dominant society and thereby prove to white people their worthiness of respect and social equality, establish a hierarchy within African America that privileges those African Americans who approximate or come closer to the mainstream norm and that rejects and crushes the subaltern African American life—life that is different, that exists outside the lines of mobility that extend into mainstream American life. (70–71)

Hogue's contention is possible and even probable as it applies to the fundamental ideas on segregation of both Johnson and his fictional character. Both use language to segregate and categorize, and both can manipulate language to position and reposition themselves in the legal context of segregation laws. Their ultimate respective choices, as they straddle blurred racial, ethnic, national, and legal borderlines, take them in different directions, and yet set them in the same ideological position with regard to segregation.

Legal scholar Cheryl I. Harris's theory on propertied whiteness is helpful in explaining Johnson's self-policing and the ex-coloured man's self-flagellation in how they negotiate the color line, whether internationally or domestically. Harris sees U.S. race laws as rooted in the successful effort to give property value to whiteness. If whiteness is thus property, passing into the white world, Harris asserts, is "not merely passing, but *tres*passing" (1711). Moreover, she states, it is trespassing with a "false passport" (1711). The idea of trespassing with a false passport is an important one, for in ignoring a third and alternative identitarian space, it assumes the internalization of a binary concept of race and subsequent segregation of the two races. While abroad, Johnson must still survey with a segregating and a segregated eye, and although he observes the porosity of race and race categories, he will only do so from a removed position. This is also the ex-coloured man's constant stance and subject position. For both, language may garner access to a more malleable identity, but the segregated self is never malleable and, in fact, concretizes his space and legal place in the world, even drawing the line that separates him from others. Language can be interpreted and translated, but culture cannot. The pull of national narratives may determine the ultimate confinement of the ex-coloured man. It may also inform Johnson's segregated and segregating language while in the Latin Americas. But Latin America and other transnational spaces within Johnson's own narratives—whether in his novel or in his memoir—rupture this very narrative and expose its politics of peoplehood as fatally flawed. Most importantly, these border crossings expose national fictions as just that.

Notes

1. The "Gomezes" are Máximo Gómez Báez: (1836–1905) and Juan Gualberto Gómez (1854–1933) respectively, and the other revolutionaries are Antonio Maceo y Grajales (1845–1896)—leader of the Mambi Army and known as "the Bronze Titan"—and Quintín Bandera Betancourt (1833–1906), his second in command. "Mambi" is from the Congo language—it is estimated that ninety-two percent of Cubans who participated in the Mambi Army were Cubans of African decent. The Mambi Army defeated Spain through two wars (1868 to 1878 and then again from 1895 to 1898), and is known as the National Army of Liberation as well as "Maceo's Army."

2. Although the Italian identity was declared legally "white" in cases such as *Rollins v. Alabama* (1922), when Johnson wrote his novel, it was also subject to questioning, exclusion, and violence. Matthew Frye Jacobson documents in *Whiteness of a Different Color: European Immigrants and the Alchemy of Race* (1998) the debate over which Europeans were and were not to be granted "white" status following mass European migration to the United States from 1840 to 1924. The Immigration Act of 1924 severely restricted the immigration of Europeans from southern and eastern Europe, and targeted Jews in particular. Virginia's "Racial Integrity" Act of 1924, rooted in the eugenics movement, banned non-white blood from the "white race."

Works Cited

Brookes, Neil. "On Becoming an Ex-Colored Man: Postmodern Irony and the Extinguishing of Certainties in *The Autobiography of an Ex-Coloured Man.*" *Illicit Sex—Identity Politics in Early Modern Culture*. Ed. Thomas Di Piero and Pat Gill. Athens, GA: U of Georgia P, 1997: 84–97.

Davis, F. James. *Who is Black? One Nation's Definition*. University Park: Penn State UP, 1991.

Harris, Cheryl I. "Whiteness as Property." *Harvard Law Review* 106.8 (1993): 1707–91.

Hogue, W. Lawrence. "Finding Freedom in Sameness: James Weldon Johnson's *The Autobiography of an Ex-Coloured Man.*" *The African American Male, Writing, and Difference*. Albany: State U of New York P, 2003. 67–92.

Johnson, James Weldon. *Along This Way*. New York: Da Capo P: 2000.

———. *Autobiography of an Ex-Coloured Man*. New York: Dover, 1995.

Pitt-Rivers, Julian. "Race, Color, and Class in Central America and the Andes." *Essays on Mexico, Central and South America: Scholarly Debates from the 1950s to the 1990s*. Ed. Jorge I. Domínguez. New York: Garland, 1994. 56–73.

Schulz, Jennifer L. "Restaging the Racial Contract: James Weldon Johnson's Signatory Strategies." *American Literature* 74.1 (2002): 31–58.

Smith, Rogers M. *Stories of Peoplehood: The Politics and Morals of Political Membership*. Cambridge, UK: Cambridge UP, 2003.

Stepto, Robert B. *From Behind the Veil: A Study of Afro-American Narrative*. Chicago: U of Illinois P, 1979.

Wagley, Charles. "On the Concept of Social Race in the Americas." *Essays on Mexico, Central and South America: Scholarly Debates from the 1950s to the 1990s.* Ed. Jorge I. Domínguez. New York: Garland, 1994. 13–27.

Washington, Booker T. *Up From Slavery.* 1901. Ed. William L. Andrews. New York: Oxford UP, 1995.

In the Crowd series, Untitled #5 (Oklahoma, 1911). Archival ink print, 14 × 11 inches. Image courtesy of the artist, Shawn Michelle Smith.

Section V

Jim Crow's Legacy

This final section explores "Jim Crow's legacy" in order to attend to the way segregation may not fit into the discrete historical era of Jim Crow segregation. This heeds Moody's crucial reminder that race segregation precedes the Jim Crow era and Harris's ominous contention in Section I that segregation persists today. To that end, Zoe Trodd considers civil rights photography to identify an aesthetic of protesting segregation, which she places in a long literary and political history that connects civil rights and abolitionist aesthetics. As Trodd imagines segregation beyond the literary and so fleshes out one way segregation's legacy is constructed and then reconstructed, Vince Schleitwiler takes a cross-ethnic approach to segregation literatures by juxtaposing an autobiographical account of racially motivated violence in Los Angeles by a second-generation Japanese American with Chester Himes's fictional accounts of similar acts in that same era. He explores how reflective forums, such as autobiography written after the end of legal segregation in America, must address the problem of remembering the end of a system whose effects are still alive and well. In this way, Schleitwiler's study most directly heeds Harris's reminder that segregation never died.

In Possession of Space

Abolitionist Memory and Spatial Transformation in Civil Rights Literature and Photography

ZOE TRODD

[P]hotographs . . . help people to take possession of space in which they are insecure. . . . In a world ruled by photographic images, all borders . . . seem arbitrary.

—Susan Sontag, 1977

In 1966, after more than a decade of demonstrations that retook the streets of Montgomery, Birmingham, Albany, and Selma, Langston Hughes celebrated Frederick Douglass's ability to "capture every street/ On which he set his feet." Affirming Douglass's ongoing participation in the civil rights movement, Hughes added: "He died in 1895./ *He is not dead*" (21).

With his description of activist feet retaking the streets, Hughes points to the battle for space that was at the heart of the movement. Whether participating in Freedom Rides, bus boycotts, sit-ins, or street demonstrations, civil rights activists battled for space. This was the physical space of buses, public schools, and lunch counters. Rosa Parks remained in her seat on a Montgomery bus in 1955, the Little Rock Nine crossed the line drawn on the street in 1957, and in 1960 Ruby Bridges integrated William Frantz Public School while four freshmen in Greensboro staged a lunch counter sit-in. But, as Hughes affirmed in another poem, the space at the heart of the desegregation battle was also *symbolic*: "There is a dream in the land/ With its back against the wall. . . . Our dream of freedom," wrote Hughes, fashioning a spatio-symbolic confinement of the "dream" by a "wall" (1964, 108). Civil rights artists, photographers and writers—including Hughes—fused these literal and figurative notions of space into an aesthetic of spatio-symbolism. The civil rights movement emerged in their protest literature as a struggle for literal, desegregated space *and* for entry into what Martin Luther King Jr., called in 1956 a "choice place" or in 1968 the "promised land" ("The 'New Negro' " 286); the site where Hughes's "dream of freedom" was unwalled.

One element of this desegregation aesthetic was the spatialization of social margins. A literary landscape of manholes, coalbunkers, sewers, kitchenettes, shacks, and boxes offered a vision of what Rob Shields terms "places on the margin . . . the periphery of cultural systems of space" (3). These holes and confined spaces in civil rights protest literature worked from the known *place* to the figurative *space*; an example of "physical extent fused through with social intent" (Smith 16). To examine civil rights protest literature for its spatio-symbolism is therefore to respond to Liam Kennedy's charge that although "our common understanding of space is that it is simply there, intangible but given," we should instead consider space as an indicator of "embedded ideologies" (8).

A second target of this aesthetic was historical marginalization: a pervasive narrative that ignored "the contribution of the Negro in American history" (41), as King protested in 1967. Spatio-symbolic representations translated Walter Benjamin's notion of *Geschichtsraum*, "the space of history" (458), into a topographic cultural symbol that remembered history's exclusions and challenged the narrative of American progress. Frequently renarrating the history of slavery, artists and writers claimed segregation as slavery by a different name. And, as well as a long history of oppression, they summoned a palpable protest past—locating the civil rights battle on a continuum with nineteenth-century abolitionism. As Hughes insisted, Douglass was "not dead." Artists and writers rejected the notion of activist discontinuity, opened access to a past that, as Douglass said in 1852, might be made "useful to the present and to the future" (366), and awakened the abolitionists in order to help narrow the space between American ideals and segregated reality. They offered *protest memory* as memory *of* protest and memory used *to* protest.

The relationship of civil rights artists to Douglass and other abolitionists runs deeper still. The deep space of black history was *itself* a history of spatio-symbolic representation. As they reimagined the spaces of segregated America, civil rights artists drew upon a key strand of the abolitionist aesthetic: the fusion of concrete boundaries with the abstract boundaries of democratic citizenship. They turned the historical memory of abolitionist literature's confined spaces into a tool for the open future. Finally, then, to uncover the hole stories of abolitionist and civil rights literature is to reveal fusions of space and historical memory that challenge Pierre Nora's famous formulations in "Between Memory and History" (1989). Nora argues that *lieux de mémoire* have replaced *milieux de mémoire*. Whereas *milieux de mémoire* had provided "environments of memory," which were "explicative," *lieux de mémoire* offer mere "sites" of memory (9, 7): memory removed from its historical context, stripped of any living presence, and used for static commemoration. But civil rights protest literature reveals a spatialized and "explicative" memory that "smoothes the transition from past to future [and] indicates what the future should retain from the past" (Nora and

Kritzman 2)—the ongoing presence of *milieux de mémoire*. Looking backward in order to move America forward, artists and writers challenged the historically segregated spaces of America's social and civic spheres with the integrated time of its living protest history.[1]

The Abolitionists' Spatial Aesthetic

Abolitionists rooted their culture of dissent in aesthetics as well as ideologies. One element of their aesthetic was spatio-symbolic representation. Whether the crevices in the tavern, the mantraps of the decaying portico, and Madison Washington's cave in Douglass's *The Heroic Slave* (1853), the "loophole" in Harriet Jacobs's *Incidents* (1861), or Harriet Wilson's descriptions of Frado's tiny L-shaped room in *Our Nig* (1861), abolitionist literature and art included an early version of the segregation trope.

For example, one series of images revolved around Henry "Box" Brown's famous escape. Updating the imagery of the Middle Passage, visual artists of the 1850s portrayed Brown climbing out of the box in which he escaped, and accompanied such lithographs with metaphors fashioning the infamous box as slavery's psychological and spiritual suffocation.[2] In one image, Brown emerges from a crate as abolitionists look on (Figure 10), whereas some lithographs depicted just the box. A variant on the theme depicted the child Lear Green escaping in a trunk. Fashioning the box as slavery's confinements writ large, Brown himself described his emergence from the box as a "resurrection from

Figure 10. "The resurrection of Henry Box Brown at Philadelphia, who escaped from Richmond Va. in a bx 3 feet long 2¹/₂ ft. deep and 2 ft wide," 1850, lithograph published by A. Donnelly, New York. *Courtesy Library of Congress, Prints and Photographs Division.*

the grave of slavery" (57) and echoed this metaphor through an observation that slavery "shuts up every avenue of hope" (45).

Brown offered a spatial reversal, too. The box symbolizes slavery's literal and social confinements but also is a site of literary resistance. While observing that he "felt much more than I could readily express" upon his "resurrection" from the box (57), the song Brown composes (which appears almost immediately after this note that he couldn't "express" everything) puns on the idea of expression: "No more Slave work for Henry Box Brown,/ In the box by *Express* he did go" (60). Reversing the idea of having no ready expression, the box moves by "express." Brown also includes the line: "Brown laid down the shovel and the hoe,/ Down in the box he did go" (60). He then explains this line in the narrative's appendix, which outlines a story. God gave mankind two bags, the black man chose the large one, "and the white man, coming up afterwards, got the smaller one." The two men untied their bags. In the large one "there was a shovel and a hoe," and in the small one, "a pen, ink, and paper" (appendix ii). By echoing the small space of the box with this description of the "small" bag, Brown implies that after laying down *his* "shovel and hoe" and entering the box, he entered the white man's space of pen, ink, and paper.

Visual artists expressed a similar faith in the power of spatial resistance and reversal. For example, in December 1860, *Harper's Weekly* published a woodcut of "Negroes and abolitionists" being chased out of a meeting in Tremont Temple, Boston (Figure 11). The purpose of the meeting, attended

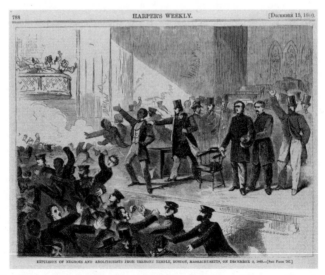

Figure 11. "Expulsion of Negroes and Abolitionists from Tremont Temple, Boston, Massachusetts, on December 3, 1860." *Harper's Weekly*, December 15, 1860. *Courtesy Library of Congress, Prints and Photographs Division.*

by Douglass and William Lloyd Garrison, was to commemorate the anniversary of John Brown's execution; however it was broken up by a mob. Expelling the abolitionists, members of the mob passed a resolution condemning Brown's raid. But the image reclaims both the public space of Tremont Temple and the history that the abolitionists had gathered to celebrate. It is composed on three different levels: ground, stage, and balcony. The abolitionists fight back as they are beaten away from the stage on the ground level. On the stage level, one black abolitionist remains standing. He lifts an arm and extends a leg, spreading himself across the three spatial levels: his right arm reaches up to the balcony, where another abolitionist's arm reaches down (as though forging a connection across the space between), and his left leg pushes down toward the ground level, where another abolitionist's fist reaches up (again, closing the space between). The image's perspective across three levels means that the space between the fist on the ground level and the leg on the stage is small—about the size of the policeman's head, which is positioned between them to the right of the fist. This connecting triangle across the space between is an expression of spatial resistance, amid slavery's confinements and the disruption of this commemorative space. In continuing to forge connections across the image's three spatial levels, the black abolitionist proclaims both that resistance victorious. He remains on stage. The empty chair at the center of the image, a conspicuously unoccupied space, suddenly seems to hold Brown's ghost.

Within the abolitionist aesthetic, the trope of confined space also revealed and challenged the country's narrative of historical progress. For example, in 1854 William Wells Brown described his "countrymen . . . groaning in the prison-house of slavery" (303). Then in 1863 Brown connected space and historical memory, explaining of Crispus Attucks: "No monument has yet been erected to him. . . . When negro slavery shall be abolished in our land, then we may hope to see a monument raised" (109–10). If not the space of a "monument," Brown's own memorialization creates a space beyond the "prison-house of slavery" in public memory. As well, in reminding his readers of the approaching emancipation (*"shall be* abolished"), Brown suggests that Attucks may well live on in the example of abolitionists. As a living history, not a static monument, the example of Attucks might help create space for slaves in history's pantheon and the future's citizenship.

Brown's discussion of Attucks was one of many abolitionist invocations of Revolutionary-era protest, many of which pointed to the gap between the Declaration's ideals of equality and the ongoing fact of slavery.[3] For example, Brown's own *Clotel* (1853) evokes the horror of July 4th for slaves. " 'You make merry on the 4th of July,' " says George. " 'Yet . . . one-sixth of the people of this land are in chains' " (225). In his autobiography, Brown also explained that the American people "boast of their freedom" but "keep three millions of their own citizens in chains." He added: "while I am seated here in sight of Bunker

Hill Monument . . . I am a slave" (103). Brown saw the risk of summoning 1776 while citizens were in "chains." Returning to America's origins as a protest nation without ending slavery made 1776 a mere stillbirth.

In spatial terms, this act of remembering a revolution without completing its process had created an "aberration within the national narrative by the trope of parenthesis," as Russ Castronovo puts it. "The structure of parenthesis," explains Castronovo, sums up "the political culture of the antebellum era. . . . 1776 became the pure, originary past, allowing America to remain in continuous temporal and ideological harmony with its own genesis" (533–34). Like other literary abolitionists, Brown wanted to lift slavery from a structure of parenthesis and to summon the "originary past" in order to change—rather than validate—the present. His narrative, written "in sight of Bunker Hill," might remove that contradiction of "freedom" and "chains."

Segregation and Spatio-Symbolism

One hundred years later, a loop of memory back to those chains under girded much civil rights rhetoric. In 1961, James Lawson observed that "after 300 years, segregation (slavery) is still a basic pattern" (1) and Marion Wright, vice president of the Southern Regional Council, suggested that every age presents a "moral issue"—slavery was that issue in the nineteenth century and its "offspring, segregation, poses such an issue in the Twentieth Century" (438). Some connected the seemingly ever-present shadows of slavery to images of confined space: Diane Nash described feeling "stifled and boxed in since so many areas of living were restricted" as a result of the "system of slavery and human abasement" (68, 69).

Black Americans still were not free. Yet, far more often than observing the continuing influence of America's slave past, civil rights rhetoric positioned the memory of slaves' courage and stamina as a stimulus for activism. Using the imagery of a dark hole in 1964, Ralph Abernathy reminded his audience that their forefathers were "kidnapped and brought here . . . to face the future in a strange land . . . to launch out in the dark and dim unknown even as . . . a fox without a hole." But, he added, even when "they were sold . . . they could envision a reunion in a land just beyond the river" (731, 732). Using historical memory in the same way the following year, the Brooklyn minister Gardner Taylor remembered scenes of slavery in the present tense and reminded his congregation that slaves would yet sing: "Before I'd be a slave/ I'd be buried in my grave/ And go home to my Lord/ And be free." Then Taylor asked that today's activists might "be equal to this issue with which our lives are met" (919). With stories of slave resistance came memories of abolitionism. In a speech about the Montgomery Bus Boycott, Horace Mann Bond noted that the abolitionists "saved America," went on to pay tribute to Lucretia Mott, John Greenleaf Whittier, Theodore Weld, and Angelina Grimké, and concluded that the movement shows "the talent we have received from the 19th century"—that it was part of a "noble heritage" (184, 186).

One function of this protest memory was to combat the use of historical memory by segregationists: "We are proud of our white blood. . . . If we are bigoted . . . so were George Washington, Thomas Jefferson, Abraham Lincoln and our other illustrious forebears who believed in segregation," noted one Association of Citizens' Councils pamphlet (n.p.). Erasing the history of black activism, another Citizens' Council pamphlet insisted that African Americans had played no part in U.S. history; had made no contribution to the Revolution, the War of 1812, the settling of the West, or the Civil War.

Still, another function of abolitionist awakenings was to counter America's confined spaces with the deep space of its protest memory. A spatio-symbolic rhetoric of confinement and immobility loomed large. Echoing the abolitionist aesthetic of space, civil rights representation both embodied the civil rights movement's struggle for space and tried to advance that struggle by expanding its scope to include an abolitionist presence. For example, setting up the stakes, numerous artists, writers and speechmakers summoned images of literal confined space and employed metaphors of confinement—turning physical space into figurative space. Some writers spatialized the idea of marginalization in the nation's founding documents. Carl T. Rowan noted that during and since slavery, African Americans have been "waiting for the day when the Constitution would be big enough to serve as a hiding place" (129). Or, like Douglass's famous memory of writing on sidewalks as a child, others saw the struggle written across the landscape. George Leonard noted that during his flight to Selma after "Bloody Sunday," March 7, 1965, he looked down, realized that the nation consisted "mostly of open space," and knew that this was appropriate for "America is still unfinished . . . a series of hopeful statements ending with question marks" (503).

For their part, visual artists repeatedly echoed the imagery of fences, walls, and decaying buildings in abolitionist print culture. In a cartoon published in November 1958, Bill Mauldin used a rundown schoolhouse as a metaphor for the disintegration of public school systems and as a commentary on the actions of Little Rock in establishing private schools to circumvent the U.S. Court of Appeals for the Eighth Circuit. Two years later, Maudlin signaled partial progress by adding a door to his confined spaces: an image from 1960 shows three tiny figures pushing open a giant door on which is written "School Segregation." The cartoonist Herb Block sounded a call to progress, too. His image "And remember, nothing can be accomplished by taking to the streets," published in

September 1963, shows a white figure pushing a black man off the sidewalk into the gutter; symbolizing the new but fragile civic space in the wake of President Kennedy's civil rights address and the Freedom March on Washington, August 28, 1963. Yet, although the black figure is pushed, his feet remain on the sidewalk, his shadow on its vast white space. And although the two figures are still surrounded by "restricted" buildings, the caption reminds us that in "taking to the streets," protestors—like the black figure in the image—have begun to confront restriction.

In addition to these speeches and cartoons, photographs performed another imaginative overthrow of segregated space. The Student Nonviolent Coordinating Committee (SNCC) image-text titled *The Movement* (1964), with text by Lorraine Hansberry, forged a space for civil rights and opened the space of abolitionist history.[4] The book opens by setting up the long history of a gap between ideal and reality, with photographs of a monument and a caption noting: "between the towns, familiar images of the Old South are conjured up" (8). In these liminal spaces of the countryside, where history has not yet caught up to the present, race relations occupy as static a space as the monument. A photograph of large house, positioned behind a wire fence follows. The area beyond the fence is overgrown and unkempt, pointing to the ongoing segregation of space—either side of a color line—in the South. Continuing the theme of historic and unchanging spatial division, another early caption observes: "The New South slams up against the Old, but the coming of industry into the Southland has not changed the problems" (13). A photograph of a bleak landscape and a dilapidated shack confirms that history is so stationary it has started to decay.

After laying out this static space of history, the book shifts direction. One photograph shows a stop sign with the word "segregation" scrawled across it (so it reads "STOP SEGREGATION") (37) and another shows a line of marchers who move past the "one-way" sign in the opposite direction (38). As though these reclamations of space have emerged out of a protest history, the text explains: "Negroes picked up the aspiration of their fathers, rekindled it, and started marching" (42). These "fathers" were abolitionists and slave rebels. Hansberry observes beneath a photograph of older protestors that the "Negro aspiration" is "integration into the fabric of a nation which our slave fathers helped to create" (50). Adding over the page that the "Movement is very old," Hansberry explains that "it took the form of sabotage, escape and insurrection" during slavery and now just has "fresh determination" (50). This series of abolitionist awakenings ends with a photograph of James Baldwin, poised in front of a microphone, his mouth open, opposite a page of quotations from a "Negro slave insurrectionist," Turner, Douglass, and a nineteenth-century "Negro minister" (50), as though the quotes have come from Baldwin's mouth.

Toward the end of the book, Hansberry fuses the middle section on historic protest and the opening message of historical stagnation into an explanation that one must counter the other. A caption notes that "the ways of the *old* order have not changed" (57) and accompanies a photograph of an Alabama state trooper with a Confederate flag on his helmet. The "ways" of abolitionist protest are therefore needed to match the ongoing Confederate mentality. The only way to combat one element of the living past—segregation—is with another: abolitionism. Concluding that the "Movement has been influenced by the spirit of Frederick Douglass, who associated the abolition of slavery with human rights everywhere" (114), the image-text situates its hope for a future end to segregated space in the memory of an abolitionist past.

Most photographers, however, worked outside the image-text medium. SNCC enlisted and trained a dozen photographers, also organizing exhibitions.[5] The Southern Christian Leadership Conference (SCLC) supported a few photographers, as did the Congress of Racial Equality. Some leaders took photographs themselves, like Wyatt Walker and Andrew Young of SCLC or James Forman and Robert Zellner of SNCC, and photographs appeared as posters, were printed in pamphlets and displayed in freedom houses. Outside the civil rights movement, Gordon Parks, Charles Moore, and Frank Dandridge photographed its events and figures for *Life,* Moneta Sleet for *Ebony,* and Marion Trikosko for *U.S. News and World Report Magazine.*[6]

Many of these civil rights photographs offered a glimpse of spatial resistance. In an image from the March on Washington, Nat Herz depicts a lone black child in the middle of a flight of steps. The vast white steps dwarf the child, and the presence of bars and a line of white policemen makes the space around him even more perilous. Herz later observed that the picture symbolized, for him, the problems that remained after the March that day. Yet the child in Herz's image holds several planks of wood, indicating a reconstruction of the empty and inaccessible spaces in the photograph.

Marion Trikosko's images from the March on Washington are particularly focused on spatio-symbolic demarcation. One is bisected at the midpoint by a storm fence, behind which demonstrators crowd (Figure 12). A sign is torn in half on the ground, with the word "right" still visible. The segregating fence visually echoes the sign: tearing across the half-way point of the image, the fence is its own symbol of "rights" destroyed. But after witnessing this fenced-off crowd and the poignant sight of a demonstrator's abandoned shoe (next to the sign on the ground), white moderates might choose to no longer "sit on the fence," Trikosko implies.[7] She followed these images from August 28 with a photograph taken on September 5, in Birmingham, Alabama (Figure 13). Again, African Americans are held behind a fence, this time warned by a sign: "Danger Keep Out." And again, Trikosko asks her viewer to enter the

Figure 12. Marion Trikosko, "Civil Rights March on Washington, D.C.," 1963. *Courtesy Library of Congress, Prints and Photographs Division.*

photograph's space as an activist. Four men have stopped to look across the barrier while two women pass by. The women are shot at the precise moment they enter the space between the three men on the left and the younger man on the right. As our embedded equivalents as viewers, the passers-by move into the empty space and join, for a split second, a tight line of bodies.

Figure 13. Marion Trikosko, "Group of African Americans viewing the bomb-damaged home of Arthur Shores, NAACP attorney, Birmingham, Alabama," 1963. *Courtesy Library of Congress, Prints and Photographs Division.*

Bob Fletcher, a photographer with SNCC, used a similar device of internal captioning to craft his spatio-symbolism. A photograph of a mother and child on a porch in Ruleville, Mississippi, includes a SNCC poster behind the figures. The poster, based on a photograph taken by Danny Lyon at the March on Washington features the word "NOW," grasped decisively by a demonstrator. All space between the demonstrator's fist and the word is closed, as though his demand has been met in the present, not delayed as a promise for the future. But the space between the mother and child on the porch remains. The mother offers a hand to her son, inviting him to step through the physical and symbolic door away from the blank space of the photograph's foreground. This juxtaposition of the poster and the mother–son pair suggests that activism will turn the child's outstretched, empty hand into the fist of the demonstrator in the poster, releasing him from the liminal space between almost-freedom and freedom "NOW."

Another photographer who crafted spatio-symbolism in his images was John Bledsoe. In one of his photographs from September 1958, African American students enter Van Buren High School, in Little Rock, Arkansas (Figure 14). The space is tight; the two male students move between a brick wall and the photographer, one boy's head is cut off by the photograph's frame, and the female student stands against a wall as the boys walk by. Behind the girl is an open window, the new space of the integrated classroom; before her is a space between the two male students, the space of activism into which she enters.

Figure 14. John Bledsoe, "Little Rock, Arkansas," 1958. *Courtesy Library of Congress, Prints and Photographs Division.*

Equally important is that while the boys face in one direction, she faces in another; collectively, the three students engage both spaces.

But of all the civil rights photographs, Charles Moore's are perhaps the most occupied with spatial limitation and liberation. On September 3, 1958, Moore photographed white officers pushing King across a police desk in Montgomery (Durham 47). King had been arrested for loitering, although in fact he had been trying to enter a crowded courtroom. Moore's image shows his bent figure forced against the countertop, sprawled and off balance. Over King's right shoulder is a glimpse of bright sunlight, blocked by a police officer. Moore went on to cover most of the movement for *Life* magazine, and many of his images fuse physical and civic space: the 1958 police-desk photograph set the tone for his spatio-symbolic constructions over the next seven years.

Charles Moore's Protest Spaces

Highlighting confined space, Moore's foregrounds are repeatedly crowded, his frames vertically bisected. The images often include heavy shadows and internal frames that further encroach upon the space of their figures. For example, Moore used the device of internal framing in a 1960 image from Montgomery, Alabama (Durham 48–49). Police attack demonstrators with clubs, and a police club and a "one-way" sign extend in the same direction, framing the space on the left and right of the image. As well, a horizontal line continues the internal frame across the image, from the club through both of the white man's elbows, the black woman's elbows and the bystander's elbow, to the arrow on the "one-way" sign. Moore repeated this device in a Birmingham image from 1963, where protestors are pinned between a store and an officer's club (Durham 114–15). Although the officer is trapped in a small space (in front of him is his motorcycle's wing mirror, and the only reflection visible is himself) and pointing fingers reach across the space toward him, the long line of the letter M in the store's sign sits above the his club in a direct parallel, framing the protestors in an even tighter internal space. Space is tight above their heads, as well, where the traffic light (reading "don't walk") almost meets the officer's hat across two different levels of perspective. This internal frame then continues in a line through the long base of the letter M.

In other Birmingham images, demonstrators appear through internal frames and are further confined by figures, shapes, and tight backgrounds. One image turns this literally confined space into a symbolic confinement (Durham 118–19). Demonstrators are herded into a police van, on their way to jail, and as they enter this confined space (where one will grip the window's bars, fingers visible, as shown in another photograph from the reel), the van's license plate is visible in the foreground: "Heart of Dixie." Explicitly labeled, this confined space symbolizes the spatial confinement at the heart of Dixie.

Another of Moore's most pointed depictions of spatial constraints came in 1965, in one of his images from Bloody Sunday, when marchers moving from Selma to Montgomery were attacked at the base of Selma's bridge (Durham 167). The image shows mounted deputies driving marchers back across the bridge. Police and cars crowd the foreground, stopping the marchers from turning around. The marchers are caught in the internal frame of the car window and the bridge frame, while to their left, light-colored cars move down the bridge, heading freely in the other direction. Signs proclaiming "speed limit" and "low clearance" frame their space even tighter. There is nowhere to go.

As well as tightening space through internal framing, Moore's photographs create the impression of confinement through their depictions of discreet space. Angles often originate from behind a shoulder or a face, so that the viewer seems to peer into a private world. In a 1962 image from Oxford, Mississippi, we look into a tight circle of police officers (Durham 54–55). The left side of the image is obscured by one man's neck and shoulder, and on the right side another man has his back to the camera. The same principle of visual trespass dominates several other images from the same shoot in Oxford. In one, the central, frontal figure appears over others' shoulders (Durham 56). In another, U.S. marshals are shot from behind tree branches (Durham 58–59), and in a third, James Meredith, surrounded by white marshals and deputies, is shot through the gap between two white men's shoulders (Durham 68).

Yet Moore's photographs don't focus solely on segregated or discreet, exclusively white space. Creating a discreet, *activist* space, a 1963 photograph of King and Roy Wilkins in Jackson, Mississippi, is shot through the bodies of two other marchers (Durham 126–27). And in numerous images of the 1963 Freedom March, activists claim their own discreet spaces. One shows the marchers gathered in a tight circle, singing "We Shall Overcome" (Durham 87). Observers mill around their circle but they are so tightly packed that Moore photographed them from above, without attempting to shoot from somewhere within. Another shows the marchers passing through a town in Georgia (Durham 83). Behind them is a sign explaining the ongoing construction of the highways on which they walk. The South is literally under construction, and in bridging the gap between the first marcher and the bystanders (including one on crutches, also under construction), the sign symbolizes the building of a bridge across the divide between activist hopes and South opinion. Confirming the constructive and "right" power of this march, an arrow sign marked "Keep right" bridges the gap between the first marcher and the second.

Depicting spatial restrictions, Moore was countering with a positive vision of black-controlled space. He repeatedly shot King in front of bright open doorways—some blocked, as in the 1958 police station photograph, but others opening out beyond his body. In another 1958 image from Montgomery, King preaches at Dexter Avenue Baptist Church (Durham 44–45). Moore shot the photograph from behind the pulpit so that King's body would appear directly in front of the open door and the bright light beyond. Or, in an image of voter registration volunteer George Ball meeting with a mother and three children, the bright light between them symbolizes a new space of activism (Durham 137), and in an image of a voter registration class in Clarksdale, Mississippi, the tiny interior space is expanded in depth by the mirror on the wall and the bright pages held by the individuals (Durham 133).

Moore even offered a vision of black-controlled space in his images from the Montgomery-Selma march. In one, black demonstrators are on their way toward the Edmund Pettus Bridge and the bloody clash with police (Durham 156–7). The figures are held within an even tighter space by the internal frame that cuts off the area above their heads: a horizontal line connects through the image from left to right, from the police officer's hat through the street sign, the store canopy, and the watermark on wall, to the fire escape rung. But some scaffolding on the photograph's right side, positioned directly behind leaders Hosea Williams and John Lewis, symbolizes the movement's work in progress. Even more important is the witness within the frame. As they cross Water Avenue in Selma, the marchers are observed by a member of the Selma police force, perched awkwardly on top of his car. Space is explicitly at the heart of the confrontation. The stamping on the car marks this particular officer as "traffic control," and visual resonances between the demonstrators and their urban environment subvert his municipal control. One woman at the center of the image has just stepped off the curb. The corner of the building behind her continues the vertical line of her draped blanket. And she also has a visual corollary in the image's most prominent lamppost: her feet and its base lie on the same horizontal plane and the color of her blanket mirrors its silver. In the photograph, at least, black activists win the battle for space. They harmonize with their environment in a way that the awkwardly positioned officer does not, and they cross "Water Ave." on their own terms (a symbolic and successful crossing of the river where they would very soon be halted).

Another of Moore's devices for opening out confined spaces was to construct spatial layering. In an image from 1964, the beauty parlor of voter registration volunteer Vera Piggy is a space reshaped across several levels for political action (Durham 132). One level of the photograph is the world of the parlor, inside the mirror. Vera's customer looks at voter registration pamphlets, while Vera perhaps explains details of the registration process. The pamphlets' fine print resembles that of the newspapers and posters on the back wall, implicating the entire space of the parlor in Vera's campaign. Another level of the photograph, within the mirror behind Vera's head, includes more framed documents. The photograph's third level is the parlor wall, which displays a large mirror and a placard that reads "STOP POLICE BRUTALITY," below a picture of a man grasping his leg as he falls to the ground. A police dog and a white officer stand in front of him, and a white-shirted man stands behind. With his back to the camera, this second man stands in for the viewer's position in relation to the beauty parlor, as though Moore is insisting on the viewer's role as a witness to the activism depicted in the placard. From the right, the angle of the image connects the photographer with the right-facing man on the ground, implicating Moore as a witness-participant, too. And, although she faces the other direction, Vera in her white shirt is another visual corollary to the man in the foreground. In her is a model of viewer–photographer response: as she educates her customer on voter registration, she takes action against racial violence in the form of forcible exclusion from voting booths.

Such layered spaces were one aspect of Moore's spatio-symbolic rhetoric. This rhetoric also involved a *temporal* layering that opened the deep space of black history within Moore's frames. For example, one of the images from Birmingham remembers sites of trauma. A boy is jumping and his apparent suspension beneath a tree branch evokes scenes of lynchings (Durham 110). But Moore's photograph adds to this memory of trauma an even deeper, resonant history of black resistance. In the tradition of artists and writers within the anti-lynching movement itself, it remembers the example of fugitive slaves. Echoing numerous nineteenth-century descriptions of the woods between the Big House and freedom, the image features a large house with a white wide porch beyond the bystanders who encourage the boys in their escape.

Moore's photographs do sometimes reveal the past as a negative living legacy. In a Greenwood, Mississippi, image from 1964, Dick Gregory has been leading a voter registration march and has been stopped by police beneath a Confederate States of America monument (Durham 130). The officers reach out arms and block the marchers' space, while the monument to the Confederacy blocks their exit behind. The figures on the monument wear the same hats as the officers, suggesting a direct line from the 1860s to 1960s—time as frozen as the hands of the clock on the tower above the scene, as static as the space of a monument. But more often, Moore's photographs offered a reusable past. Another image, taken in June 1963, expresses history's open loop of repetition *with difference* (Durham 139). The photograph displays a gothic Southern space, complete with a swamp that symbolizes the ongoing mires of race relations while recalling numerous nineteenth-century scenes of slave resistance and escape. On June 21, three civil rights activists had been jailed and released later that day, only to be hunted down and killed. Moore's shot of deputies trolling the swamps for the bodies includes a train of light that runs from the image's foreground to its midground, a bisection emphasized by the top of the tallest man's hat, which further divides the body of water that is already traversed and the dark unknown ahead. This juxtaposition of known and unknown, along with the branches and shadows on the water, crowds the scene with gothic hauntings, but the water mark on the tree offers a trace of time's passage across the years between the 1850s and 1963. While the deputies move through a Southern swamp rich with slave history, and the image echoes numerous nineteenth-century scenes of the "dismal swamp," the scene reveals a change over time and a shift in race relations. Of the three dead men, one was black and two were white: behind the image are the intertwined civil rights struggles of blacks *and* whites.

These signs of change amid a usable past suggest that in reaching for black space within America's public history, Moore's images were also reaching for black space in the country's civic future. Taking up this theme, many photographs depict demonstrators on the move. One 1964 image captures voting rights activists leading a line of potential voters toward a Greenwood, Mississippi voting booth (Durham 128). The image is bisected at its midpoint and the foreground is crowded with people, cars and a building. But here, in a linearly organized photograph, the marchers look ahead as they move from an even *more* crowded background, filled with rooftops, trees, and power lines. They are emerging from a constricted space, moving toward a new civic space at the voting booth. An internal caption, the store sign that reads "fair deal," labels that space as rightfully theirs. Equally important, their leader looks directly at the camera, as though inviting the viewer to join his protest line as witness-participants, and the photograph includes internal witnesses (a boy in a yard, two adults on a porch).

In fact, Moore's images often have internal witnesses that mirror their *own* audience. And although the viewer of the image depicting a store and an officer's club is positioned on the side of the officer, here in the 1964 image we join the observers who face the scene as members of the local community. Still another photograph confirms that there are two kinds of witnesses: active and passive. In Birmingham, in 1963, seven people watch the clash with police from a store window (Durham 111). A woman on the left shields her eyes, and is positioned above an incomplete internal caption ("Fried Chic"). But this incomplete act of witnessing is countered by the man on the right, who offers the only direct gaze of the seven figures at the window.

Moore shot a series of photographs exploring this space between activists and observers. Sometimes the space remains a vacuum—unbridgeable and empty. In a photograph of marchers resting in Georgia, Sam Shirah tries to shake hands with a local, who keeps his hand away (Durham 85). The space at the very center of the image, between the two hands, remains unbridged, whereas more than half of the frame is filled with the restless space of shifting clouds. But the opposite dynamic appears in another Freedom March image, this time shot in Chattanooga, Tennessee, where an observer fully enters the activist space (Durham 76–77). As a bystander watches the marchers pass her home, the photograph's angle places her at the spatial level of the march in the background, so that she appears to be the last marcher in the line. Here, the space between activists and observers is bridged, the literal empty space of the chair nearby her porch symbolizing a space left behind as she—visually at least—joins the marchers' line.

Across Moore's body of civil rights work, such witnessing gazes make visible the demonstrators' performance of activism *and* turns the internal witnesses themselves into engaged observers. For example, one image from the march to Montgomery, which began again on March 21, 1965, shows black onlookers at some distance back from the road (Durham 198). Some wave and one woman raises a hand in blessing. Between the observers and the marchers are four young children. Two boys stand facing the road and two girls crouch on the ground. One girl grasps the other's arm and watches the march, while the second girl twists her body away from the road and stares at the observers. The Janus-faced pair, looking backward and forward, bridges the space between marchers and observers.

A more physical connection between marchers and observers in another image, taken in 1963, confirms their fusion in an activist space (Figure 15). Moore captured the back of a young activist as he walks down a city street filled

Figure 15. Charles Moore, "Georgia," 1963. *Copyright Charles Moore/Black Star.*

with antique stores. Two old women stand at either side of a store entrance, surrounded by the repeated internal caption "Antiques" (the word appears four times, along with one iteration of the word "relics"). The marcher's shadow fills the space between them and even enters their store, blending with the dark space inside. He extends to one his right arm. The twist of his body suggests that he draws the women into his protest, as does the first woman's tight hold on his fingers (the muscles in her right forearm are visibly strained), and the second woman's bent hips, lifted foot, and look of anticipation. She is ready to take his hand. Like the two girls on the ground in the 1965 image, the handshake and promised handshake function as a witness-participant connection that bridges the witness/activist divide.

Moore's images even embed a discreet space of activism between marchers and observers. There is a square between the marcher and the women in the 1963, marked by their linked, straight arms and the marcher's shadow along the square's top and bottom, and their two bodies along the square's sides. And although it is an open space of activism, the space is also a temporal fusion. Another internal caption, "the route," confirms this space as a fusion of past ("antiques"), present (the marchers) and future (the destination of the "route"). Equally, there is a neat rectangular space between the children and the marchers in the 1965 image, marked by the girls' heads at its bottom, the marchers' line at its top, the boy's straight body at its right side and the stiff hand/white pole at its left (Durham 198). And the girls looking backward and forward between witnesses and marchers have bridged a spatial but also a temporal gap between the elderly observers and the marchers. The discreet space within this image fuses past (the elderly observers), present (the passing marchers), and future (the destination of the march and the future of the watching child). Between observers and activists in both photographs is a space of possibility—the birth-place of future activism.

ဦ≫

President Kennedy once said that the eloquence of civil rights photographs exceeded that of "explanatory words" (Fairclough 138). Senator Jacob Javits believed that photographs hastened the Civil Rights Act and Arthur Schlesinger claimed that they "did as much as anything to transform the national mood and make legislation not just necessary . . . but possible" (Durham 32). Burke Marshall at the Department of Justice claimed that photographs of the Birmingham campaign "stirred the feelings" of most whites (Dudziak 170).

But it was King and Moore who struck notes of spatio-symbolism in their assessments. King repeatedly explained that visibility was vital to success, noting in 1964 that the activist should "force his oppressor to commit his brutality openly . . . with the rest of the world looking on," instead of "submitting to surreptitious cruelty in thousands of dark jail cells and on countless shadowed street corners." He went on to reference the media's coverage of the Birmingham campaign, and explained: "The brutality with which officials would have quelled the black individual became impotent when it could not be pursued with stealth and remain unobserved. It was caught—as a fugitive from a penitentiary is often caught—in gigantic circling spotlights. It was imprisoned in a luminous glare revealing the naked truth" (*Why We Can't Wait* 37, 39). Sure enough, with the "luminous glare" of their lens and flashes, Moore and other photographers had imprisoned segregation itself within a "penitentiary" space.

As for Moore, he later insisted that "pictures can and do make a difference," for they demand that "we all move forward together" (Durham 6). His photographs had offered a series of activist spaces that fuse observers and activists, past and present generations, historical memory and the "forward" thrust. Alongside civil rights and abolitionist art and literature, his images overthrew the confined space of America's civic and physical spheres, turning the marginal no-place into a space of protest history and a site of resistance.

Notes

1. This article builds on Werner's contrast between the African American narrative of excavation and the Faulknerian narrative of repudiation. Although he doesn't root his analysis in the civil rights movement, Werner argues that excavation narratives attempt to redeem the complexity of formerly unknown or unacknowledged pasts. See also Harris who uses survey responses to explore whether memories of the Scottsboro trials, the Brown decision, the murder of Emmett Till, and the Montgomery Bus Boycott had any impact on collective action. Harris posits: "With the exception of the Scottsboro trials . . . blacks' knowledge of historical events . . . had positive consequences for black activism" (32).

2. On how Brown's narrative revised the imagery of the middle passage, see Wolff.

3. For more on antebellum memory see Bethel's argument that African Americans reached "for a new body of tradition" in the form of a "self-consciously constructed historical myth of a collectively 'remembered' past" (168, 169).

4. For a rare analysis of *The Movement,* see Blair, 201–223.

5. For more on SNCC and photography, see Raiford's argument that SNCC members "understood the importance of photographs . . . as visual bricks in the raising of the new integrated free world" (1139).

6. For two rare considerations of civil rights photography, see Willis (2003) and Willis (2005).

7. For a brief discussion of how other photographs asked a similar question, see Johnson on the Birmingham Campaign: "The stark contrasts contained in the photographs summoned white moderates to respond to the question 'What side of the line are you on?' . . . making it impossible . . . to 'sit on the fence' " (6–7).

Works Cited

Abernathy, Ralph. "Love and Race Relations." 1964. *Rhetoric, Religion, and the Civil Rights Movement, 1954–1965.* Houck and Dixon, 730–37.

Association of Citizens' Councils. "Why Does Your Community Need a Citizens' Council?" Undated. Citizens' Council Collection, University of Mississippi, container b1f18.

Benjamin, Walter. *The Arcades Project.* Cambridge, MA: Harvard UP, 1999.

Bethel, Elizabeth Rauh. *The Roots of African-American Identity: Memory and History in Free Antebellum Communities.* New York: St. Martin's Press, 1997.

Blair, Sara. *Harlem Crossroads: Black Writers and the Photograph in the Twentieth Century.* Princeton, NJ: Princeton UP, 2007.

Bond, Horace Mann. "A Cigarette for Johnnie Birchfield." 1956. Houck and Dixon, 178–87.

Brown, Henry. *Narrative of the Life of Henry Box Brown.* Manchester, UK: Lee & Glynn, 1851.

Brown, William Wells. *The Narrative of William W. Brown.* 1847, London: Charles Gilpin, 1849.

———. *Clotel.* London: Partridge & Oakey, 1853.

———. *The American Fugitive in Europe.* Boston: J.P. Jewett, 1854.

———. *The Black Man: His Antecedents, His Genius, and His Achievements.* 1863, New York: Johnson Reprint, 1968.

Castronovo, Russ. "Radical Configurations of History in the Era of American Slavery." *American Literature* 65.3 (1993): 523–47.

Douglass, Frederick. "What to the Slave is the Fourth of July?" 1852. *The Frederick Douglass Papers Series One, Vol 2.* Ed. John W. Blassingame et al. New Haven, CT: Yale UP, 1987. 359–88.

Dudziak, Mary. *Cold War Civil Rights: Race and the Image of American Democracy.* Princeton, NJ: Princeton UP, 2000.

Durham, Michael, ed. *Powerful Days: The Civil Rights Photography of Charles Moore.* New York: Stewart, Tabori & Chang, 1991.

Fairclough, Adam. *To Redeem the Soul of America: The Southern Christian Leadership Conference and Martin Luther King, Jr.* Athens: U of Georgia P, 1987.

Harris, Fredrick C. "It Takes a Tragedy to Arouse Them: Collective Memory and Collective Action During the Civil Rights Movement." *Social Movement Studies* 5.1 (2006): 19–43.

Houck, Davis and David Dixon, eds. *Rhetoric, Religion and the Civil Rights Movement 1954–1965.* Waco, TX: Baylor UP, 2006.

Hughes, Langston. "Dream of Freedom." *Wayne State University Graduation Comment.* July 1964. 108.

———. "Frederick Douglass: 1817–1895." *Liberator*, December 1966: 21.

Johnson, Davi. "Martin Luther King Jr.'s 1963 Birmingham Campaign as Image Event." *Rhetoric & Public Affairs* 10.1 (2007): 1–25.

Kennedy, Liam. *Race and Urban Space in Contemporary American Culture.* Chicago: Fitzroy Dearborn Publishers, 2000.

King, Jr., Martin Luther. "The 'New Negro' of the South: Behind the Montgomery Story." 1956. *The Papers of Martin Luther King, Jr., III*. Ed. Clayborne Carson et al. Berkeley: U of California P, 1997. 280–86.

———. *Why We Can't Wait*. New York: New American Library, 1964.

———. *Where Do We Go From Here: Chaos or Community?* New York: Harper & Row, 1967.

Lawson, James. "Eve of Nonviolent Revolution." *Southern Patriot* 19 Nov. 1961: 1.

Leonard, George. "Journey of Conscience." *Nation* 10 Nov. 1965: 502–5.

Morin, Mary. "Oral History: Charles Moore." S.I. Newhouse School of Public Communications Civil Rights Symposium Archives, Syracuse University, 2004. n.p.

Nash, Diane. "Interview," 1961. *Let Freedom Ring: A Documentary History of the Modern Civil Rights Movement*. Ed. Peter Levy. Westport, CT: Praeger, 1992. 68–70.

Nora, Pierre. "Between Memory and History: Les Lieux de Mémoire." *Representations* 26, (1989): 7–24.

——— and Lawrence Kritzman, eds. *Realms of Memory*. New York: Columbia UP, 1996.

Raiford, Leigh. " 'Come Let Us Build a New World Together': SNCC and Photography of the Civil Rights Movement." *American Quarterly* 59.4 (2007): 1129–57.

Rowan, Carl. "The Cradle (of the Confederacy) Rocks." 1957. *Voices in Our Blood: America's Best on the Civil Rights Movement*. Ed. Jon Meacham. New York: Random House, 2003. 129–50.

Shields, Rob. *Places on the Margin: Alternative Geographies of Modernity*. New York: Routledge, 1991.

Smith, Neil. *Uneven Development: Nature, Capital, and the Production of Space*. New York: Blackwell, 1991.

SNCC. *The Movement: Documentary of a Struggle for Equality*. New York: Simon & Schuster, 1964.

Taylor, Gardner. "Some Comments on Race Hate. 1965. Houck and Dixon, 914–19.

Werner, Craig. *Playing the Changes: From Afro-Modernism to the Jazz Impulse*. Urbana: U of Illinois P, 1994.

Willis, Deborah. "Exposure." *Only Skin Deep: Changing Visions of the American Self*. Ed. Coco Fusco and Brian Wallis. New York: International Center on Photography, 2003. 275–81.

———. "Visualizing Political Struggle: Civil Rights–Era Photography." *American Visual Cultures*. Ed. David Holloway and John Beck. New York: Continuum, 2005. 166–73.

Wolff, Cynthia Griffin. "Passing Beyond the Middle Passage: Henry 'Box' Brown's Translations of Slavery." *The Massachusetts Review* 37.1 (1996): 23–44.

Wright, Marion. "The Minister as Citizen." 1961. Houck and Dixon, 437–45.

Into a Burning House

Representing Segregation's Death

VINCE SCHLEITWILER

> But white Americans do not believe in death, and this is why the darkness
> of my skin so intimidates them.
>
> —James Baldwin, *The Fire Next Time*

As long as the promises of integration remain unfulfilled, it is premature to
inquire after segregation as if it were over. If anything, it's the former whose
time may have passed, for these promises, in all their deliberate speed, are rarely
encountered these days outside the refuge of a museum. Perhaps it would be
better to speak of segregation's death, if you are prepared to think of death as
other than the end. For segregation haunts an officially antiracist and multicul-
tural society in undeniably material forms. So long as segregation's death defies
its ending, so too do all the forms of death by which segregation has been
manifested, whether metaphorical or literal, spiritual or corporeal.

For students of African American culture, to begin a historical inquiry
from such haunted premises should recall a familiar precedent, which Saidiya
Hartman terms "the time of slavery." Reading an inscription outside Ghana's
Elmina Castle that celebrates "the redressive capacities of memory," Hartman
is troubled by "the confidence it betrays in the founding distinction or break
between then and now," and asks, "Can one mourn what has yet ceased hap-
pening?" (758). At the same time, it is necessary, somehow, to take measure of
the distance between then and now—a point Octavia Butler makes in dramatic
fashion in her novel *Kindred*. As her protagonist Dana is repeatedly dragged
back in time to her ancestors' slave plantation, she learns that the annihilation
of this distance would, quite literally, demand her death.

To take measure of the distance from segregation's death, following Hartman, is not "to assert the continuity or identity of racism over the course of

245

centuries" (758), but to consider its transformations. This task not only is historical, but political, epistemological, and aesthetic. Why, Angela Davis recently
remarked, do we think of racism as formerly "overt," as if it is somehow "hidden"
in the post-civil rights era? What *instructs* us to do so? For some, this training
suffices to make racism imperceptible, as in the successful police defense in the
Rodney King case, which Patricia Williams describes as less a rationalization
than a painstaking lesson in an "aesthetics of rationality" (54). The assertion that
segregation actually *is* over is not uncommon and is symptomatic of a peculiar
epidemic of blindness. In current ideological terms, this is called "colorblind-
ness," a condition that has somehow been confused with those gifts of second
sight to which visionary black political movements have often aspired. Instead,
it might be understood as just another mutation of racism's aesthetics—a set
of enabling constraints on the perceptions of the senses.

In speaking of segregation's death, I refer simultaneously to its displacement as the dominant ideology of a racial regime, from World War II through
the mid-1960s; its ongoing manifestation as the capacity to constrict life[1]; and
its termination of a field of representation, how it sets perceptual limits that
enable knowledge and expression. In the post-civil rights period, U.S. national
community is constituted through the celebration of segregation's death, in all
three senses. Its passing as ideology is reconciled with its *de facto* material presence
through rituals of commemoration that train the nation to perceive segregation's
death as the negative image of its cherished freedom. These rituals transmit two
messages, logically contradictory but mutually reinforcing: segregation has ended,
segregation will never end. These messages work in tandem to construct the
racial order as natural and inevitable. They are reconciled not through rational
explanation but the experience of terror, as an aesthetic training that conditions
rationality. These rituals restage the birth of an exceptional nation: as racism
disappears, the nation emerges, its destiny manifested as a beacon of freedom,
beset on all sides by darkness. But this darkness aligns the innocent victims of
past racism with the spectral figures of present-day racial threat (the criminal,
the alien, the terrorist) who must be subjected to incarceration, banishment,
and preemptive violence—to every possible form of death. To peer into this
darkness, in what Fred Moten calls a "glancing [that] is the aversion of the
gaze" (233), is to experience a transfixing terror, which trains perception. Terror of the darkness keeps the nation's subjects in their separate and unequal
places, by marking unfreedom as vulnerability to violence and envisioning the
privileges secured by violence as freedom's only possible form. Commemorating
segregation's death convinces them that they are free.

In this essay, I consider a representation of segregation's death from what
may appear a distant location, a brief memoir by the Japanese American writer
Hisaye Yamamoto. Read alongside other historical and cultural texts, including a novel by Chester Himes, the memoir demonstrates how the passing of

segregation as an official ideology, and the transformation of the racial order this entails, turns on a series of links between African American and Japanese American racialization. Although these processes incorporate non-white subjects into a national community by distinguishing between tokens and threats, they pivot on a point of divergence external to the nation. In his work on diaspora, Brent Edwards theorizes such connections outside a national or imperial structure as an articulation through difference, discrepancies, or gaps, which he terms *décalage* (*Practice* 13–15).[2] If the racial subjects that appear in the memoir are bound together as differential forms of unfreedom through their relation to segregation's death, the links between them (understood as *décalage*) point to a domain outside and opposed to an imperial nation, something it excludes or that eludes it.

If national commemoration casts this domain beyond the limits of representation, how is it possible to bear witness to a call for justice that issues from it? The technical resources of black cultural traditions may be consulted here. Although their engagement with racism's aesthetics has most often been analyzed in literary studies as a paradox of hypervisibility and invisibility, they cannot be reduced to the visual, or to any single sense. If they have challenged racism in the name of a reality beyond shared racial delusions, that reality is never self-evident or unmediated, but merely postulated, as nagging doubt or longed-for prize, at the point of struggle where politics and poetics converge. "We can agree, I think," writes Toni Morrison, "that invisible things are not necessarily 'not-there' " (11)—beyond the limits of what can be rationally known, of what can be perceived by the senses, which is another way of saying beyond death.

વ≻

First published in a Japanese American newspaper in 1985, Hisaye Yamamoto's "A Fire in Fontana" considers the deaths, forty years earlier, of an African American family who had recently moved into an all-white neighborhood outside Los Angeles. Just days before the fire that claims their lives, the father, a man named Short, seeks protection from the threats on his family by contacting the local black press. Although the fire causes a minor uproar, an official investigation concludes it was accidental, and further protest is ignored or suppressed. A "White priest" who writes a play about the murders, for example, is abruptly reassigned to a distant parish in Arizona (154).

For the narrator, the task of representing segregation is first encountered in her failure to defend the family from death. As a young employee of a small black newspaper, the *LA Tribune*, she had taken down Short's account, but her inadequate response still haunts her. Reading the memoir in the wake of the 1992 LA riots, however, King-Kok Cheung celebrates it for "effectively

expos[ing] a long-forgotten crime," comparing it to both the priest's play and
the Rodney King video ("Dream" 127). Equating justice and representation,
Cheung contends that the memoir triumphs by "writing/righting the wrong"
(128). Redeeming her earlier failure, Yamamoto "has vindicated and reclaimed
her own voice" by permanently engraving the crime into the historical record,
"ensur[ing] that this disturbing event will never be forgotten as mere 'news' "
("Dream" 128).

Yet if the crime was effaced in the proceedings of the law, it had already
been entered into the historical record, both as "news" (O'Day Short's cause
was taken up by numerous crusading journalists)[3] and as literary art. *Trial by
Fire*, written in 1946 by noted Jesuit activist George H. Dunne, and based on
his original reporting for *Commonweal*, was performed nationally over the next
decade. In September 1954, when the *Chicago Defender* reported on the lifting
of Jim Crow housing restrictions in Fontana, it assumed its readers would recall
the town *because* of the play.[4] On the terms of Cheung's argument, the play's
success would exceed that of the memoir. Unless these acts of representation
are collapsed into a single, repeated event, one must presume some decisive
historical shift in the conditions of representation endows Yamamoto's text with
a greater, retroactive power.

By 1985, however, to expose the deaths of the Short family as a racist
crime no longer requires any appreciable moral courage, perceptual acuity,
or rhetorical art. This historical shift does not facilitate the transit between
representation and justice, but rather impedes it. If Yamamoto is tasked with
any political or aesthetic challenge, it arises from her readers' familiarity with
stories of segregation's death. Her autobiographical "voice" is not triumphant but
strained; nowhere in the memoir does she represent herself speaking confidently
and effectively against racism. Indeed, the memoir carefully obscures details of
Yamamoto's biography that might attest to her literary and political agency. For
example, after leaving the *Tribune*, Yamamoto gained national recognition for
her short fiction, but turned away from this budding career to enter a Catholic
Worker community (Crow 77).

In the event, the memoir acknowledges the failure of representation to
achieve justice for the Short family. The inadequacy of her initial response,
"a calm, impartial story, using 'alleged' and 'claimed' and other cautious jour-
nalese," haunts her for decades. For, she explains, "Anyone noticing the story
about the unwanted family in Fontana would have taken it with a grain of
salt" (154).[5] That the more courageous efforts of writers like Dunne did not
ultimately change the outcome does not assuage her shame, nor does her
characterization of her condition as a *lack* of agency. Her statement is framed
by a recollection of two neighborhood characters from prewar Little Tokyo, a
street-corner preacher and a disabled boy. She writes, "I should have been an
evangelist at Seventh and Broadway, shouting out the name of the Short family

and their predicament in Fontana. But I had been as handicapped as the boy in the wheelchair, as helpless" (155). Yet if the boy's disability represents his deficiency as a political subject, the preacher's speech is compared to that of a beast: "from a distance, it sounded like the sharp barking of a dog" (154). They are further linked by the boy's "Japanese military-style" haircut and the man's "uniform" and "military-type cap" (154), underscoring the condition of helplessness with heavy irony, for this desperate, pathetic militancy alludes to a prewar history of racial identification that became virtually unspeakable in the aftermath of internment.

By the end of the text, after decades of repression, the narrator succeeds in fashioning a different representation of the scene of the fire. This is made possible through a narrative operation whereby the memory of Fontana reappears as the precursor to a later event: the 1965 Watts riots. Note that it is not a celebration of the civil rights movement's triumph over Jim Crow that enables representation, but the violent revelation of segregation's afterlife in the geography of urban abandonment. The narrator only experiences this violence via television, from the security of a home in a neighborhood that restricts African Americans; the distance between her middle-class domesticity and urban racial violence has conditioned her recollection.

James Lee reads this as a "[c]ynical distance" that rationalizes the writer's disavowal of political agency, diagnosing Yamamoto's irony as a disabling intellectualism that blinds her to "ideology's control" (91). The narrator rigorously exposes not only the racist hypocrisy of her white and Asian American neighbors, but also her own complicity in resegregation through suburban flight (156–57)—the very movement denied to the Short family twenty years earlier. Nonetheless, Lee notes that her greater awareness does not correspond to any change in her actions, which evidences a politically debilitating limit to literary representation. In contrast, I argue that the memoir's political task is not to portray transformative action, but to project a call, seeking to gather and bind a collectivity in the act of response. In the following, I return to this scene to read the effacement of the narrator's agency and the emphasis on the distance between subjects racialized as token and as threat as part of a representational strategy negotiating the perceptual limits established on segregation's death. But in order to avoid reifying this distance, blinding yourself to the ways that structural disparities in a racial regime are naturalized as "common sense," it is necessary first to ask, how was this distance *historically* produced?

ે❧

The memoir begins: "Something weird happened to me not long after the end of the Second World War. I wouldn't go so far as to say that I, a Japanese American, became Black, because that's a pretty melodramatic statement. But some kind of transformation did take place, the effects of which are with me still" (150). Her account is contrasted with two tales from the realm of black music. First, she recalls a novel about a white trumpeter's tragic association with "Negroes" ("in 1985," she adds, "how odd the word has become!"). Next, she recalls a "real life" figure, Johnny Otis, a musician who became "the pastor of a church in Watts" (150). To the narrator, Otis's life "represents a triumph"—an assessment she will not make of her own story:

> Because when I realized something was happening to me, I scrambled to backtrack for awhile. I continued to look like the Nisei[6] I was, with my height remaining at slightly over four feet ten, my hair straight, my vision myopic. Yet I know that this event transpired within me; sometimes I see it as my inward self being burnt black in a certain fire. (150)

Given the text's emphasis on the historical specificity of racial naming, it is curious that otherwise sensitive readers have ignored the lowercase "b" of the word "black" here, disregarding her caution that this is *not* a story of how a Japanese American became "Black."[7] If you simply take her at her word, the memoir's pursuit of some mysterious "event" or "transformation," recounting a series of pivotal differentiations between Japanese Americans and African Americans, takes measure of the historically dynamic distance between racial subjects. This distance, furthermore, provides a history of Japanese American racialization as such. In other words, her memoir is not about how she became Black, but about how she became *Japanese American.*

The task of representing this weird event is impeded by its causal and chronological instability. She continues, "perhaps the process, unbeknownst to me, had begun even earlier," recalling a wartime trip on a Greyhound bus out of Chicago (150). Along the way, she encounters Jim Crow, not directly, but through a chatty white woman's "glee" over the refusal of service to a black passenger at an Illinois restaurant (151). She is unable to reciprocate the sentiment, associating it with internment—she is, it happens, on her way to rejoin her family in an Arizona concentration camp. Unsure how to respond, she somehow expresses dissent, to the surprise of her previously friendly seatmate. But as the bus swings through the South, she decides to try using the "White" toilets herself, and is unchallenged—except for the "long look" she is given by a black cleaning woman, which haunts her (151).

This anecdote, initiating a motif of transport that links circuits of migration and movement from local to national levels, alludes to a historical detail that Yamamoto does not stress: what is she doing on a Greyhound bus *headed back* to an internment camp? Accounts of Japanese American incarceration generally feature a different journey—the forced removal of entire West Coast communities to makeshift detention centers like the Santa Anita racetrack, or the subsequent voyage on shuttered trains to remote interior locations. But the bus trip references a later migration—the resettlement programs by which the War Relocation Authority sought to reintroduce internees into society, to empty camps that increasingly embarrassed a nation aspiring to postwar hegemony in Asia. Like the better-known efforts to draft Nisei into segregated military units, resettlement demanded the careful processing of an incarcerated population, most notoriously through a so-called "loyalty questionnaire," to identify model subjects of Japanese American rehabilitation. Qualifying internees were encouraged to depart for colleges and jobs in the Midwest and East Coast, and discouraged from "self-segregating" into Little Tokyo communities. Despite this advice, resettlers generally concentrated in a few areas, particularly Chicago, where they encountered another wave of migrants—African Americans from the Jim Crow South. As Jacalyn Harden has shown, the sponsors of resettlement saw a rigorous differentiation between the two groups as crucial to their assimilationist project (89–91).

Returning to the anecdote, it becomes clear that what is novel and disturbing to the narrator is not the experience of anti-black racism, but the neighborly invitation to a shared pleasure in its observation, which seems incommensurate with her internment. The liberal engineers of resettlement gambled on such ignorant hospitality in dispersing resettlers into regions where everyday racism was not shaped against a significant Asian population. Rather than taking it for granted, however, the narrator poses it as a puzzle, a missed omen of the weird transformation she seeks to understand. Confessing her rationalization of the bathroom encounter with dismaying irony—"I decided, for the sake of my conscience, that the Negro woman had never seen a Japanese before" (151)—she alludes to the prior, ongoing histories of race with which she was freighted, which resettlement could not dispel.

Despite the efforts of the War Relocation Authority (WRA), most internees returned to their West Coast communities after the war, where they were reintroduced to forms of segregation that were not simply self-induced, but rigorously enforced through restrictive covenants as well as less formal, sometimes violent means. As in Chicago, black and Japanese migrations intersected in Los Angeles, but this time a massive increase in African American population took up residence within a "race problem" previously mapped as Japanese. In a segregated housing market, the influx of black war workers was largely absorbed by areas emptied by internment. Little Tokyo was reborn as Bronzeville, but the new name did nothing to improve housing conditions, particularly after the internees began to return. Surveying the situation, and perhaps dazzled by the southern California sunshine, a 1946 *Ebony* spread titled "The Race War that Flopped" proclaimed "a miracle in race relations . . . the wedding of Little Tokyo and Bronzeville" (3). Behind this cheeriness lay a more sober agenda, promoting a postwar "Negro-Nisei" interracialism forged in a shared struggle against segregation, whether "Jim Crow" or "Jap Crow" (7). As evidenced by a photo of earnest young "Negro and Nisei vets" planning a "Fair Employment Practice Committee" (9), the strategy was to draw on the ideological capital wartime loyalty was supposed to provide.

This postwar liberal project explains why the narrator's first job out of camp is at a black newspaper. As the narrator explains, she was hired to "attract some Japanese readership," so that "maybe there would be the beginnings of an intercultural community" (152). She tersely dismisses the project's failure, concluding, "It didn't work out that way at all, because I'm not one of your go-getters or anything" (152).[8] The friction Negro-Nisei interracialism entailed is demonstrated in her initial discomfort with the "inexhaustible" conversations about race that now surrounded her: "I got a snootful of it. Sometimes I got to wondering whether Negroes talked about anything else. . . . More than once I was easily put down with a casual, 'That's mighty White of you,' the connotations of which were devastating" (152).

As on her trip from Chicago, the narrator finds herself situated on the privileged side of a white–black binary. Following the deaths in Fontana, however, she finds a new discomfort in the race talk of non-black friends and family. Now she's the one who seems oversensitive, "a curmudgeon, a real pill" (155). But chronology and causality remain uncertain:

> It was around this time that I felt something happening to me, but I couldn't put my finger on it. It was something like an itch I couldn't locate, or like food not being cooked enough, or something undone which should have been done, or something forgotten which should have been remembered. Anyway, something was unsettling my innards. (154)

This confusion persists as the narrative stumbles from one recollection to another, organized instead by the continuing motif of transport. On a bus, she witnesses an incident of racist name-calling that shakes her deeply; sometime later, also on a streetcar, she is overwhelmed by a desire to keep riding, recalling the feeling she'd had years earlier driving to her mother's funeral. Weeks afterward, she quits the paper with a vague "excuse about planning to go back to school" (156). Instead, "after a time," she gets "on trains and buses that carried me several thousand miles across the country and back. I guess you could say I was realizing my dream of traveling forever (escaping responsibility forever)" (156). What she figures here as aimless wandering, flight without destination, she glossed at the beginning of the text as *scrambling to backtrack*: to retrace her steps, to return to a path she was on before getting lost. The past she is seeking, back before the mysterious event that transformed her, is, in the end, a past that never was.

In February 1943, authorizing the creation of a segregated Nisei military unit, Franklin Roosevelt proclaimed: "The principle on which this country was founded and by which it has always been governed is that Americanism is a matter of the mind and heart; Americanism is not, and never was, a matter of race or ancestry" (qtd. in Fujitani 244). This retroactive insistence, on what *never was*, neatly captures the temporal confusion of loyalty for the Japanese American subject who, as soldier or resettler, is called to prove what has supposedly *always been*—the antiracist ideal that makes the nation exceptional. Perhaps knowing better, but no doubt aware that as a loyal Nisei she is nothing if not a good sport, the narrator goes gamely off in search of this *never was*. Instead—in Massachusetts, New York, New Jersey, Maryland—she finds it *is not*: in each location, just as on the bus to Arizona, she comes across supposedly obsolete forms of anti-black racism that are traveling, too.

Settling back in LA to raise "a passel of children" (156), she finds them again in the dynamic of desegregation and resegregation that motors local development. According to Daniel Widener, between 1946 and 1952, the year of her departure, Japanese American "inroads" into white areas served as "a wedge subsequently broadened" by black families, while desegregation efforts were often coordinated by groups like the Japanese American Citizens League (JACL) and NAACP (170). By 1965, however, as the narrator discovers, this wedge looked more like a buffer. Thus, just as she achieves a facsimile of that "American Dream" where domestic bliss is a litany of gendered labor—"in between putting another load of clothes into the automatic washer, ironing, maybe whipping up some tacos for supper"—the Watts riots appear on her TV set (157). She watches, "sitting safely in a house which was located on a street where panic would be the order of the day if a Black family should happen to move in—I had come there on sufferance myself, on the coattails of a pale husband" (157): the distance she's traveled in twenty years, from her days at the *Tribune*, is dramatic. Why does it seem so natural to contemporary readers?

Looking back, one clue appears in a January 1966 article in *The New York Times* by sociologist William Petersen, published in the wake of the riots. Frequently cited in Asian American studies as a key text in the popularization of the notorious "model minority" thesis, "Success Story, Japanese-American Style" is a surprisingly vigorous exposé of the racist history endured by Japanese Americans. Petersen insists that they suffered "the most discrimination and the worst injustices," limiting the question to "persons alive today" (20)—thereby differentiating them from "problem minorities," whose unfortunate reaction to "well-meaning programs" is "either self-defeating apathy or a hatred so all-consuming as to be self-destructive" (21). Rehabilitated as the model minority by signifying the repudiation of black protest, the Japanese American is welcomed into the racial community of the nation. Following the logic of resettlement, this is racial comparison as a severing or disarticulation, although Petersen crucially revises assimilation theory to celebrate a reified Japanese cultural difference. In setting the terms of a post-civil rights racial regime, the distance between Watts and the Nisei home is naturalized.

But for Yamamoto's narrator, to be released, *on sufferance*, from urban segregation is not triumph but continued defeat, not freedom but its substitution by degrees of racial privilege.[9] This entails, first of all, the privilege of being terrorized—of sharing in the communal "panic" by which her neighborhood is consolidated against black incursion. Hence, her first reaction to the televised scene: "Appalled, inwardly cowering, I watched the burning and looting on the screen and heard the reports of the dead and wounded" (157). By locating this fear as "inward," the text demonstrates the disciplinary function of racism's aesthetics of terror. The vision of an alien violence intruding upon domestic security threatens to betray other forms of difference rendered invisible by the dominant racialized form of community. If the token (Nisei) secures racial privilege by displacing the image of threat onto others (blacks), the risk of being recognized in that alien image and made vulnerable to the community's retaliatory violence keeps her in her place. Nonetheless, underneath her internalized terror, the narrator discovers and exposes the very evidence of her identification with the violence from outside: "But beneath all my distress, I felt something else, a tiny trickle of warmth which I finally recognized as an undercurrent of exultation" (157). It is this confession that generates, in the text's final lines, the narrative representation of the fire *last time* in Fontana.

Yamamoto's recasting of racial comparison corresponds with a parallel gesture in an earlier literary exploration of racialized terror in Los Angeles, Chester Himes's *If He Hollers Let Him Go* (1945).[10] The novel begins with the anxious dreams of Bob Jones, a migrant from Cleveland, who awakens to a state of pervasive, visceral fear: "Every day now I'd been waking up that way, ever since the war began. And since I'd been made a leaderman out at the Atlas Shipyard it was really getting me" (3). Something weird has transpired inside him, scrambling chronology and causality. But this fear, he reasons, didn't bother him in his prewar experiences with racism:

> maybe it wasn't until I'd seen them send the Japanese away that I'd noticed it. Little Riki Oyana singing "God Bless America" and going to Santa Anita with his parents the next day. It was taking a man up by the roots and locking him up without a chance. Without a

trial. Without even giving him a chance to say one word. It was thinking about if they ever did that to me, Robert Jones, Mrs. Jones's dark son, that started me to getting scared. (3)

Like Yamamoto's narrator, Jones can only narrate his experience of a shift in racism by reflecting on a differently racialized figure. "After that it was everything," he adds, "It was that crazy, wild-eyed, unleashed hatred that the first Jap bomb on Pearl Harbour let loose in a flood" (4). This incursion of racialized violence into the domestic space of the nation generates a panicked desire for retaliation. On one hand, the racial crisis of war with Japan allows African Americans access to previously unprecedented degrees of privilege, of inclusion in a community constituted by terror. On the other, this privilege depends on an unstable distinction between a model minority and a racial threat: "I was the same colour as the Japanese and I couldn't tell the difference. 'A yeller-bellied Jap' coulda meant me too" (4). Indeed, when Jones loses his token position as the first black leaderman at the shipyard, he immediately thinks of the incarcerated Japanese (30).

In making this interracial articulation, Jones, like Yamamoto's narrator, is *not* proclaiming an identity; he is locating a site of substitution, a switching point. Their metaphors of visual indistinguishability (*I was the same colour and couldn't tell the difference, a yeller-bellied Jap coulda meant me, my inward self was burnt black*) turn precisely on the articulation of difference—of the discrepant histories that racism renders invisible. For Yamamoto's narrator, the deaths of African Americans in racialized violence conjure the suppressed history of Japanese American racialization, and the vulnerability to the same violence by which it marks her. For Jones, the incarceration of little Riki reminds him of his own, overwhelmingly gendered and sexualized racialization, that fraught history of black maternity and masculinity condensed in the phrase, *Mrs. Jones's dark son*. Although the figure of the incarcerated Japanese is largely absent in the rest of the novel, it initiates a remarkable inquiry into the crisis of the U.S. racial order in the cauldron of wartime LA, demonstrating Himes's acute awareness of the particular, shifting racialized conditions of Filipinos, Chicanos, Jews, poor white Southerners and "okies," and a local black elite anxious to distinguish themselves from the migrants of Little Tokyo.

Himes was writing in the wake of the unprecedented commercial success of Richard Wright's *Native Son* (1940), which transposed an older lynching narrative from the rural South to the urban North. In a 1943 *Crisis* article, "Zoot Suit Riots Are Race Riots," Himes makes a similar point in his dramatic final sentence: "But the outcome simply is that the South has won Los Angeles" (225). The novel, however, makes a different argument. If the plot rehearses the lynching narrative, as Madge, a white migrant from Texas, accuses Jones of rape, its conclusion is strikingly revised: instead of being killed by a mob or by the state, he is released by a judge on the condition that he enlists in the army. Rather than assert the continuity of Jim Crow, the novel identifies wartime desegregation not as a false or faltering step toward freedom that ends in failure, but as a crucial transformation in the racial regime. Against the optimistic liberalism of Roosevelt and the WRA, *Ebony* and the JACL, it represents military service not as the proof of loyalty that will secure inclusion into an antiracist nation, but as a new manifestation of racial coercion, of the nation's boundless appetite for terror and violence.[11]

As Yamamoto's narrator gazes at her TV in 1965, what she perceives is not an image that threatens her freedom from outside, but an internal sensation that longs for its release. To understand this alien agency emerging from within, whose movement makes the narration of a memory possible, it may help to locate the text in its moment of production. Grace Hong persuasively situates the memoir in the context of the Japanese American redress movement, which in 1985 was approaching its greatest triumph—an official federal apology for internment, along with financial reparations (307).

Taken as a critique of redress, which banked on the equation of representation and justice, the memoir's scattered references to an "inward self" may be read as an allusion to a subject redress could never recover. Neither a patriotic Nisei nor an alien saboteur, her *indeterminate* loyalty was the effect of state action. You might call her the "non-alien," recalling the now-iconic Civilian Exclusion Orders posted in West Coast communities, demanding the appearance of all "persons of Japanese ancestry, both alien and non-alien." A euphemism for U.S. citizens subsumed within the enemy Japanese, the "non-alien" is a double negative (*no–no*), a liminal category whose ambiguity threatened domestic security.[12] She is terrifying not because her race conclusively proves disloyalty, but because her race simultaneously invokes a threat and conceals it from perception.[13] Neither expelled beyond state borders nor included within a national community constituted against her, she was internally segregated, held in indefinite detention while her fate would be determined elsewhere. From her perspective, the WRA questionnaire—and all those subsequent processes of interrogation by which the loyalty of Japanese Americans came to be established as historical fact—may be understood as the repression of the internment itself, along with the history of anti-Japanese racism that produced it. To be called to prove her loyalty is to deny the very state action that demanded her appearance; her only possible response is to vanish.

Banished from sight, she continues to haunt the rehabilitated Japanese American, most of all in the latter's possession by an inkling of vulnerability, a racialized terror that keeps her in her place. But the narrator's references to an "inward self" may indicate a different manifestation of haunting. The quavering or quickening of the shade, as an unlocatable *itch*, a misplaced memory or duty, like undigested food, *anyway something was unsettling my innards*, rises

from beneath a *cowering* as *a tiny trickle of warmth, an undercurrent of exultation.*
These phrases may be read as a "flickering interiority," akin to the twinge of a
phantom limb stirring to life after being severed above the joint.[14] Her vision
of *an inward self burnt black in a certain fire* does not represent a Japanese
American freely choosing to forego or disavow her privilege, but a non-alien
emerging from the grave, whose desire for revenge binds her to those other
figures of death that conjured her forth.

The word "certain," paradoxically, renders uncertain just which fire is
being referenced; but what distinguishes Fontana from Watts is the shift in
identification from the subject to the object of violence. In postwar Japanese
American culture, the trope of consuming flames is most frequently associated
with scenes of immolation, set between Pearl Harbor and internment.[15] What is
burned, by parents and their children, are the irreplaceable traces of an immigrant past—letters and books in Japanese, photographs, toys, heirlooms—that
might be misperceived or threateningly unreadable in the eyes of state officials.
You might read this as an act of commemoration against all hope, secreting
what is precious in a domain beyond perception. Generally, however, these
scenes stage a desire for recovery through representation by the children or their
descendants, who hope to redeem their inheritance by producing cultural texts.
But in linking this trope both to the immolation in Fontana and the conflagra-
tion in Watts, Yamamoto's memoir critiques this desire, turning it back toward
risk and destruction, gambling the legacy redress sought to recover against the
chance, beyond hope, of justice.

Although justice cannot arrive in the text, across the measure taken by
narrative, it may be useful to consider some of the forms by which its fugitive, utopian domain has been imagined. One stock of figures, with a rich and
varied history across the syncretic range of black religious traditions, foresees an
intervention from the realm of the afterlife. Not surprisingly, perhaps, this is
the strategy taken by Fr. Dunne in his play about the Fontana fire. In a curious
funeral scene, a bodiless "Voice," addressing the stage through a loudspeaker but
apparently unheard by the actors, caustically proclaims, "No restrictive covenants
in heaven, mister" (2–24). This disruption of the play's documentary aesthetic
is authorized by black music, by the materiality of its sound: a sung spiritual
that falls away from words into humming provides the aural medium for the
scene's detour into the fantastic. Put differently, Hartman's insistence that "we
are coeval with the dead" (759) incites such prophetic desires: in the realm of
freedom, the claims of the dead will be heard.

Another stock of figures awaits the arrival of justice from across earthly
borders. Although James Baldwin staked his faith on a radical demand for
national integration, in *The Fire Next Time*, reflecting on perspective of the
Nation of Islam, he phrased that famous question of the 1960s: "Do I really
want to be integrated into a burning house?" (127). This house is inhabited

by an imperial nation, heir to a Western civilization understood as white supremacy; *outside* it waits for a different figure of interracialism, which came to be known as the Third World. In his 1966 article, Petersen explained the criminality of a young Sansei through what he considered a bizarre association with black Muslims (40). Yet in Chicago in 1942, some eighty-five members of a variety of black nationalist organizations, including Elijah Muhammad, were arrested on charges of sedition and draft evasion—as pro-Japanese traitors. African American sympathies for imperial Japan, imagined as a potential "champion of the darker races," can be traced as far back as the Russo-Japanese war, and were more widespread during World War II than elites were willing to admit.[16] Indeed, Himes's Bob Jones remarks offhandedly that "at first" he "wanted Japan to win" (38).

These apparitions of *disloyal* interracialism, of a black-Asian convergence outside and against a white nation, haunted each of those projects that sought to exclude it—resettlement assimilationism in Chicago, Negro-Nisei liberalism in Los Angeles, model minority theory after Watts. Although they do not appear in Yamamoto's account, they are positioned, just off stage, at both ends.[17] My point is not to endorse, or even evaluate, the specific political programs enumerated in the name of the "darker races" or "Third World," but to emphasize how these figures point to a range of utopian desires outside the representational field of imperial nationalism.

In any case, the memoir does not portray a promise of paradise or a call for Third World revolution. It does not foreclose these desires, but it cannot translate, or carry over into representation, what waits beyond the measure of its narrative. In the end, it seeks only to accept the task that the narrator had been given by the man named Short: not to depict an ethical or political triumph, but to publicize a call for help. As an individual, a Nisei woman might have been no less "helpless" before the forces of segregation than a Negro man, but his appeal is addressed to a power beyond her, in the collectivity that might gather in response to the call. The writer's task is to mediate and amplify this call under conditions that threaten to render it inaudible, to fashion a representation whose material form might gather into itself both sides of an antiphonal structure. The task remains, decades later, complicated not only by the family's death but by the transformation of the field of representation, thronged by images of similar deaths whose ritual commemoration would absolve a nation's guilt and silence the claims of the dead. The task thus involves a kind of improvised training of perception. For to pursue responsibility, to be capable of response, requires first of all, as in the biblical exhortation, that you have the ears to hear.

This training is performed, in the memoir's final depiction of the fire, as a straining against the material limits of multiple media, which foregrounds the artificiality and insufficiency of representation to point to what lies beyond its borders. Like the hum of grief interrupting Dunne's play, this passage might be understood, borrowing Nathaniel Mackey's phrase, as "eroding witness." Brent

Edwards glosses the term as responding to "an aesthetic imperative to test and break the limits of what can be said," describing a "fascination with edges, with extremes, with erosion, with modes of expression that strain against themselves" that is "ultimately less involved with the particularities of the media involved" than "with the task of pressing or distending elements of those mediums . . . to bear witness—'eroding witness'" ("Notes" 572). Here is the final passage of the memoir:

> To me, the tumult in the city was the long-awaited, gratifying next chapter of an old movie that had flickered about in the back of my mind for years. In the film, shot in the dark of about three o'clock in the morning, there was this modest house out in the country. Suddenly the house was in flames and there were the sound effects of the fire roaring and leaping skyward. Then there could be heard the voices of a man and woman screaming, and the voices of two small children as well. (157)

Yamamoto underscores the stumbling, mixed-media metaphors that frame the memory with a peculiar rigor, from the spectacle of televised news to the linearity of a novel or history book to the flickering of a film screened only in the interiority of misplaced consciousness. No actors are visible, neither criminals nor victims, much less the belated agents of local law or the triumphant cavalry of national justice, only the stolid nighttime exterior of a house suddenly consumed by flames. The impediments to vision are joined to the artificiality of *sound effects*. Then something crosses over: the sound of four specific voices, which have fallen away from or exceeded speech—for if words could be discerned, they are not recorded. This sound was never actually heard by anyone who lived, yet it is phonographically reproduced on the page, beckoning the reader to follow, into and through the burning house, to cross the threshold of death. Words cannot do justice: it is the sound of a man, a woman, and two children being killed.

If this is all that can be achieved in the text, if the inadequacy of representation only marks the deferral of justice, you must remember that no one has been saved. Nonetheless Yamamoto's literary recording of the sonic materiality of segregation's death, what Fred Moten might term her "terribly beautiful music" (5), improvises a different training or dissonant tuning of perception, in preparation to hear a call. Response, and responsibility, still waits.

Notes

1. See Ruth Wilson Gilmore's definition of racism: "The state-sanctioned production and exploitation of group vulnerabilities toward premature death" (qtd. in Best and Hartman, 13n6).

2. Edwards contends that diaspora should be approached as a political project, manifested in practices that operate through difference. Similarly, Hartman's work on "roots tourism" persuasively argues that the trope of common ancestry is insufficient to attend to the nonequivalent positions of diasporic subjects. Diaspora theory is instructive for comparative studies of U.S. racial formation that ask how unevenly positioned subjects are ethically and politically bound neither in the pluralism of an imperial nation nor in a claim to a common ancestry.

3. For further discussion of the case, see Bass 135–36 and M. Davis 399–401.

4. On the play's reception, including two glowing notices by Langston Hughes, see Dunne's memoir, *King's Pawn* 132–36 and 171–74. The *Defender* report first appeared in a Hollywood column (Levette), one week before a front-page story whose headline alludes to the play's title ("Lynch by Fire Town Reforms").

5. See Grace Hong's reading of this passage as a critique of a "journalistic objectivity" that trains perception in accordance with "the language of the state" (305).

6. "Nisei" refers to the "second-generation" children of Issei immigrants, who, like their own Sansei children, were endowed with U.S. citizenship by birth. The Issei were barred from naturalization on racial grounds until 1952.

7. See Cheung, "Introduction" xii, and Lee 69, 77. Both Cheung ("Dream") and Lee then read this as figure as exemplifying a variety of multiculturalism—a matter of celebration for the former and dismay for the latter. By contrast, Otis, whose "Greek heritage" Yamamoto notes (150), indeed claims to have become "Black"! See his *Listen to the Lambs*, a remarkable memoir written in response to the Watts riots.

8. In an analysis of Negro-Nisei interracialism in postwar Los Angeles, Scott Kurashige points out that the "liberal white and Nisei assimilationists" who championed it "were the elements who rank-and-file Japanese Americans felt had most betrayed them during the war" (19). In the 1940s, a Nisei "go-getter" would most likely be a leader in the JACL, whose controversial ascent to community dominance was enabled by its collaboration with the internment regime.

9. On the terms of mid-century liberal sociology, the memoir's strongest evidence that a "race problem" has become a "success story" is the figure of interracial marriage, the zero-point on the scale of "social distance" between minorities and whites. As it happens, Yamamoto's "pale husband," Anthony DeSoto, is Latino; by allowing him to pass as white in the text, she underscores, rather than disavows, the narrator's distance from African Americans. Caroline Simpson argues that the emergence of the Japanese war bride in 1950s popular culture, following the failure of resettlement, served as a crucial "prototype" for the model minority (174).

10. Lee also juxtaposes this novel to Yamamoto's memoir, to different ends. For another reading of interracialism in Himes, see Itagaki.

11. I am grateful to Ji-Young Um for sharing her insights on imperial wars and the racialized soldier in Himes.

12. The term "no–no boy" refers to internees deemed disloyal on the basis of their responses to nos. 27 and 28 of the WRA loyalty questionnaire. For Mae Ngai, this paradox exemplifies what she terms "alien citizenship."

13. Arguing against the return of internees to California, Governor Earl Warren warned, "no one will be able to tell a saboteur from any other Jap," explaining that his

position "isn't an appeal to race hatred" but "an appeal to safety" (qtd. in Cho 118). See Cho for a detailed analysis of his support for internment in relation to his later career as chief justice.

14. The phrase in quotes and its relation to the figure of a phantom limb is borrowed from Wagner 123; cf. Butler.

15. For an early, canonical example, see Sone 154–56.

16. See Allen and Lipsitz.

17. Guarding both wings is the figure of S.I. Hayakawa, whom she invokes as a kind of precedent for her job at the *Tribune* (152). The Canadian-born Nisei was hired by the *Chicago Defender* in 1942, after the sedition trials; in a typical column ("Second Thoughts"), he not only proclaimed his own loyalty, but chided those African Americans more sympathetic to Japan than to white liberals. Although famous as a semanticist and jazz critic for decades, by 1985 Yamamoto's readers would remember him as a Republican senator from California, flamboyantly opposed to redress, whose sharp rightward turn began when Governor Ronald Reagan named him president of San Francisco State to put down the Third World students' strike.

Works Cited

Allen, Ernest, Jr. "When Japan Was 'Champion of the Darker Races': Satokata Takahashi and the Flowering of Black Messianic Nationalism." *Black Scholar* 24 (1994): 23–46.

Baldwin, James. *The Fire Next Time*. 1963. New York: Dell, 1964.

Bass, Charlotta A. *Forty Years: Memoirs from the Pages of a Newspaper*. Los Angeles: Charlotta A. Bass, 1960.

Best, Stephen and Saidiya Hartman. "Fugitive Justice." Ed. Stephen Best and Saidiya Hartman. "Redress." Spec. issue of *Representations* 92 (2005): 1–15.

Butler, Octavia E. *Kindred*. 1979. Boston: Beacon, 1988.

Cheung, King-Kok. "The Dream in Flames: Hisaye Yamamoto, Multiculturalism, and the Los Angeles Uprising." *Having Our Way: Women Rewriting Tradition in Twentieth-Century America*. Ed. Harriet Pollack. Lewisburg, PA: Bucknell UP, 1995. 118–30.

———. "Introduction." *Seventeen Syllables and Other Stories*. Revised and expanded edition. By Hisaye Yamamoto. New Brunswick, NJ: Rutgers UP, 2001. ix–xxi.

Cho, Sumi. "Redeeming Whiteness in the Shadow of Internment: Earl Warren, *Brown*, and a Theory of Racial Redemption." *Boston College Third World Law Journal* 19 (1998–99): 73–170.

Crow, Charles. "A *MELUS* Interview: Hisaye Yamamoto." *MELUS* 14.1 (1987): 73–84.

Davis, Angela Y. "Civil Rights and Human Rights: Future Trajectories." U of Washington, Seattle. 17 Apr. 2007.

Davis, Mike. *City of Quartz: Excavating the Future in Los Angeles*. New York: Vintage, 1990.

Dunne, George H. *King's Pawn: The Memoirs of George H. Dunne, S.J.* Chicago: Loyola UP, 1990.

————. *Trial by Fire*. Washington, DC: National Theatre Conference, 1946.

Edwards, Brent Hayes. "Notes on Poetics Regarding Mackey's *Song*." *Callaloo* 23.2 (2000): 572–91.

————. *The Practice of Diaspora: Literature, Translation, and the Rise of Black Internationalism*. Cambridge, MA: Harvard UP, 2003.

Fujitani, T. "*Go for Broke*, the Movie: Japanese American Soldiers in US National, Military, and Racial Discourses." *Perilous Memories: The Asia-Pacific War(s)*. Eds. T. Fujitani, Geoffrey M. White, and Lisa Yoneyama. Durham, NC: Duke UP, 2001. 239–66.

————, Geoffrey M. White, and Lisa Yoneyama, eds. *Perilous Memories: The Asia-Pacific War(s)*. Durham, NC: Duke UP, 2001.

Harden, Jacalyn D. *Double Cross: Japanese Americans in Black and White Chicago*. Minneapolis: U of Minnesota P, 2003.

Hartman, Saidiya. "The Time of Slavery." *South Atlantic Quarterly* 101.4 (2002): 757–77.

Himes, Chester. *If He Hollers Let Him Go*. 1945. New York: Thunder's Mouth, 2002.

————. "Zoot Suit Riots Are Race Riots." 1943. *Black on Black: Baby Sister and Selected Writings*. New York: Doubleday, 1973. 220–25.

Hong, Grace Kyungwon. " 'Something Forgotten Which Should Have Been Remembered': Private Property and Cross-Racial Solidarity in the Work of Hisaye Yamamoto." *American Literature* 71.2 (1999): 291–310.

Itagaki, Lynn M. "Transgressing Race and Community in Chester Himes's *If He Hollers Let Him Go*." *African American Review* 37.1 (2003): 65–80.

Kurashige, Scott. "The Many Facets of Brown: Integration in a Multiracial Society." *Journal of American History* 91.1 (2004): 56–68.

Lee, James Kyung-Jin. *Urban Triage: Race and the Fictions of Multiculturalism*. Minneapolis: U of Minnesota P, 2004.

Levette, Harry. "This Is Hollywood." *Chicago Defender* 4 Sept. (1954): 21.

Lipsitz, George. " 'Frantic to Join . . . the Japanese Army': Black Soldiers and Civilians Confront the Asia Pacific War." *Perilous Memories: The Asia-Pacific War(s)*. Eds. T. Fujitani, Geoffrey M. White, and Lisa Yoneyama. Durham, NC: Duke UP, 2001. 347–77.

"Lynch by Fire Town Reforms." *Chicago Defender* 11 Sept. (1954): 1.

Moten, Fred. *In the Break: The Aesthetics of the Black Radical Tradition*. Minneapolis: U of Minnesota P, 2003.

Morrison, Toni. "Unspeakable Things Unspoken: The Afro-American Presence in American Literature." *Michigan Quarterly Review* 28.1 (1989): 1–34.

Ngai, Mae M. *Impossible Subjects: Illegal Aliens and the Making of Modern America*. Princeton, NJ: Princeton UP, 2004.

Otis, Johnny. *Listen to the Lambs*. New York: W.W. Norton, 1968.

Petersen, William. "Success Story, Japanese-American Style." *New York Times Magazine* 9 Jan. (1966): 20–21, 33, 36, 38, 40–41, 43.

"The Race War that Flopped." *Ebony* 1.8 (July 1946): 3–9.

Simpson, Caroline Chung. *An Absent Presence: Japanese Americans in Postwar American Culture, 1945–1960*. Durham, NC: Duke UP, 2001.

Sone, Monica. *Nisei Daughter*. Seattle: U of Washington P, 1979.

Wagner, Bryan. "Disarmed and Dangerous: The Strange Career of Bras-Coupé." Ed. Stephen Best and Saidiya Hartman. "Redress." Spec. issue of *Representations* 92 (2005): 117–51.

Widener, Daniel. " 'Perhaps the Japanese Are to Be Thanked?' Asia, Asian Americams, and the Construction of Black California." *positions* 11.1 (2003): 135–81.

Williams, Patricia J. "The Rules of the Game." *Reading Rodney King/Reading Urban Uprising.* Ed. Robert Gooding-Williams. New York: Routledge, 1993. 51–55.

Yamamoto, Hisaye. "A Fire in Fontana." 1985. *Seventeen Syllables and Other Stories.* Revised and expanded edition. By Hisaye Yamamoto. New Brunswick, NJ: Rutgers UP, 2001.150–57.

———. *Seventeen Syllables and Other Stories.* Revised and expanded edition. New Brunswick, NJ: Rutgers UP, 2001.

Afterword

CHERYL A. WALL

As I read the richly varied articles collected in *Representing Segregation,* the case of the Jena Six made headlines. Its images of the lynching tree, the manacled black male body, and the self-righteous agent of an unjust justice system resonated with my memories of the Jim Crow era. I was not alone. The images evoked a powerful action: demonstrators by the thousands—most too young to remember segregation but haunted by its history nonetheless—marched on the tiny Louisiana town, where they were met with the same charge of "outside agitator" that had been hurled fifty years before. Yet even as some proclaimed the beginning of a new civil rights movement, they faced a situation that was at least as different as it was similar than that confronted by their predecessors. These twenty-first-century marchers arrived by chartered bus with every expectation that they would spend several hours at most in Jena. I suspect that few of their mothers wept in fear as they saw them off, an experience recounted by many veterans of Freedom Summer in 1964. In 2007, the hangman's noose remained empty. The stakes were not life and death, except perhaps for the six young men initially charged with attempted second-degree murder and a conspiracy count for beating a white classmate; for them the death in life that constitutes long-term incarceration still threatens.

But the stakes are high for the rest of us as well. Our visceral response to scenes from Jena—as from New Orleans and Jasper, Texas—indicates how alive the legacy of segregation is.

Although scholars have explored extensively the impact of slavery on the literary imagination, they are just beginning to explore the ways that segregation's legacy informs the work of most twentieth-century black writers. From Charles Chesnutt and Ida B. Wells-Barnett at the turn of the last century to Richard Wright and Lorraine Hansberry at its midpoint, these writers grappled with the challenge of how at once to represent and to resist the logic of segregation. The concept of race as a fixed identity, visible in its marking and permanent in its effect, was the premise on which Jim Crow rested. If on the one hand, the texts analyzed here show how completely these writers reject that premise, they remind us as well how pervasive the system was and how impenetrable to change it seemed. As the readings of Frank Lloyd Brown's *Trumbull Park* and *A Raisin in the Sun* confirm, the system disciplined interior as well as exterior space. Yet there was room to resist. Hansberry's ideal of "genuine realism," writing that encompassed "not only what is, but what is possible" captures the aesthetic to which many of these texts aspire.

Wright is this volume's exemplary figure, as he charts first the physical and psychological terror of segregation in the South in his short stories and in *Black Boy*, and then maps the segregated precincts of Chicago's Black Belt in *Native Son*. "A Survey of the Amusement Facilities of District #35," an archival find, suggests how social realities fired his imagination. Segregation was also constraining. As the article, "Black is a Region," demonstrates, Wright remained trapped by its boundaries even as he traveled the world. He was convinced that the concerns of African Americans were too particular, too narrow, to be taken up in a global forum. His stance may give specialists in African American literature pause, as we consider how to situate ourselves in the now globalized world of literary study.

The signs of Jim Crow, linguistic and literal, demarcated an impassable color line; consequently, the photographs and visual texts reproduced here are centrally important. So much depended on how African Americans read and were read visually. It is hardly surprising that black writers made poetry out of invisibility. Re-viewing the cartoons in "American Graffiti" and the photographs in "A Negative Utopia" reminds us that African Americans refused to be locked into the social identities they were assigned. Shawn Michelle Smith's images that explore the legacy of lynching for white women invite us to think about the psychological burden placed on those who would not or could not escape their social identities.

Writers from multiple locations take up the paradox of claiming citizenship in a nation that remains substantially segregated even after the victories of the civil rights movement. Published in 1985, Hisaye Yamamoto's "A Fire in Fontana" suggests the complex connections between writing by African Americans and writers of color whose texts are in conversation with theirs. Whether belongingness can register as something different from assimilation is a question members of most communities oppressed by white supremacy face. So too is the moral challenge posed when one's belongingness comes at the expense of an even less favored group. Chang-Rae Lee's *Native Speaker* is one of the most compelling recent novels that explore these issues. Significantly, a primary intertext for *Native Speaker* is *Invisible Man*.

The articles collected here suggest questions that we might pose of texts in multiple literary traditions across lines of race/ethnicity, genre, period, and region. As critics and scholars continue the conversation that Brian Norman and Piper Kendrix Williams have so ably begun, we must continue to hone a mode of critique that:

1. explores the response to segregated communities on both sides of the color line and reads Faulkner alongside Wright and Hurston, Bellow and Mamet alongside Ellison and Hansberry and Chang-Rae Lee alongside John Cheever (I can think of numerous white writers who are aware of the color line that segregates their characters' experiences; for example, Tillie Olsen and Jonathan Lethem come to mind. But we should ask what it means when writers fail to acknowledge that the spaces they imagine are segregated.);

2. registers the psychological as well as physical terror that polices the borders of segregation;

3. acknowledges the creative and sustaining cultural expressions produced by oppressed people without minimizing the injustice and exploitation at the core of oppression itself; and

4. analyzes the strategies of representation that these historical conditions produced and provoked.

Contributors

Elizabeth Abel is professor of English at the University of California, Berkeley. Her books and edited volumes on gender, race, and psychoanalysis include *Virginia Woolf and the Fictions of Psychoanalysis* (1989), *Writing and Sexual Difference* (1982), and *Female Subjects in Black and White: Race, Psychoanalysis, Feminism* (with Barbara Christian and Helene Moglen, 1997). Recent articles have appeared in *Representations*, *Critical Inquiry*, and the *African American Review*. The essay in this volume is drawn from her forthcoming book, *Signs of the Times: The Visual Politics of Jim Crow* (University of California Press, 2010).

GerShun Avilez is a PhD candidate in English at the University of Pennsylvania. His work focuses on African American critical culture and the social meanings attributed to black embodiment. He is completing his dissertation on the artistic legacy of the black arts era.

Ruth Blandón earned her doctorate in English from the University of Southern California. Her dissertation is titled, "Trans-American Modernisms: Racial Passing, Travel Writing, and Cultural Fantasies of Latin America."

Tess Chakkalakal is assistant professor of English and Africana Studies at Bowdoin College and her book manuscript, *Novel Bondage: Slavery, Marriage and Freedom in Nineteenth-Century American Literature*, is forthcoming.

Eve Dunbar is assistant professor in the Department of English at Vassar College. She specializes in African American literature and cultural expression, black feminism, and theories of black diaspora. Dunbar is completing a book project on the aesthetic and political ties that bind literary genre, American nationalism, and black cultural nationalism in the works of mid-twentieth-century African American writers writing from abroad.

Michelle Y. Gordon is assistant professor of English at the University of Southern California. Her current research focuses on the aesthetic and grassroots relationships between twentieth-century black literary movements in Chicago and African American freedom struggles.

Trudier Harris is J. Carlyle Sitterson professor of English at the University of North Carolina at Chapel Hill (UNC). Her more than twenty authored and edited books include *Exorcising Blackness: Historical and Literary Lynching and Burning Rituals* (1984), *Fiction and Folklore: The Novels of Toni Morrison* (1991), *Saints, Sinners, Saviors: Strong Black Women in African American Literature* (2001), *The Oxford Companion to African American Literature* (1997), and *Reading Contemporary African American Drama: Fragments of History, Fragments of Self* (2007). Her memoir, *Summer Snow: Reflections from a Black Daughter of the South*, appeared in 2003 from Beacon Press. Her several teaching awards include the UNC System Board of Governors' Award for Excellence in Teaching (2005). Her latest book is *The Scary Mason-Dixon Line: African American Writers and the South* (2009).

Elizabeth Boyle Machlan is a lecturer in English at Princeton University. Her book manuscript, "Panic Rooms: Architecture and Anxiety in New York From 1900 to 9/11," is under contract for the Urban Life, Urban Landscape series at Ohio State University Press. Her work addresses intersections between literary form, architectural history, and urban studies. Her work also appears in *Studies in the Novel.*

Joycelyn Moody is the Sue E. Denman Distinguished Chair in American Literature at the University of Texas at San Antonio, where she teaches courses on early African American literature and culture. She served as editor of *African American Review* (2004–2008). Her publications include *Sentimental Confessions: Spiritual Narratives of Nineteenth-Century African American Women* (2003) and *Teaching with The Norton Anthology of African American Literature* (2004). She has lectured on U.S. black women in slavery at the University of Washington-Seattle, Hamilton College, the Harvard School of Divinity, Southern Methodist University, and numerous other institutions.

Brian Norman is assistant professor of English at Loyola University Maryland where he teaches American and African American literature. His is the author of *The American Protest Essay and National Belonging: Addressing Division* (2007). His other work appears in *African American Review, Canadian Review of American Studies, differences, Frontiers, MELUS,* and *Women's Studies,* and collections on James Baldwin, Emmett Till, and Malcolm X. He is working on projects on Jim Crow in post-civil rights American literature, dead women talking, and American stories of class descent.

Birgit Brander Rasmussen is assistant professor of American Studies at Yale University. She is co-editor of *The Making and Unmaking of Whiteness* (2001). Her article "Negotiating Treaties, Negotiating Literacies: A French-Iroquois Encounter and the Making of Early American Literature" won the 2007 Norman Foerster Prize for Best Article in *American Literature*. Other work appears in *Interventions: International Journal of Postcolonial Studies*, *Mississippi Quarterly*, and on MediaCommons: A Digital Scholarly Network. She is completing a book manuscript entitled *Queequeg's Coffin: Indigenous Literacies and the Making of American Literature*.

Anne P. Rice, assistant professor of African and African American Studies at Lehman College, CUNY, edited *Witnessing Lynching: American Writers Respond* (Rutgers UP, 2003). She is working on a book entitled *Dangerous Memories: Lynching and the American Cultural Imagination*.

Lori Robison teaches American literature and is the academic director of the Composition Program in the Department of English at the University of North Dakota. Recent publications include an essay on *Iola Leroy*, sentimental discourse, and race in *Genre* and an essay on race and region in Blackwell's *Companion to the Regional Literatures of America* (2003).

Vince Schleitwiler is assistant professor of English at Williams College. His current research examines the intersections of African American, Japanese American, and Filipino migrations across U.S. imperial domains.

Shawn Michelle Smith is associate professor of visual and critical studies at the School of the Art Institute of Chicago. She is the author of *American Archives: Gender, Race, and Class in Visual Culture* (1999) and *Photography on the Color Line: W.E.B. Du Bois, Race, and Visual Culture* (2004), and co-author, with Dora Apel, of *Lynching Photographs* (2007). She has exhibited her photo-based artwork in a number of venues throughout the United States.

Gary Totten is associate professor of English at North Dakota State University. He is the editor of *Memorial Boxes and Guarded Interiors: Edith Wharton and Material Culture* (2007). His essays on late nineteenth- and early twentieth-century American literature and travel writing appear in such journals as *African American Review*, *American Indian Quarterly*, *American Literary Realism*, *Dreiser Studies*, *MELUS*, and *Pedagogy*.

Zoe Trodd teaches in the history and literature program at Harvard and is currently a Mellon Foundation fellow. She researches American protest literature, especially the literature of abolitionism and civil rights, and her books include *Meteor of War: The John Brown Story* (with John Stauffer, 2004), *American Protest Literature* (2006), *To Plead Our Own Cause: Personal Stories by Today's Slaves* (with Kevin Bales, 2008), *The Long Civil Rights Movement* (2008), and *Modern Slavery* (with Kevin Bales and Alex Kent Williamson, 2009).

Cheryl A. Wall is Board of Governors Zora Neale Hurston Professor of English at Rutgers University. She is the author most recently of *Worrying the Line: Black Women Writers, Lineage, and Literary Tradition* (2005).

Piper Kendrix Williams is assistant professor of African American studies and English at The College of New Jersey. Her article, "Gendered Migrations: Black Woman's Return to Africa," appears in *Frontiers*. She is currently working on a book-length thematic study of the formation of black identity in African American literature.

Eric Wolfe teaches American literature and is the director of graduate studies in the Department of English at the University of North Dakota. Recent publications include an essay on Charles Brockden Brown, ventriloquism, and democracy in *American Literature* and an essay on William Apess, melancholia, and rhetorical sovereignty in *Studies in American Indian Literatures*.

Index

Note: Page numbers in *italics* indicate figures.

273